MY LIFE AND EASY TIMES

Also by Patrick Campbell

A LONG DRINK OF COLD WATER

A SHORT TROT WITH A CULTURED MIND

AN IRISHMAN'S DIARY

LIFE IN THIN SLICES

PATRICK CAMPBELL'S OMNIBUS

COME HERE TILL I TELL YOU

CONSTANTLY IN PURSUIT

HOW TO BECOME A SCRATCH GOLFER

THE P-P-PENGUIN PATRICK CAMPBELL

BREWING UP IN THE BASEMENT

ROUGH HUSBANDRY

ALL WAYS ON SUNDAYS

A BUNCH OF NEW ROSES

GULLIBLE TRAVELS

THE COARSE OF EVENTS

THE HIGH SPEED GAS WORKS

PATRICK CAMPBELL'S GOLFING BOOK

WAIVING ALL EXCUSES

FAT TUESDAY TAILS

35 YEARS ON THE JOB

A FEAST OF TRUE FANDANGLES

MY LIFE AND EASY TIMES

by

PATRICK CAMPBELL

produced by
Vivienne Knight

PAVILION
MICHAEL JOSEPH

For My Mother

This edition published in Great Britain in 1988 by
PAVILION BOOKS LIMITED
196 Shaftesbury Avenue, London WC2H 8JL
in association with Michael Joseph Limited
27 Wrights Lane, Kensington, W8 5TZ

First published in Great Britain in 1967 by
Anthony Blond Limited

Jacket Design by Fraser/Morgan

British Library Cataloguing in Publication Data

Campbell, Patrick, 1913-1980
My life and easy times.
1. English literature. Campbell, Patrick, 1913-1980
I. Title
828'.91409

ISBN 1-85145-316-4

Printed and bound in Great Britain by
Biddles Ltd, Guildford and King's Lynn

Introduction

The title page of this book is a little unusual. It reads:

My Life and Easy Times
by
Patrick Campbell
Produced by
Vivienne Knight.

Vivienne did produce this book. We discussed each chapter
before I wrote it, and I wrote each chapter from the detailed
notes she made of our discussions.

This was comparatively easy. We had worked together by the
same system on film and television scripts for more than ten
years. But in producing this book she had an additional and
much more difficult task; that of causing me to look at the
realities of my life, and to write them down as honestly as I
could.

It was a new experience for me, and often an exhausting one
for her.

I'm very, very grateful to her for her intelligence, for her
understanding and, most of all, for her superhuman persistence.

She even married me before we had quite finished the book.

P. C.

Chapter One

M Y mother said to me on the telephone from Dublin, "I don't want to talk too loudly because I think he can hear me, but you'd better come over. He had a bad night and he's very feeble."

I said I'd come at once.

I found I was neither shocked nor sad, but only excited. My father, Lord Glenavy, was going to die. It would be an event of some importance in Dublin and I, as the inheritor of the title, would be playing a leading part in it.

At this moment it wasn't possible to guess what the effect of his death would be. Death to me was an unknown quantity.

My sister had been killed by a flying bomb towards the end of the war in London, but we hadn't seen one another for a long time. The only emotion I could remember was a disgruntled feeling of waste. Her husband was killed at the same time and they hadn't been married long enough to have any children, so that one of the things I wasn't going to be was an uncle. But behind this familiar selfishness was the grey melancholy of knowing I'd never see my sister again.

I supposed I'd feel the same sort of thing about the Lord if, indeed, he was going to die. He'd already made, at the age of seventy-eight, an astonishing recovery from a major abdominal operation and when I'd last seen him a couple of months ago he'd been talking about playing golf again and buying a small boat.

No one ever spoke of the reason for the operation. The Lord himself called it, with a cheerful good-humour that didn't look faked, "Just straightening out the guts." Perhaps he really didn't know, but everyone else could only believe that it was cancer. The Old Lord had died of it, too, although he was eighty-eight.

They were always known in the family, and to the few close friends who ventured into it, as the Lord and the Old Lord. My mother, however, referred to my father as Gordon and his sister called him Charlie, while my brother and I spoke to him as

Lordship. His infrequent letters to us were signed in the same way.

I know, for my part, that this use of 'the Lord' and 'Lordship' in place of 'my father' or 'Daddy' was to relieve us of an intimacy that would have been embarrassing to both. The Lord liked to keep everyone at a safe distance from him and particularly those that he didn't know well. Whenever I brought new friends to the house he'd refer to them for months afterwards as 'the Paul' or 'the David', de-personalising them for curious reasons of his own. Once the 'the' was dropped they were in.

And now it seemed that he was dying, and I was going to have to face the fact of his death. But all that I had at this moment was the feeling of excitement, of much to be done, of taking over the leadership of the family.

I rang the traffic manager of Aer Lingus in Regent street, with whom I'd had dealings in the past, and told him my father was dying and that I had to get over to Dublin as quickly as possible. The feeling of excitement and importance had risen to a warm glow.

The traffic manager seemed to share it. He said he would ring their people at London Airport and tell them to do everything they could to help me. It wasn't the best time, he said, with the August Bank Holiday and the Dublin Horse Show coming up, but he was sure they could find me a seat.

The Aer Lingus representative at the airport got me one on the very next plane although, as he told me, "There's ninety-three people standing by." It was not unpleasant to be the Hon. Patrick Campbell, receiving V.I.P. treatment on the way to the bedside of his dying father, Lord Glenavy.

A hired car, sent by my mother, was waiting for me at the airport in Dublin. It was a large and derelict Dodge which must have been used that morning for a wedding because the back seat was full of confetti and the smell of stout. It was strange to think that two people had got married while my father was dying, but then they'd probably never heard of either of us.

The battery of the Dodge was almost flat, but the engine fired on its last dying revolution. I hoped the driver wouldn't stall it, because I was suddenly sure that the Lord would die while we were stuck in one of the side streets around Ringsend Basin.

He stalled it on the hill up to the traffic lights in Blackrock, a couple of miles away from home. The only way we could get it going was to push it back down the hill in reverse, but there was a queue of cars behind us. I jumped out to wave them past and found I knew at least one of the people in each of the first three cars. They were pleased and amused to see me. As I pushed the old Dodge back down the hill one of them called out, "Give you a grand bit for the *Sunday Times*, Paddy, what?" Several more car-loads gave me a cheer as they went past. When the engine fired and I got into the back again I found I no longer believed that my father was dying. People lived for ever in Dublin. The informality, the easy laughter, the complete lack of pressure kept everyone going until they were ninety.

I remembered my mother had told me on the phone that the Lord had taken her and her sister, Marjorie, to dinner in the Royal Irish Yacht Club only a week ago, and that he'd driven the car himself.

He, too, would live to be ninety and we'd be playing golf together again soon. He'd had relapses before, but he was made of leather. No one ever died in careless, irresponsible Dublin.

We turned off the sea road in Sandycove into the horribly named Ballygehin Avenue, and there was the house, looking small and ordinary in the sunshine.

For fifteen years or so my father and mother had lived in Rockbrook, a large house in the Dublin mountains. If the weather was very clear you could see the whole city laid out beneath you, and the shadow of the Mountains of Mourne eighty miles away to the north.

A brown mountain stream ran through the grounds in a series of natural waterfalls. My father had planted hundreds of trees an shrubs around the swimming pool, which he'd had blasted out of solid rock that sparkled with quartz. On a summer's day it was a magic place, a thousand miles away from the uproar of cities and people. But in the winter, when the wind and the rain howled down from the ruins of the Hell Fire Club above, it was peculiarly lonely and desolate, and full of dying.

The news of my sister's death came to Rockbrook, and of the death of Ralph Brereton Barry, my mother's inseparable friend. Two favourite dogs had died there and a few miles farther up in the mountains was the Military Road with its lonely crosses, marking the places where men had been shot during the Civil War. In the winter it was too far from Dublin, and too close to death. My father sold it and bought this much smaller house,

called Rockall, on the sea road in Sandycove, on the outskirts of
Dun Laoghaire.

There was a tiny croquet court at the back, overlooked by
terraced houses, but in the front only the garden and the sea
road separated it from Dublin Bay.

My mother's taste and highly developed capacity for home-
making had, at least, made it comfortable and original inside,
even if the back of the house was the only part that got the sun.

The sun was shining now as the derelict Dodge left me outside
the gate. The door was open and the house seemed to be empty.
I called out several times, "Anyone there?" but there was no
reply.

I was sure that my father had had another of his miraculous
recoveries and that he and my mother and Marjorie had gone
out for a drive in the sunshine. Just to make sure I went upstairs
to my father's room and opened the door and saw the most
frightening thing I'd ever seen.

A shrivelled little old man was propped up against a lot of
pillows in my father's bed. The face was yellow, and the bones
were protruding through it. The right forearm was resting on top
of the head in the position of someone trying to think of something, when the thought won't come. The figure was motionless,
as still as death.

I was staring at it, paralysed, when a pretty little blonde girl
in a white coat came round the end of the bed. I saw she must
be the nurse, and that she was as startled as I had been.

I said, "I'm Mr. Paddy—his son." She said, confusedly, "I
knew you would be." Then I found myself sitting on the chair
beside him. I took his hand. It was very small and bony and
cold. I said, not knowing what I was saying, "You're a great
man. You're a great man."

His eyes were opaque, completely unseeing.

The little nurse bent down and spoke clearly and precisely into
his ear. "It's Mr. Paddy. It's your son."

My father stayed absolutely motionless. He seemed not even
to be breathing. "It's me," I said. "Paddy. How are you?"

The little nurse spoke to him again. "Just squeeze his hand,"
she said. "Tell him you know he's here."

The cold, bony little hand lay lifelessly in mine.

"I think he knows," the nurse said to me. Then she spoke to
him again. "Just move your finger," she said. "Tell him."

I believe I felt the faintest little flutter.

The little nurse looked down at him with a gentleness which seemed to come from more than just a familiarity with death. "He knows you're here," she said. Then she said suddenly, "He was a lovely man. We had the grandest laughs."

I realised then for the first time that I'd never talk to my father again. "He *was* a lovely man." Very soon now he would be wholly dead.

I said, "I'd better go." I didn't have the courage to wait to see it happening. I said to the nurse, "Is my mother in?" She said she thought she was in the garden.

She was sitting on a bench, very composedly looking out at the sea, waiting for it to happen, as she'd been waiting for nearly a year.

"Hello," I said, "it's me."

"Darling," she said, "it's lovely to see you."

I said, "I thought you'd all gone out for a drive and then I went up to his room. It's awful."

Both of us struggled for a moment with tears and then she said, cheerfully, "He was grand last night. Dr. Werner, of the Eye and Ear Hospital, came out to see him and he brought a bottle of champagne. Werner didn't know how ill he was. I think the Lord was delighted that someone from the Eye and Ear had turned up at last. I think he thought they'd forgotten all about him."

(My father had been chairman of the hospital for years.)

"They had a long talk all about racing," my mother said, "and the Lord had a glass of champagne. I don't think it was very good for him. He had a bad night and now—"

We struggled with tears again. Then I said, tritely, "It's a good way for him to go, having a glass of champagne and talking about racing with that pretty little nurse looking after him."

"I used to hear peals of laughter coming from the room," my mother said. Neither of us looked up at the curtained window.

"She told me they had the grandest laughs," I said. "He was a great man."

"I've just remembered," my mother said, "we got married fifty years ago tomorrow. When we knelt down at the altar everyone saw that Gordon had a huge hole in the sole of his shoe.

Malcolm came to the wedding in a top-hat, with a tennis racquet." (Malcolm was her brother.)

We both laughed and then my mother said, "I'm sure Michael would like to be here, but he'd never be able to get back in time."

My brother was on holiday in Elba. I became efficient. I said I'd send him a telegram, asking him to ring us. I asked her if there was anything else I could do. I was getting another disagreeable glow of pride at being the head of the family.

We couldn't think of anything else. We went into the house, to find that Marjorie had come back from posting letters. Then I suddenly remembered Dorothy, the other sister.

They'd both arrived in Dublin some weeks before, Marjorie from her home in New Zealand, and Dorothy from South Africa. They came home to Dublin every five or six years, so that their arrival had nothing to do with the Lord's illness, but I was very glad that they were here now. And then I remembered about Dorothy, again. A couple of weeks ago she'd had a stroke, watching racing on television with the Lord, and was now in a Dublin nursing home.

"Dorothy!" I said. "How is she? I'd forgotten about her."

"No one knows yet," my mother said. Then she laughed, but it was sadly. "Everyone seems to be falling to pieces," she said.

The three sisters had always adored one another, and comforted one another with endless, vivid letters from their three corners of the world. Dorothy and my mother had been painters for more than fifty years. Marjorie played the piano as though it were part of herself. Sometimes, while driving along in the car through the mountains that they'd known so well as girls, they'd burst spontaneously into operatic arias, singing all the parts, including baritone and tenor, in perfect harmony until they broke down in laughter. Together, they were the happiest people I'd ever known.

The three of us had lunch and talked in a desultory way about the latest Dublin gossip, while we listened for a sound from upstairs.

The little nurse came down soon after three o'clock. She stood quietly in the door of the sitting-room for a moment and then said, "I'm afraid his Lordship's gone."

We all stood up, but then the nurse said to Marjorie, "I think you'd better come upstairs a minute, Mrs. Tweed."

My mother and I sat down again, glad in a frightened way

that Marjorie was there. She was a doctor's wife. We hoped she must be familiar with the arrangement of death.

Marjorie came down a few minutes later and said, "It's all right now. He's nice and tidy." She was composed, but looked rather white. We went upstairs to my father's room.

He looked smaller than ever now, so small that he wasn't really there at all. His head was sunk on his chest and the arm that had lain across it had been lowered to his side.

I held the hand and now it was icy. Marjorie suddenly leant over and kissed the top of my father's head. My mother looked astonished, and then she kissed him, too.

There was nothing we could do. Marjorie went to her room and my mother and I went downstairs, where the nurse joined us a couple of minutes later, to express her sympathy.

My mother, who'd been crying silently, suddenly lifted her head and said, "There's some champagne in the kitchen. They didn't finish it."

"We'll drink it for him," I said.

When I came back with the champagne Marjorie had joined us. There was just enough left for the four of us. I raised mine rather formally and said, "Here's to a great man."

I realised I'd been calling my father a great man ever since the first shock of seeing him that morning, and I knew why I was doing it. I was telling him something I'd always half-known, but had never said openly before.

We drank our champagne, but it wasn't really a tribute. It was just something to do for the moment, until the next thing began.

The nurse, who had been perhaps a little shocked by the champagne, and at the same time preoccupied with what she had to do, went back upstairs. Marjorie followed her, I didn't know whether to help her or to go to her own room.

After a while my mother said, "It was very queer, but every time I sat with him he used to ask, 'Where's Marjorie? Where's Nurse?' As if I was a stranger. I just felt so glad that there were people like the nurse and Marjorie that he wanted."

There was a small bump on the floor upstairs. It could not be ignored. My mother said, as if it was a small joke, "I wonder what she's doing to him."

I shook my head quickly, to tell her—without saying it—that we didn't have to pay any attention to the practicalities of death.

2—MLAET

Suddenly, then, I said, "I don't feel he's dead at all. He's all around everywhere. He's pottering about in the garden or playing croquet or watching the yachts. I'm sure that death really isn't anything."

But it wasn't true. I did feel that his spirit, the essence of him, and the memory of him, were indestructible, but the true reality was that a huge, empty hole had suddenly opened up in my life for the first time—a hole that would never be filled again.

"I know what you mean," my mother said. "But it's extraordinary, I just feel relieved that it's all over. It's been such a long time and it's marvellous to know that he won't suffer any more."

I had that aching in the jaws, almost like rheumatism, that comes from trying to hold back tears, and I could see my mother had it too. And yet she was profoundly happy because the man with whom she had lived for fifty years was now out of pain for ever, and had died comforted by the presence of her sister from New Zealand and a little nurse from Dublin. The fact that he had seemed to feel no need for her in his last days gave her no feeling of rancour, no feeling that her life might have been wasted. She regarded it, rather, as an emotional phenomenon, a fascinating quirk in human nature to be discussed objectively, to be respected for itself.

I remembered, when my sister had been killed, that an elderly cook we had at the time had complained to me, "Her Ladyship doesn't suffer right." The cook had been looking forward, with Catholic fervour, to my sister's portrait being draped in black, the blinds in the house drawn, the whole family convulsed in solitary grief. Yet everyone was sitting out in summer clothes in the patio at the back of the house, and there was even laughter, at small things.

My mother had said to me, with complete simplicity, "The worst thing that can happen to anybody is to lose a child," and then she had begun to talk about Biddy playing in goal for the Irish lacrosse team 'with a queer thing like a fencing mask all over her face'. A moment later she said, "I was sure the poor child was going to be killed." We both laughed, because it was so very much the wrong thing to say. But the memory of the fencing mask, and the emotions it had created, were too strong to be censored.

In fact, I could never remember anything being censored in

our family. There was always an atmosphere of lively discussion, of absorbed curiosity in the motives of others, usually led by my mother, with her favourite introduction, "I thought it was terribly interesting when—"

And yet the Lord was always a little apart from these free-for-alls. There was never any question of a stern, Victorian father-figure, yet I always felt that the things that my mother and Biddy and I found 'terribly interesting' seemed to him to be merely frivolous and self-evident. He had read Spengler, Nietzsche and Schopenhauer and seemed to have found much in common with these sombre philosophers. At Sunday evening suppers he would discuss them at length, and with the appearance of excitement, when someone turned up whom he considered was worth talking to. Yet he had no conscious pride in his own intellectualism. I shall never forget the wounded look on his face when he came into the room and heard me say to Biddy, "I was talking to Schopenhauer and he said Spengler was an eejit." I was about twelve at the time, but he seemed to take it as though an adult had criticised the quality of his mind.

My mother, almost certainly not having read him, was a stern anti-Spengler woman. "All that about the decline of the West," she would say. "It's nonsense. The world's getting better all the time."

Neither my mother nor the Lord ever seemed to be parents in the way that I'd seen other mothers and fathers being parental. There was never any feeling of discipline. Rather, there were things you could do that were anti-social, that caused annoyance or inconvenience to others, and there was a kind of unspoken indication that it would be better if you didn't do them again. But here again, the Lord was different. He left what little discipline there was to my mother, seeming to have a set of principles of his own that were too lofty and too austere, even to him, to be applicable to ordinary human beings.

Suddenly, my mother, sitting by the fire, said, "I never really knew what sort of man he was."

She, too, had been remembering the past, looking back over many more years with the Lord than I had known.

The noises from the room upstairs had ceased. It seemed to be the right time for this kind of examination, almost a formal board meeting to consider the evidence and to come to conclusions, the old, insatiable curiosity over again.

"Neither did I," I said. "What did he do, for instance, when he went to the Bank?"

She gave a small, rather helpless laugh. "I could never imagine," she said.

Hundreds of people all over Ireland—businessmen, farmers, trades union officials, cattle dealers, industrialists, politicians— all of them certainly knew more about my father's commercial capabilities than I did.

All that I knew of his working life had been what I'd read in my mother's voluminous scrap books, cuttings of every kind which she'd kept since the first war.

I knew that he'd been a barrister in London before 1914, and during it had worked under Churchill in the Ministry of Munitions. I knew, like his father, who'd become Lord Chancellor of Ireland and later Chairman of the first Irish Senate, that he could have had what is always called a brilliant career at the English Bar, but that he'd given it up and come home to Ireland to do what he could to assist the first Irish Government, under President Cosgrave. In this he became Parliamentary Secretary to the Ministry of Industry and Commerce, a job he held until Cosgrave lost the election to de Valera.

This return to Ireland had always seemed to me to be a strange sacrifice for a man who liked being successful and who had enjoyed in the literary life of London the serious, cultivated kind of discussion that he never really found in sufficient measure in Dublin.

In fact, he frequently railed against 'the cretinous slobs who pass for people of intelligence in Ireland'. Once, when I asked him, "Why did you come back here, then?" he shook his head— an instinctive gesture that said the question was out of order.

The truth was, of course, that he'd come back to Ireland because he loved Ireland, and loved the idea of taking part in the formation of what he thought of, romantically, as being a new and ideal Free State. One of the first tastes he got of the new and ideal Free State was when the I.R.A. burnt down our house on Christmas Eve, 1922, and it seemed for a long half hour that they were going to execute him on his own front lawn.

I never knew how he made the transition from politics to

business. I must have been at school in England when it happened, or at Oxford or in Germany, but when I came home again the Lord was a director of the Bank of Ireland, Chairman of the Great Northern Railway and of the Royal Hibernian Insurance Company, and on the board of a number of other companies he never mentioned.

I formed the idea—and literally formed it, almost out of nothing, because I had to have one—that he was a kind of financial mystic or seer, the kind of genius who can be shown the balance sheet of an unknown company and can diagnose its ills an hour later.

Mysterious figures from the world of international finance would occasionally come to the house on Sunday evenings. Large, weighty Swedes or silent Englishmen with big foreheads. More often than not my mother, by her own passionate enthusiasm, would draw them into some discussion of painting or the theatre in which everyone except the Lord would join.

With increasing frequency he'd sit by himself at the window, looking bored and more and more resentful of what he'd come to describe as 'women's kitchen gossip'. Soon, we were able to identify 'kitchen gossip' as any form of emotional communication, any expression of subjective opinion that was not based upon knowledge or reasoned thought.

Once, trying to compensate the Lord for a particularly bitter and silent evening, I asked him, "Why do all these experts from the World Bank or whatever it is come all the way to Dublin to see you?" He gave the self-deprecating grin that wasn't deprecatory at all and said, "They come to get straightened out."

Probably much of his time in the Bank of Ireland was spent in wondering whether to allow a farmer in Mullingar to increase his overdraft by another £1,000 or in trying to talk the bank clerks' leaders out of another strike, but I do believe he had a visionary sense of money. It was his form of art, a desire to see money irrigating the affairs of individuals or companies to the best possible effect. In exchange for this service, however, he never seemed to receive very much of it for himself.

For as long as I can remember the family lived in considerable comfort—on the very edge of bankruptcy. An unnecessary shovelful of coal on the fire, or a stove left on in an empty bedroom, would bring on the Lord's grim look and the statement, "You people simply don't understand the value of money." My mother often said, "The Lord's always telling me I'll be scrubbing floors in the workhouse but I wouldn't mind it at all. I've been scrubbing floors all my life."

This refusal to be depressed by the constant threats of bankruptcy seemed to the Lord to be the essence of feeble-mindedness and irresponsibility, and then he'd go to the races or buy a new, if modest, car.

We never knew where we were, and the Lord's certainty that we were incapable of understanding the fearful position we were in meant that he never took the trouble to explain it in any realistic detail.

In this he was abetted by Archie Robinson, who'd been the family solicitor for as long as anyone could remember. But Archie was more than a solicitor. He was the silent, dedicated guardian of the lifeblood of the family. It always seemed to me that the whole of his working day, every day, must have been concerned exclusively with our affairs, whatever they might be. In this, he and the Lord were one, and particularly in the belief that there was no point in inviting interest or understanding on the part of the rest of us.

The only other person I knew of who had the Lord's confidence in matters of money was Willy Ganly, despite the fact that Willy was at least twenty years younger.

He was one of a huge family of Ganlys, most of whom were in the cattle business in Dublin. He'd first come into the Lord's life as a friend of mine and particularly as a friend of my sister, Biddy.

Willy was direct and forceful and a very astute businessman. Like my father, he loved fishing and any kind of outdoor life. He was also incorruptibly honest, a quality that the Lord admired, in business, above all others. Before long, he took Willy into the Bank of Ireland as the youngest director the Bank had ever had. In one day Willy said of my father, "He's the only completely incorruptible banker I've ever known," and my father said of Willy, "You could trust him with your very last shilling."

Though Willy and I were close friends I never learnt anything from him about the hidden, commercial side of my father's life. It was as though he had complete respect for the Lord's certainty that his wife and children were incurable imbeciles where money was concerned. And I have no doubt that this unquestioning respect, as much as Willy's other outstanding qualities, went a

long way to warm the Lord towards him. Unquestioning respect
was not one of the things he enjoyed in his own household.

The little nurse came into the room, dressed in her outdoor
clothes. After hesitating for a moment, she said, "Everything's
arranged, so I'd better catch the bus."

My mother thanked her for all she had done, and the nurse
said again, "He was a lovely man." When she saw what this
did to us she left the room at once. We heard the front door
close.

My mother said, "I think I'll go upstairs and lie down for a
bit." I helped her to her feet—she was very tired—and I said,
very quickly and as simply as I could, "Don't go and look."

She said, "I won't," and thanked me with a little smile.

Alone in the sitting-room, I sat in the Lord's chair by the
window, looking out at Dublin Bay. His race glasses—I think
they'd belonged to his father—were on a stool beside the chair.
I picked them up and tried to focus on a small collier steaming
out of the Liffey past the Poolbeg Lighthouse, but the image was
blurred.

Suddenly, I got into a state of desperation. Everything was
slipping away. The feeling that I'd known nothing about his
business life became unbearable. It was idle, ungrateful, unforgivable. And now all the memories of him were becoming
shadowy and confused. I had to arrange them, file them away,
before it was too late.

I got up and went out of the house, through the front garden
and to the sea road and down to the rocks at the Forty Foot, a
roughly concreted enclosure that had been a bathing place for
Gentlemen Only for many years. The Lord had sometimes
bathed here before breakfast in the very early morning, loving
the feeling of solitude, the sun coming up over the Hill of Howth
and the clean, new sea.

He said, "I lurched into the Forty Foot the other morning and
when I came out I found I'd begun to grow a whole new crop
of hair."

It was true. In the last year of his life—perhaps it was some
manifestation of the disease that killed him—grey and bristly
hair had begun to sprout all over the top of his scalp. He was
proud of it, and massaged it constantly while he was reading.

I tried to remember some of the other, human things, to make up for my lack of knowledge of what he'd done for a living.

Years ago, he'd written a play called *A Treaty With the Barbarians*. It was produced at the Abbey Theatre one Sunday night. I had a vague memory of having read it. It had a flavour of Shaw, but without Shaw's vitality. My mother said, but not in his hearing, "There seemed to be an awful lot of talk."

A few years before he died he astonished me by sending to me, in London, written on thick, lined paper in his beautiful handwriting, 'six television plays for Charlie Drake'. In a rare burst of enthusiasm he'd spoken of Charlie Drake as 'more imaginative, more of an all-round comic character than Chaplin'.

The plays were written under the pen-name of Carl Hendry, though he'd taken the name of Richard Erroll for *A Treaty With the Barbarians*. They were beyond hope. Some of them might have played for ten minutes, others for about twenty. In the majority of them it was impossible to tell which was the role intended for Charlie Drake. The style in places was reminiscent of the stage Irishry of Donn Byrne, in others it was no more than an attempt to imitate the comic business in a pre-war music-hall sketch. In a covering note he said I was sure to know someone in the BBC who'd be interested.

I thought first of all of sending them back, with some convincing words of praise, but qualified by reminding him of the tight time-factor in television. Then it seemed to be unfair not to give an airing to something on which he'd worked so hard, so I sent them to Eric Maschwitz, who was then Head of Light Entertainment at Television Centre. In a letter, I explained the unusual circumstances.

Eric was very good. He sent them back with a note that said, "While your friend Carl Hendry shows very considerable promise as a writer of comedy for television, he still has something to learn about the technical matter of length. I should be delighted to see any revisions he might care to make."

I posted the six plays back to Dublin, with Eric's letter, and heard no more about them for a year or more. Then, talking about something I'd written for television, The Lord said to me, "I still think my stuff would have worked." He didn't like to be beaten by anything.

But this wasn't the kind of thing I wanted to remember,

standing on the rocks at the Forty Foot, looking out at Dublin Bay where we'd sailed every Saturday afternoon before the war, racing in an old 21-foot cutter called the *Garavogue*. The Lord would never give up, even long after the evening breeze had died away into a flat calm and the ebb had begun to carry us south past Dalkey Island, getting farther and farther away every minute from the finishing line in Dun Laoghaire Harbour. "We'll just hang on a bit longer," he'd always say. "There'll be a puff of wind sooner or later."

My sister and I, with a party to go to in Dublin, would beg him to let us get the sweeps out and row ourselves back into the harbour, and the Lord would put on his grim and injured look. Once again we were being irresponsible and feeble-minded.

He loved sailing and was for ever inventing methods of marking the sheets with coloured thread so that, after we'd won a race, almost entirely by luck, we'd be able to reproduce the same winning trim again.

He had a passion for games of every kind and, failing the proper equipment, he would improvise a completely new one out of an old biscuit tin, a piece of wood and a tennis ball and play it with a fanatical regard for the rules which we invented as we went along.

He could read three detective stories in an evening with such complete absorption that he might have been under a general anaesthetic and when he'd finished them he could give you neither a glimmering of the plots nor the name of a single character. He relied on the girls in Switzers Library to give him one he hadn't read before and when they slipped up he'd read as many as twenty pages before realising what had happened.

He adored the company of pretty women, without going too far out of his way to look for it. He had a teasing, flirtatious way with them that often reduced the less resilient to tears. Their failure to appreciate that this teasing was a form of love-making left him feeling injured and depressed, so much so that he would sometimes, during the weekends, retire to bed with his detective story as early as four o'clock in the afternoon.

Once, he astonished me by saying, "When it comes to kissing the Campbells run away." In his case it was almost certainly true.

Or perhaps it wasn't.

I never really knew him at all.

I never even knew whether he was disappointed to find that neither my brother Michael nor I had any capacity for business or banking. Michael did make an attempt at a professional career by being called to the Irish Bar, after studying law in Trinity, but he never practised. Like myself, he was eased into a job on the *Irish Times* by the Lord, who was an old friend of the editor, Robert Smyllie. Indeed, if it hadn't been for the *Irish Times*, it's difficult to tell what would have become of either of his sons.

Yet the Lord's disappointment—if disappointed he was—never took the conventional, demanding form. He did say to me once that he should perhaps have been fiercer with me, making me train for a profession, and with Michael, compelling him to go on with the law. But being fierce with people was never his way. I think he laid out in his mind an ideal course of behaviour for everyone he knew and cared about and felt personally injured when they failed to live up to it. And to get them back on the rails he used persuasion so oblique and delicate, and with such concern for their *amour propre*, that it was often difficult to perceive that the process was going on at all.

I suddenly remembered an old gardener who'd got into an incomprehensible tangle with a seed merchant, ordering enough bulbs to fill the whole of Phoenix Park. My father straightened out the mess in a couple of minutes. The old gardener paid him a tribute straight from his heart.

"His Lordship," he told me with love, "could mind mice at a crossroads."

The sun was going down behind the Dublin Mountains. The sea, washing round the rocks of the Forty Foot, was turning grey and cold. I began to walk back to the house.

It seems to be extraordinary, looking back upon it now, but on the night of my father's death my mother and I, and Marjorie, went to a party—a wedding reception for Willy Ganly's daughter, Clodagh.

There wasn't any discussion about it. We just went.

The party took place in a hotel about a mile away. There must have been a hundred or more people, nearly all of whom I'd known for years, and yet I can't remember one of them speaking to me about my father, who'd died that afternoon at

3.30. Willy must have told some of them about it, yet no one mentioned his name.

Or perhaps I wasn't aware of it. I was still totally preoccupied with the business of trying to file away, permanently, everything I could remember about him, in the hope that by doing so I could fill in the enormous gaps in my knowledge of what he had been, and of what he had done.

For a long time I got trapped in a corner by one of those ancient, over-dressed and over-painted Protestant ladies who seem to decorate the Dublin social scene for ever. She wanted to tell me, without stint, that nothing I'd written since had been one half as good as the stuff I used to write in the Irishman's Diary column in the *Irish Times*. It was almost a pleasure to have this babble going on, because it was so familiar. It made no intrusion upon my private filing process. At one moment I said to the lady, "Irish people can't bear a fellow Irishman to make the smallest success in another country," but I was really remembering how gloriously funny my father had been.

There was a Sunday supper party and an actress friend called Shelagh Richards had been talking at length about another old friend, Alan Duncan. Alan had long ago retired from Dublin and was living in considerably disordered poverty in Paris, on a tiny British Army pension.

"And then," said Shelagh, in full flood, "poor old Duncan met me at the Gare du Nord—"

The Lord's intervention was perfectly timed, the note of haughty reproof most beautifully performed.

"Captain—from you, please," he said.

I must have been about eleven or twelve at the time, but I remember with absolute clarity the instant of silence that fell upon everyone, and then the great roar of laughter that followed.

And then I remembered something else. A couple of days later the cook, a savage old woman with a beetroot-coloured face, had been talking to me about 'all the queer lookin' people that does be comin' to this house', and suddenly—and splendidly—I heard her say, "What ever happened to that fella wit' the long hair on him—wasn't it Misther Duncan?"

"Captain—from you, please," I said.

I was astonished a moment later to receive a belt on the ear from Bridie that knocked me flat on my back on the kitchen table.

I never had the time or the opportunity to tell the Lord about that, like so many other things, but I almost knew how he would have taken it. He wouldn't have tried, as many other people would have done, to extract still more juice from it by analysing, however amusingly, the various attitudes involved. He would just have grinned, the sad eyes would have lit up and we would both have had a moment of perfect pleasure.

I found my mother and Marjorie standing beside me. They looked strained and exhausted. It had been a long day. I said, "We'll have a quick dinner downstairs in the restaurant and then we'll go home."

It was better than sitting down to eat in our own dining-room, with whatever the nurse had left behind in the bed upstairs.

The restaurant was full, but the head waiter said he would have a table for us in a few minutes, if we'd like to have a drink at the bar.

"What name is it, sir?" he said to me.

Neither my mother nor Marjorie looked at me, but the three of us knew that this was the time—the very first time—to try it out.

"Lord—" I said, and then my stammer came against me. It was an appreciable second or two before I could say, "Glenavy".

"Thank you, my lord," said the head waiter, and went away.

My mother gave a little laugh that might have been the product as much of pride as of embarrassment.

"You'd better get used to being it," she said.

But I knew I never would. I knew now with certainty that my father had been the last, real Lord Glenavy, as his father before him had been a real Lord. They had been great men, with soberly distinguished careers, who by large and public services had merited, in full, the honours and dignities that had come to them.

The disagreeable glow of self-importance had altogether gone.

To keep up my own end as Patrick Campbell would be the best I could manage from now on, and however good it turned out to be I knew I could never take over from the second Baron Glenavy, even if I lived, like him, to be almost eighty years of age.

Nor did I, any longer, feel like the head of the family. The sense of being the busy, efficient organiser and arranger had gone. From now on the most that I was there to do was to try to help my mother.

I met her outside the Lord's room the following morning.

"Did you—go and look at him—during the night?" she asked me.

"No."

"Neither did I."

We went downstairs to breakfast.

Archie and Willy arrived about an hour before the hearse. They were calm and efficient, hiding their own private grief. I couldn't even guess at the amount of work that Archie had done, in arranging the funeral. I tried to thank him, for everything. He said, "That's all right."

When the hearse arrived, backing into the short drive in front of the house, they went upstairs with the undertaker. My mother and I sat in front of the fire in the living-room. I talked about last night's party, trying to distract her attention from the noise above.

After rather a long time we heard the bumping of the coffin being carried down the narrow stairs, and then the sound of feet on the gravel outside.

After a few more minutes Archie came into the living-room, with Willie behind him. They were both very quiet, keeping a tight control on themselves. Willie's face was ghastly. I could almost imagine what he'd gone through upstairs.

Archie said, "The hearse is just leaving."

My mother said, "I don't think I want to see it."

I said, "Come on. We'd better."

My mother stood up. "You're quite right," she said. "One should always see everything."

The hearse was brilliantly black in the narrow drive, and seemed to be almost completely covered with flowers.

My mother said, "Look at all the flowers. Where did they all come from?"

The back doors of the hearse were still open. The coffin, inside, was very shiny, in some light wood, like oak. The whole equipage seemed to be much too highly polished, for the Lord.

Very clearly, in my own mind, I said to my father, "Get up out of that silly thing and come and play croquet."

Then the undertaker closed the doors and the hearse drove away, along the shore of Dublin Bay, to the church in Dun Laoghaire.

My mother went straight upstairs to my father's room, pulled the curtains back and opened all the windows. Then she pulled the bed away from the wall, turned it round and put it with its head against the one opposite.

In the living-room I gave her an inch of brandy, with a little soda. She sat in her usual place by the fire. She sipped her drink. Suddenly, she said, "He just got tired of wearing that old overcoat."

I was surprised. It didn't sound like her. She smiled apologetically. "That nice young clergyman, Mr. Day, said it last night." Then she made one of her positive judgements. "I think it's rather good."

After a moment I said, "That's what it was. Just tired of wearing his old overcoat. That's all that happened."

Chapter Two

ABOUT an hour before my father's funeral service my mother said, "Perhaps I can't go to the church looking like this."

Her hat and coat were lying on the arm of the chair. Two shades of beige. Her dress was of the same oatmeal colour. I'd once referred to her exceedingly modest wardrobe as 'variations on the theme of porridge'. She'd thought the description exact, and felt not at all wounded. For years her only interest in clothes had been that they should be comfortable and anonymous.

"I never go out anywhere," was her contention, "so I don't really need them."

In fact, she did go out quite often, to lunch parties, art exhibitions or the theatre, but on these occasions she could have worn an old dressing-gown without anyone noticing. Her own burning interest in what was going on, her hungry curiosity, her passionate concern with the world outside herself meant that it didn't matter in the least what she wore.

She was telling me once about an opening at the Royal Hibernian Academy and said, "there was poor ———, wearing a hat looking like a beehive splattered with custard and thinking everyone was looking at her when just behind her on the wall was a hideous but terribly interesting picture by Louis le Brocquy."

But now, probably for the first time for as long as she could remember, she felt the pressure of convention.

"But I never had anything black in my life," she told us.

Marjorie, always completely competent in any emergency, said, "Dorothy left a coat behind. Come on and we'll try it."

She'd always had a passion for dressing up. There were dozens of earlier photographs of her in the family albums wearing the Lord's clothes, or a bowler hat with an immense walrus moustache. Before moving into her comparatively decorous sixties she'd always been a marvellously funny clown, keeping always the true dignity of a clown—a rare capacity in a woman.

"Come on," she said to my mother, "and we'll see what we've got."

They went upstairs and for ten minutes or so I heard giggles and laughter and protestations. They might have been dressing up for one of the charades that Marjorie had always revelled in. Then there was rather a long silence, and after it the sound of my mother coming slowly downstairs.

I turned to face the door, preparing for the shock of seeing her, for the first time, in funeral clothes.

She came into the room wearing the familiar oatmeal dress and over it an even lighter coat. She gave me an embarrassed smile, which was also apologetic.

"I looked a fool dressed up in black," she said, "so I'll wear this. Anyway, I'm not a widow—I'm a bride."

I remembered that she and my father had got married fifty years ago on the previous day.

"You'll do grand like that," I said. Then I remembered something else. "I haven't got a black tie," I said. "I'd better go out and buy one."

My mother said, immediately, "The Lord's got dozens of them up in his room. He was always going to funerals."

After a moment, I said, "I think I'd better go out and buy a new one."

I walked up Ballygehin Avenue to the bus route, to the small haberdasher's on the corner, thinking that this was the way the Lord had come every weekday morning, on his way in to the Bank.

He'd travelled to the Bank by bus for years, sharing them—at 10 o'clock in the morning—with housewives going shopping with yelling babies, the essence of discomfort, to my mind. But he always found it more agreeable than driving a car in Dublin traffic, and he had this strange affinity with very young children.

When they were living at Rockbrook he used to drive the seven or eight miles down to the bus terminus in Terenure. He told me once, with great pleasure, "Two little boys outside Doyle's cottage on the corner have it in for me. Every time they see the car coming they yell, 'Dere's Dord Dendavy—t'row de mud.' And they do."

His normally gloomy face shone for a moment with pure delight.

And this, now, was the small suburban road he'd walked up

every weekday morning, with the whizzer probably already beginning to do its work.

It used to take him the best part of a couple of hours to have breakfast in bed, get up and shave and have a bath. It was the time he did his thinking, about the farmer in Mullingar or about the approach of yet another weighty Swede. And suddenly, then, he'd find it was later than he thought and he'd come hurrying downstairs in a state of disorder, his hands full of papers and telephone messages and the gardener's wages and for several minutes he'd deliver a stream of instructions to anyone who happened to be present, the right forefinger bent and stabbing the air for emphasis.

Most of the things he wanted done had been done already, or were things that only he could do. Everyone waited patiently for the storm to subside, while making gentle and meaningless sounds of assent.

The Lord would then shoot a desperate look at the big clock in the hall. It was always kept twenty minutes ahead of the real time, but it never got him out of the house before ten. Then, wearing his strange, grey Homburg hat—the only Homburg I'd ever seen that was turned down in the front—he'd stride into the dining-room and, still with the hat on his head, dive into the drink cupboard in the corner.

In the recesses of this cupboard he'd pour himself a large glass of gin, throw in a splash of lime juice and lower the whole lot in a single gulp. He never drank very much but this 'whizzer', as he called it, a little defensively, was as much a part of his morning routine as the brushing of his teeth.

That strange, grey Homburg hat. I'd always felt he'd invented his own clothes. They had an odd, home-made look about them. The white bawneen trousers he'd bought in Galway that were like two large and solid cylinders from ankle to waist. The heavy, practical shoes that his feet twisted into their own unique shape within a week. And the suit.

One evening the Lord came home from the Bank looking, for once, almost elegant in a dark-blue suit—a sharp change from his usual, shapeless grey. No one had seen him leave the house in the morning, so that for a moment I thought he must have bought it in Dublin. But there was something odd about it. It didn't look new.

He sat in his usual chair by the window and settled down to

the extreme pleasure of analysing the racing results in the *Evening Herald*.

After a moment he gave one of those convulsive sneezes which were his speciality, and reached for the handkerchief in his breast pocket, while continuing to read the paper. He couldn't find the handkerchief.

My mother and I had both been watching him, but she was the one who was brave enough to speak.

"Your handkerchief's on the other side," she said.

Slowly, the Lord looked up over the top of his paper with the look of puzzlement, and of indignation, which was normal to him when interrupted in his reading. He looked at my mother, as though trying to work out in his own mind whether or not she was speaking English.

"Your handkerchief," she explained. "It's in your breast pocket —on the other side."

The Lord reached for the handkerchief, as if he'd known where it was all along, blew his nose and resumed his study of the paper.

It was not a thing that my mother could let go. Her curiosity, as usual, was too great to allow her to be diplomatic.

"I thought men's breast pockets were always on the left," she said. "Why is yours on the right?"

The Lord put down his paper. He addressed us with board-room solemnity. "I had Paddy's suit turned," he said, and sat there fully armoured against whatever might happen next.

I was so surprised that I, too, forgot to be careful.

"Where did you find it?" I asked him.

"It was wrapped up in a parcel in the hall."

"But I was going to give it to Mrs. Donovan, for her husband," my mother said. "I thought she'd taken it. He's out of work."

'There's plenty of good wear in it still," said the Lord, and went back to the *Evening Herald*.

What a strange and lovely man.

In his honour, in the little haberdasher's shop, I bought a horrible, shiny, string-like black tie for 5s. 11d. It was the only one they'd got. Rather than wear such a thing himself—he hated all synthetic fabrics—he would probably have tried to make one out of some piece of black cloth, sewing enormous, irregular stitches in the privacy of his bedroom and throwing it away, with a sense of injury, when he found it didn't work.

Back at the house Willy and Archie had once again arrived, bringing with them, as usual, the comforting sense that all the details of the funeral had been attended to. Now all that my mother and I had to do was to endure it.

Marjorie came downstairs, wearing a black coat and a small, black straw hat. The coat was probably the one belonging to Dorothy that my mother had rejected.

Archie had one brief, troubled look at my mother's oatmeal ensemble, but he said nothing.

Marjorie, my mother and I got into the chief mourner's car, a shiny black Cadillac of endless length dating from the years when they still had the giant tail-fins. We drove slowly and in silence along the coast road, to the church in Dun Laoghaire.

There seemed to be a lot of people, mostly men, standing about outside the church in their best clothes. At the gate, talking to one another confidentially, were two high-ranking—by the scarlet flashes on their collars—officers of the Irish Army.

My mother, Marjorie and I got out of the huge car and stood uncertainly for a moment on the pavement. The two officers approached us. One of them went straight up to Marjorie and saluted gravely.

"I represent the President, my Lady," he said. "He wishes me to present his deepest sympathy."

Marjorie stared at him in astonishment.

It was my mother who saw what had happened. Marjorie, dressed in black, must surely be the widow.

My mother put out her hand. *"I,"* she said in a stately voice, "am the Dowager Lady Glenavy."

The Colonel—we discovered his rank next day from the *Irish Times*—was so taken aback that it seemed for a moment he was going to take off his cap. Then he changed it into a kind of half-salute and finished up by bowing over her hand.

"Please tell Mr. de Valera," said my mother, "I'm very grateful."

The other Colonel also bowed. "Mr. Sean Lemass," he said, "and the other members of the Government wish me to add their condolences to those of the President."

The mix-up over Marjorie didn't matter any longer. I was overwhelmed to find that my father had been recognised by the

President and by the Prime Minister of the Irish Republic, although of course I should have expected it. But it seemed to take him away from us, to turn him into some kind of monument.

For as long as I could remember the Lord had been corrosively scathing about de Valera and his Fianna Fail party, talking about 'the utter hopelessness of trying to get a bunch of ex-gunmen to understand even the rudimentary basis of economics', and here now de Valera and Sean Lemass were presenting their sympathy on his death.

It made him into the public figure that he'd been for many years, the public figure we'd never really appreciated or understood.

I took my mother's arm and we walked slowly into the church. The first thing I saw was the shiny, pale coffin, with its head pointing towards the altar. I looked away instinctively, knowing that the Lord wouldn't like to feel that his family were watching him, giving so public a performance, and then I saw that the church was full, right into the gloom of the last row of pews. I saw a few familiar faces, but most of them were strange to me. They were the faces of the businessmen, the farmers, the trades union officials, the cattle dealers, the industrialists and the politicians—all the men who'd known the value of his public life so much better than I.

My mother and I, with Marjorie beside us, knelt for a moment in the front pew and then we sat back, unable to take our eyes off the coffin, now that it stood so squarely in front of us.

I became aware of organ music and looked to see where it was coming from. There was a small organ on the left of the altar. Above it I could just see the small, polished bald head of my mother's cousin, Jack Elvery. He was playing a strange kind of preoccupied, thoughtful lament that rose at times to a note of strident but controlled protest, before resuming its grumbling theme. The music went on and on, showing no sign of approaching a finale.

I whispered to my mother, "What's Jack playing?"

She whispered back, "He's making it up."

"It sounds exactly like the Lord talking."

She nodded, and we both struggled with tears. But even through the tears I was thinking with pleasure of the Lord's astonishment, if he could have heard what Jack was doing for him.

Ever since I'd been a child Jack had been in charge of the Elvery's shop in Nassau Street, a sports outfitters that sold everything from trout rods to remarkably dowdy cardigans for elderly ladies. There was another branch in O'Connell Street which was looked after, to even less effect, by Jack's brother, Fred.

The Lord moved in on the business, to try to resurrect it, for the good and sufficient reason that my mother, as an Elvery, held a substantial proportion of the shares. If the dividends could be increased by better business methods it would be another small insurance against the bankruptcy that seemed to threaten us every day. And yet in this, as in all his commercial enterprises, the Lord was not seeking only personal profit. He was also thinking of all the other Elvery sisters and brothers and cousins, all over the world, who needed even more urgently a boost in their incomes.

He ran head on into Jack Elvery. For centuries, it seemed, Jack had been sitting behind the huge, littered desk in the back part of the shop in Nassau Street, getting in the way of better business methods, and insisting on the continued employment of ancient assistants who should have been pensioned off years ago. "They know where the stuff is," Jack would say, indicating the mass of broken cardboard boxes that littered every shelf in the place.

"I went in there the other day," the Lord told me once, "wanting to buy a couple of golf-balls, and there was Jack behind the desk scratching away in a mound of papers, looking for something that didn't matter a damn to anyone. I asked him for a couple of Dunlops and he went on rootling through his papers. Then he looked up and said, absolutely cheerfully, 'Dunlops? My dear chap, we haven't seen a Dunlop in weeks. Same thing with Silver King. Simply can't get 'em. Tell you what you do, though. Just nip round the corner to Hely's. They've got boxes and boxes of them there. Dunlops *and* Silver Kings'."

Hely's were then Elverys' only competitors in the sports goods trade in Dublin.

Jack was equally provocative at board meetings, into which the Lord had inserted two capable directors of his own choice. "We'd at long last," he said, "got something straightened out, some practical proposal agreed to, and then we'd ask Jack for his opinion. He only had one. 'I'm not satisfied,' he'd say. 'I'm not satisfied at all.' Utterly hopeless," the Lord would say, with gloomy but profound relish. And then he'd go on to add, with even deeper satisfaction, "Jack also turned down the Irish agency for the Yo-Yo. He said no one would want to buy a fiddlefaw like that."

But here now was Jack Elvery, who was never satisfied, who never had any golf-balls and who had turned down the Yo-Yo, playing a lament for the Lord on the organ, a lament that sounded exactly like the Lord's own voice.

I could just see his small, pale face below the polished, bald head. Jack must have been nearly eighty years of age but he was composing and playing his music with fire and passion, all the emotions of a young man.

The Lord, I thought, would have been well satisfied. One of his many ineffective methods of attacking kitchen gossip was suddenly to shout, in a lull, "You lot—either tell me a thing I didn't know before, or didn't think you were capable of saying!"

Almost certainly, he never would have thought that Jack was capable of saying what he was saying now.

Mr. Day, my mother's 'nice young clergyman', began to recite the funeral service, and all at once I found there was a new aspect of my father to be considered.

I hadn't been inside a church since compulsory attendance at school. I'd forgotten about, or ceased to be consciously aware of, the faith that insists that we are all children of God.

It was extraordinary to hear my father referred to as— 'Gordon Glenavy, Thy son'. I'd never thought of him as being anyone's son, not even the Old Lord's. But on the other hand I was very much his. However little I might have known about his public life, at home he was my father beyond any possible doubt. Though we might laugh at turned suits and incomprehensible instructions, he always had the fundamental dignity and authority of a father, and a father's generosity in the dispensation of gifts to his children.

I must have been nearly fifty when I'd last played golf with him, yet he'd come out of the pro's shop with a couple of new golf balls for me.

"Better put those in your bag," he said, with the diffidence that afflicted him when he was giving us any kind of present. Then he added, even further to reduce the importance of the gesture, "They might come in useful."

In the bar afterwards he insisted on buying both rounds of drinks. "And," he told the barman, "you'd better give my son another large one. There's a lot of him."

As the words of the funeral service unfolded I began to get a frightened feeling—or it was nearly fear—that the Lord and I had missed something, had deprived ourselves of something that might have nourished us a very great deal, by standing away from religion. It might have warmed both our natures, where warmth was not an outstanding ingredient.

It was too late for me now. The habit of irony was too deeply ingrained. But the sense of living with a missing limb persisted.

The educated, Protestant voice of Mr. Day filled the church :

"I know that my Redeemer liveth, and that he shall stand at the latter day upon the earth. And though after my skin worms destroy this body, yet in my flesh shall I see God : whom I shall see for myself, and mine eyes shall behold, and not another."

It didn't sound like a belief that the Lord, with his objective intellectualism and high capacity for amusing self-mockery, could have held. That self-mockery of his didn't come from humility, but from what always looked like a pretty solid conviction that he was invulnerable to criticism and was therefore in a position to provide entertainment by criticising himself, in flights of fancy that bore less and less relation to the truth, with advancing years.

The moment passed. My heart closed up again. Wherever the Lord was now, I thought, and whatever might be the nature of the inquisition he was facing, he was dealing with it in his thoughtful, calm and rational way which, for all its calm and rationality, still contained an emotional element of injury—almost injured innocence—as though only people of malicious disposition could find a motive for questioning him.

But it still wasn't much consolation for something which I knew—and would always know from now on—that we'd both missed.

Suddenly, Monk Gibbon was standing at the lectern, looking strangely smart in a dark suit, his vigorous, grey-white hair unusually neatly brushed.

He began to read, in an emphatic, powerful, actor-like voice.

"Remember now thy Creator in the days of thy youth, while the evil days come not, nor the years draw nigh, when thou shalt say, I have no pleasure in them—"

After my parents had moved to Sandycove, Monk, who lived round the corner, had become an indispensable part of my mother's life.

As a writer, he kept her in touch with the world of books, pouring out his opinions in a non-stop, bounding flood. Even before he became ill, the Lord had been a somewhat morose companion. Monk provided my mother with the vitality, the running commentary on the life of Dublin, even the kitchen gossip, that she loved.

"And the splendid thing about Monk," she told me, "is he's completely uninsultable."

Monk's uninsultability was fairly frequently put to the test. At times my mother, whose delight it was to keep open house for everyone, would suddenly feel that she was being put upon, being used by people who weren't properly appreciative.

"You," she told Monk, in one of these unexpected flare-ups, "you and your enormous family only use this house for eating and drinking, and some of you don't even speak while you're doing it."

That broadside caused Monk to disappear for a week. Then he came bounding round the following Sunday evening, with news too vital to be kept to himself.

A woman's body had been found in the sea near the Forty Foot a couple of nights before, with her stocking tied round her throat.

"Beattie," Monk boomed from the door, his eyes alight with joy, "I don't want a drink and my family aren't coming to dinner, but we've all just been interrogated for hours by the police."

"I know," said my mother, in a satisfied voice. "They came here first and I sent them round to you."

The two friends were friends once more.

Monk's great voice echoed round the church.

"Or ever the silver cord be loosed, or the golden bowl be broken, or the pitcher be broken at the fountain, or the wheel broken at the cistern. Then shall the dust return to the earth as it was, and the spirit shall return unto God who gave it."

Once again the feeling came to me that my father had been taken over by other people, that his death had made him public property.

If, for instance, the Lord had been alive I don't think Monk would have got very much further with his reading from Ecclesiastes.

The Lord, who was probably envious of Monk's inexhaustible vitality and equally inexhaustible good nature, treated him, openly, as a small and noisy boy, to be tolerated only when he was silent and even then only for short periods of time.

If Monk had been reckless enough to begin reading aloud in his presence, the Lord would certainly have watched him for a moment over the top of his detective story, softening up the victim, and then have said, in the gentle voice that reduced the pretty women to tears—the gentle voice that contained so much more malice than he really intended—"Monk, why don't you go and do that in the garden? In your own garden, I mean."

"The preacher sought to find out acceptable words: and that which was written was upright, even words of truth. The words of the wise are as goads, and as nails fastened by the masters of assemblies, which are given from one shepherd."

The choice of this last chapter of Ecclesiastes had been made by Monk and my mother. It was as exactly right as Jack's music.

It seemed to me that all the people who'd been wary of the Lord, and specially wary of his tongue, had in fact loved and understood him, and it was sad that he had to be dead before they could tell him so.

Once again, these convoluted admonitions sounded so like my father talking.

"The words of the wise are as goads, and as nails fastened by the masters of assemblies, which are given from one shepherd."

I didn't know what it meant, but it was the Lord all right. He was certainly the master of the assembly that was gathered every Christmas Day around the remnants of the lunch table. The assembly consisted of my brother and myself, and it was convened by the Lord in his usual diffident and conspiratorial fashion.

Before lunch he'd say to me, very privately, something like, "We'd better have a bit of a chat about money, after lunch. If you could get Michael to stay . . ."

Like myself, Michael would not have missed these occasions for anything.

The subject under review was the avoidance of death duties, and the imperative need for the Lord to hand over to Michael and myself the monies held in the Glenavy Trust. The Lord always called them 'the monies', probably with the intention of giving them the sacrosanct and untouchable quality of the Crown Jewels.

He would begin, every Christmas Day, by reviewing the history of the Trust, Michael and I having another brandy and the Lord pouring himself a second bottle of stout.

The opening theme was always the hopeless situation that had been created by the Old Lord's will. So far as Michael and I could make out, the old Lord, in the last years of his life, had lost a great deal of money on the Stock Exchange, but had taken no account of this in his will. In fact, he hadn't left sufficient 'monies' to cover his numerous bequests.

At this point Michael would sometimes say, in a carefully casual manner, "How much did he leave?"—and the Lord would reply that he'd come to that in a moment.

The next and equally appalling facet of the situation was the clause in the Old Lord's will that said that 'the monies' in the Trust should go to the holder of the title of Lord Glenavy.

"This," said the Lord, with evident satisfaction, "has given Archie and myself some fearful headaches. Legally, you see, Paddy, I can't give it to you until you're Lord Glenavy and—" the bent forefinger would come out, gently stabbing the air— "you won't be Lord Glenavy until I've passed on."

He would look at both of us intently, to see if we had any glimmering of understanding of this abstruse and complex point.

Michael and I would nod, our brows furrowed in concentration, trying not to meet one another's eye.

"But, you see," the Lord would go on, "if I—pass—on before —doing something about it, you and Michael are going to be absolutely bankrupted by the appalling death duties."

"They'd be pretty big?" I'd suggest.

"Yes. So Archie and I have been working night and day to try to find some way out of the mess. I must say, Archie's been marvellous, but it's killing him. He's not looking at all well. At this rate he'll go before I do and then we'll all be finally ruined."

At this point Michael and I knew we would be safe in sitting back and abandoning for another year all hope of discovering anything about our financial prospects. The Lord had worked himself into his favourite morass, buried so deeply in a pit of troubles that he could see no gleam of hope anywhere, and determined to make it impossible for either of us to do anything else except join him.

For the next half hour he would give us a review of the prohibitive cost of running the house. "Beattie's got to have a car and the cook's wages have gone up and the fence has fallen down in the lower field . . ." From these domestic burdens he would pass to more serious matters. They were always centred around his certainty that in the next couple of months he would be stripped of all his directorships. "They don't like Protestants, you see, and they can't wait to get me out." In this welter of approaching disaster, however, he was prepared to give us one piece of good news. "I suppose the Bank would probably keep me on, as I'm the only person that knows anything about it." But it was instantly neutralised by the threat of a greater catastrophe than any we'd been faced with yet—the threat not merely of personal bankruptcy, but of bankruptcy on a national scale.

"This present Government," the Lord would say, savouring every word, "simply hasn't got the faintest idea what it's doing. Lemass is all right but the rest of them couldn't run a village shop in—in Ballyslumgullion. The trade figures are appalling. They're recklessly importing every kind of trivial foreign luxury at prohibitive cost and all they can do in exchange is send a few flea-bitten cows to England. Within the next couple of months you'll see the biggest economic crash here since the American Depression and then God knows what will become of Beattie—"

Michael and I always knew that the prospect of Beattie scrubbing floors in abject penury was an indication that the Lord was feeling better and that the talk had almost come to an end. This would be confirmed when he'd suddenly say, "Anyway, you and Michael don't have to worry. There's plenty of money there."

In some curious way this reassurance seemed to be the logical outcome of all that had gone before. Then the Lord would say, reaching for the brandy, "Give me a swash of that stuff there." He'd pour himself half a glassful, throw it straight down, and say, "I suppose we'd better try a bit of croquet before the rain."

Another assembly had come to an end, leaving Michael and

myself as totally ignorant of the financial situation and of what, if anything, was going to be done about it, as before.

Then an extraordinary thing happened. One day, in the bar of the Grange Golf Club, the Lord suddenly said to me, out of the blue, "Well, it seems that the Campbells are solvent at last."

I could only imagine that the news was so good that for once he was unable to keep it to himself, or to turn it into his usual recital of despair.

I said, "What's happened?"

"It's these marvellous stockbrokers. They've been making some pretty useful investments."

"How much have we got?"

But the question was too direct. Like a flat-fish, menaced by the approach of some predator, the Lord began to scuffle himself into the sand.

"Very difficult to say. You see, these appalling death duties. It's a very difficult situation. I'll probably have to go and live in England or Tahiti or somewhere. Archie and I are working at it night and day."

"Have one on me, anyway, to celebrate our solvency."

"No, no," said the Lord, taken by surprise and suddenly concerned. "I'll do this. You keep your money. You'll probably need it."

"Let us hear the conclusion of the whole matter," Monk read in his powerful voice. "Fear God and keep His commandments: for this is the whole duty of man. For God shall bring every work into judgement, with every secret thing whether it be good, or whether it be evil."

He stood at the lectern for a moment, looking down at the big Bible. Then he closed it. It was the last thing he could do for Gordon Campbell. I guessed he was sorry he'd been unable to do more.

I can't remember the rest of the service. Perhaps it came to an end then. But all at once I was holding my mother's elbow as we walked out of the church behind the coffin.

It seemed almost unnecessary to disturb the Lord again, after his peaceful and solitary night in the church. It was as though we'd buried him there, with Jack's music and the funeral service and Monk's requiem, but the coffin had still to be put into the ground in Glasnevin, where soon there would be a headstone with my mother's beautiful lettering saying that the second Lord Glenavy was now lying here beside the first.

Very shortly there would be only a grave, and memory, and nothing else. It was impossible for us to restrain our tears.

My mother got into the back of the car with Marjorie. The door was still open when Eric Mieville, almost running, came out of the churchyard. He seized my mother's hand. He was unable to speak. The tears were running down his face.

My mother pressed his hand. She, too, could say nothing. Then Eric shut the door and the long, black car moved off.

Eric Mieville was one of the few people for whom the Lord had expressed unqualified admiration and affection. The fact that they met infrequently no doubt assisted their relationship a good deal.

Eric was all the things that the Lord wasn't and would probably have liked to be, if he hadn't been himself.

"He's the perfect Renaissance man," the Lord said to me. "The complete all-rounder."

Before the Hitler war Eric had been a major in the French Foreign Legion, and still retained the uniform for special public occasions in Dublin. During the war he'd been one of those mysterious, lone-handed adventurers that every war throws up. In his maddeningly evasive and mock-modest way he'd tell us of his part in the kidnapping of Otto Scorzeny from his prison in the Italian Alps and then go on, as though it were part of the same story, to sketch in a gun-running deal with an Arab state that was never precisely named.

The Lord would listen to him in silent glee, with a look almost of pride on his face. He very much liked Eric's laconic, allusive way of telling a story of heroism and dangerous adventure. It was the way he would have told it himself, if he'd ever become involved in such escapades.

Eric seemed to have known every beautiful woman in Europe. He spoke every European language and could talk art, literature, religion and philosophy as profoundly as the Lord himself.

He'd come to Ireland at the end of the war to create, at Bally-keane, a stud-farm of incredible elegance and efficiency, drilling his yard-boys and farm-hands into a condition of Swiss cleanliness and precision that was unique in a country with no great partiality for either of these virtues.

The Lord had a passion for rough gardening, breaking up old rockeries or tearing out patches of brambles. The result was never quite perfect, but it made him happy to know that he'd done it all by himself. Eric's capacity to give orders to Irish labourers and to see them achieve a result almost beyond perfection was always a source of wonder and pleasure to the Lord.

"I swear to you," he said to me, "the gravel in front of Eric's house must be raked three times a day by men on hands and knees, with hair-combs. I don't know how he gets them to do it."

He probably didn't realise that his own gardeners and casual labourers were just as devoted to him, and might have achieved the same kind of result if he'd been as stern with them as Eric was with his. But that wasn't the Lord's way. He could only give an order by roundabout suggestion, making it seem, if possible, that it was the man's own idea. And, always, the whole enterprise would be so wrapped in humorous fantasy that no one could be quite sure if he meant it or not.

"In the end," he would say, "we'll probably have to borrow a couple of pile-drivers from the Great Northern Railway, but you have a go at it with your shovel first."

They'd touch their caps, laughing delightedly, and then hold anxious deliberations among themselves after he'd gone.

My mother and I were walking along a path in Glasnevin Cemetery towards an untidy pile of earth and planks that looked very like one of the Lord's major reconstructions. The grass on either side of the path was long and ragged. It would have given him the greatest pleasure in the world to bring it to order, strewing the scene with all manner of lawn-mowers, shears and scissors, working away on his own on a summer evening, long after the sun had gone down, and long after he'd been summoned to dinner.

In the sunshine, and amid the litter left by the grave-diggers, the burial service was quick and seemed unnecessary. The young clergyman in his white surplice looked altogether out of place in this rough and ready garden, the symbolism of the sprinkling of the earth altogether too perfunctory.

My mother and I just wanted the whole thing to be over now, and grass growing on whatever was left in the coffin. I took her back to the car before the grave-diggers began to fill in the earth. I think it was the most desolate moment that either of us had yet endured.

Back home again she took her usual place in the sofa by the fire, and I gave her her inch of brandy and soda. After a moment I saw that she was smiling. When she saw me looking at her she said, "I was just thinking—Dev must have had a terrible job to find two Protestant Colonels in the Irish Army."

It meant that the time had come to begin again, that the tears were over and that we now had to try to find out what the house would be like, what life would be like, now that the Lord had left it for ever.

Archie and Willy again appeared, Archie with the keys of the small safe which had sat for years in the ground-floor room which my mother used as a studio.

Archie said, "I don't suppose there'll be anything in it. Your father and I went through all the papers that were of any importance some time ago. Oh, by the way, you'd better sign this."

It was a death certificate. It said that my father had died of cancer, of the stomach and liver. It was impossible to imagine how he'd kept himself alive for so long.

Willy, as one of the Trustees, followed me into my mother's studio. Archie opened the safe. There were a number of sheets of lined foolscap paper, covered with my father's beautiful handwriting. They looked quite like the six television plays he'd sent me for Charlie Drake.

Archie glanced through them.

At the back of the safe I found a small ring with a cheap stone in it, almost the kind of thing a young girl might buy for herself in Woolworths. There was nothing else. I put the ring back in the safe. It didn't matter any more.

Archie said, "These are only some notes your father made about the question of death duties. They don't apply any longer."

He tore up the sheets of foolscap.

There was nothing left of my father's private life.

The business of the funeral had caused my mother, for once, to forget to order anything for dinner. Marjorie said she'd go into Dun Laoghaire and buy a chicken.

My mother said, "Paddy could drive you, in the Lord's car.

He usually leaves the keys in the little tray on his dressing-table."

She still didn't fully realise he was dead.

Marjorie and I went to to his room. It was impossible not to have a feeling of intrusion, despite the open windows and the sunshine and the bowl of fresh flowers on the table.

In the little tray where the keys should have been there was only a broken pipe and a kind of home-made, brass cigarette lighter.

Marjorie was very brisk and businesslike, making it better for both of us. "Have a look in his suits," she said. "I'll try the drawers." She began opening them, one by one.

I went through the pockets of my father's clothes, the shapeless grey tweed suits, the corduroy gardening trousers, the white bawneen pair from Galway, as stiff and cylindrical as ever. I was glad not to find my own turned suit. But there was no trace of the car keys. All the pockets were completely empty, a strange neatness in a casually untidy man. He must have cleared them out himself, perhaps one afternoon when the pain had driven him to bed, and he'd guessed what was coming.

"There's nothing here either," Marjorie said. Then she looked up at the ceiling, pretending to be stern. She and the Lord had always had great fun together, more like a couple of brothers than a man and a woman.

"Look here, Gordon," she said to the ceiling, "I know you hate people driving your car, but where are the blinking keys? You old nuisance," she added, after a moment.

"He's hidden them," I said. "It's just like him."

Marjorie gave me a very gentle smile. "I'll have a look downstairs," she said.

She left me alone in my father's room. I opened the two top drawers of his dressing-table. One of them was empty. The other contained a couple of pipe cleaners, a device for sharpening razor blades and a member's badge for Leopardstown race course.

There was nothing else. No personal jewellery, no passport, no letters, no keepsakes, no photographs—no mementoes of any kind.

Perhaps he'd never needed the things by which other people set such store.

Perhaps because he was a truly great man.

Chapter Three

SOME time after the Lord's death I attended a literary party in London and got trapped for half an hour in a corner by a very literary young man. I defended myself as best I could, until he suddenly burst out, "I simply cannot understand it. You've been making a good living for at least twenty-five years by writing and yet you don't know the first thing about English literature. I don't know how you've got away with it."

I managed to get away from him, but on the way home I did begin to think about the nature of my education. It was one of the most formal kind—prep school, public school and Oxford, however briefly. But it was quite true that in some inexplicable way it had failed almost entirely to make a mark on me, or me on it.

I must have endured the process of being educated for at least fourteen years. My life-long fear of authority must have caused me to work hard enough to avoid punishment. I have no memory of trailing behind any class I ever attended and must, indeed, have been comparatively bright. But now, as an established writer of more than fifty years of age, I had to admit that I'd hesitate to bet £10 on Keats—or Shelley—being the author of the poem about the nightingale. Nor could I name with any conviction the novel in which any one of Dickens' characters appeared, with the exception—of course—of such cast-iron certainties as Dombey and his son, or Oliver Twist.

The longer I thought about them the wider the gaps in my knowledge became. Even a rudimentary account of the plot of any of the plays of Shakespeare was beyond me. I never seemed to have read a word of the great masters like Thackeray, Carlyle, John Donne—or Thomas Hardy. Nor, indeed, could I add to the list of the names of the great masters of English literature without a good deal of thought.

I realised I felt neither pride nor humility in such total ignorance. It merely left me stunned.

But how could it have happened?

My father was an educated man. He'd won literary prizes at
Charterhouse. He'd become a barrister. His knowledge and
appreciation of English literature was as wide as anyone's I've
ever known. But not the faintest shadow of it had rubbed off on
to me.

Presumably he'd tried to stimulate my mind into the enjoy-
ment and therefore the benefits of the formal education that had
cost him so much money down the years. He always had a
marked family pride. Once, he described us as being 'slightly
upper-middle class'.

Surely he should have worked harder on me?

Though the gap is supposed to be narrowing, education or the
lack of it discriminates as sternly between the classes as first and
third railway tickets, and the Lord always had an instinctive
tendency towards travelling first.

I'd have thought that an educated son would have been almost essential to his *amour propre*. But perhaps the imposition of
the discipline that this involved would have been repugnant to his
reserved and diffident nature—diffident, at least, where personal
relationships were concerned.

In the matter of my education my mother could have been of
little help to him.

The only formal teaching she'd ever received had been in
learning to draw at the Dublin School of Art, and later on at the
Slade. To this day she counts on her fingers, and her spelling is
an extraordinary scramble of phonetic sounds or, at any rate, of
sounds that she believes to be phonetic.

And, finally and always, she's believed that there is no point in
pushing people, particularly children. For them she's always been
certain that 'it will all come right in the end'.

The Lord, at least, pushed me into Crawley's Preparatory
School, St. Stephen's Green, in Dublin. He'd gone there himself,
and was proud of his academic record, but the only memory I
retain of Crawley's is a dark cellar and terror so dreadful that the
only way I could contain it was by trying to stand outside myself,
telling myself that it must come to an end, that sooner or later I
would be safe on the top deck of the No. 15 tram, going home.
Crawley's was a day-school, or I might not have survived it.

The trouble was two enormous brothers. To me they looked
like fully grown men. One had flaming red hair, and a temper

that became more and more demoniac the longer he persecuted me. The other was dark and sinister, and invented new tortures for his brother to carry out.

These ceremonies—they had the feeling of ceremonies in their set form and fixed dénouement—were conducted in the cloakroom, a cellar in this old Georgian house, and they terminated in my head being shoved into a revolting lavatory bowl by the red-haired brother, while the dark one pulled the chain.

I'd imagine they picked on me because I was very tall and very thin, and my stammer made me almost completely inarticulate.

But those possessed and dreadful brothers did one thing for me. They gave me a life-long conviction that anger and violence are an actual waste of time. I remember I had to walk half a mile every morning from our house to the tram terminus in Terenure, and then sit in the tram for another half hour, with the brothers and the lavatory bowl getting nearer every minute, and the only thing I really objected to, in an utterly numb and miserable way, was this waste of time.

I could have been doing anything else, but here I had to sit on top of the tram as it lurched and howled down the long drabness of Rathmines Road, waiting for the moment to come when I walked into the cellar to hang up my coat, and to provoke the brothers to their inexplicable furies—furies that no appeal to reason could disperse.

It was a comfort, on top of the tram, to look forward to my approaching misery as a waste of time—a period of hours in which no nice or funny or interesting thing would happen, a time of limbo, of non-life.

Years later, at a party in London, a jolly psychiatrist in an eccentric but exceedingly smart suit, heard me telling someone that I regarded anger as a waste of time.

"But what would you prefer to do with this time which is wasted, as you say, upon anger?" he wanted to know.

"Live it," I said, to my own satisfaction but not, as it turned out, to his. He thought it stemmed from a subconscious refusal to accept reality, but then he hadn't known the demon brothers and, at his prices, I wasn't prepared to lay their record before him.

Neither was I prepared to tell my mother, nor anyone else, about them. It seemed to me that the three of us had a secret so shameful that we could only keep it to ourselves. I don't remember any other boys being involved, or even being in the cellar, while we were conducting our rites, but I suppose many of them must have known what was going on.

And my mother must have guessed, because one afternoon she called for me at the school apparently by accident, saying she'd been shopping. I was outside on the pavement, when she arrived, with a number of boys of my own class. When we got home she said to the Lord, "We'll have to find Paddy another school. He's getting much too tall for Crawley's. When I saw him this afternoon he looked like a tree surrounded by a lot of little dogs."

I left Crawley's, and went to a gentlemanly boarding school on the outskirts of Dublin called Castle Park.

The headmaster was W. P. Toone, and he ran Castle Park on the lines of an English public school. The school motto was *Mens Sana in Corpore Sano*, and we were expected to live up to it.

In fact, it was a very good and enlightened prep school, and W. P. Toone was an outstanding headmaster, but I arrived too late. I had only a year at Castle Park, in place of the normal four, and regarded it—when I thought about it at all—merely as a temporary resting place.

W. P. Toone had a passion for cricket, and there was a beautiful ground right in front of the school. But the only cricket I'd played had been scratch games at Crawley's playing fields, which we'd reached on bicycles.

Quite soon I saw that *Mens Sana in Corpore Sano* was going to demand a sense of duty and a regard for principles that threatened to be beyond me, and I think W. P. Toone saw it himself. On the last speech day I spent at Castle Park I heard him say to my father that it was a pity I had not come to Castle Park at a more formative age, and I'm sure he was right.

It was the first time in my life I'd been exposed to personal discipline, to have set before me a course of behaviour which, if obeyed to the letter, would not only have educated me but would also have given me a genuine regard for the necessary virtues of truthfulness and industry.

As it was, these benefits didn't have time to take hold. Castle Park did teach me one thing—that I was not the sort of person to hold power or authority over anyone else. I made this discovery in the last week of my last term. I'd been made a prefect in this last term, having been at Castle Park for less than a year.

It was an honour which had certainly not been gained either by long service or by merit, but was probably merely a part of W. P. Toone's crash course to turn me into a gentleman.

One morning another prefect came to me, more or less convulsed with laughter, to tell me, "Someone's gone and peed his name all over the wall in the outside lavatory."

I cannot remember what inspired such a reaction, but I took a stern turn against this gross infringement of the school motto. It might have been because the other prefect was younger than I, and I thought he wasn't taking his duties sufficiently seriously by laughing at such bestial behaviour. Or, much more probably, I saw in this minor offence an opportunity to exercise my authority as a prefect for the first time. It seemed unlikely there would be another one, with only a week to go till the end of term.

With the other prefect, who was already frightened by the turn things had taken, I went to inspect the offence.

Someone had, indeed, 'peed his name all over the wall', in a fine and flowing hand. Not without difficulty, I was able to decipher the name of a plump and sloppy little boy whose appearance and mannerisms had displeased me several times in the past. I remember being surprised at the time to find that he had it in him to make so masculine a gesture, and in such copious profusion. He'd even managed, though shakily, to underline his signature. I did not, however, allow these merits to weigh with me.

"We'll have to have a prefects' meeting over this," I said. "This is serious."

We held the prefects' meeting in an empty classroom after lunch, under the chairmanship of the Captain of the School. He was a very correct boy, whose name I've forgotten, but he was the perfect example of W. P. Toone's beau idéal.

He began on a stern note. "This is the first time for many years," he said, "there's been a prefects' meeting at Castle Park." He looked straight at me as he made this announcement, making me feel for a moment as though I had committed the offence myself.

"The whole school knows," he said, "this meeting is going on."

And presumably, I thought, the whole school knows who's called it, and for what reason.

At once, I wished I hadn't started it. For the first time I was playing a leading part in an official matter, and already I knew that everything was whirling out of control.

"As far as I'm concerned," the Captain went on, "I don't think the offence is serious enough to be considered by a prefects' meeting, but on the other hand any prefect, acting on his own judgement, can call a prefects' meeting at any time."

I stared back at him seriously, prepared to play my part, however distasteful it might be, in the dispensation of justice.

"Now that the meeting has been called," he continued, "it is my duty to tell you what our powers are. We can give the offender not more than five hundred lines. I, myself, with the consent of all of you, can give him six strokes with a swagger stick. That is the limit of our authority. But," he added, with new solemnity, "there are two other things we can do."

He cleared his throat and once again looked me straight in the eye. "We can report the offender," he said, "to his Housemaster or, in the most extreme case of all, to the Headmaster himself. I have to tell you," he added, "that I do not believe that a prefects' meeting has ever reported directly to the Headmaster in the whole history of the school."

I knew, then, that that was what we had to do. It was totally unjust, and even vicious, but I was absolutely set upon it. It was the first time I'd ever taken a decision that would bring down punishment on someone else, but I was determined to go on with it. And at the same time I couldn't even look at my own motives, though I had a fairly clear idea what they were.

There was, firstly, the excitement of calling upon W. P. Toone as an equal, of finding myself for a while on the same level as the masters.

There was, secondly, the undeniable satisfaction—one that I'd never even guessed at before—that comes from wielding power, from talking other people into doing what you want them to do, however fearful the consequences may be.

There was also the certainty that I'd gone too far now to turn back. I felt, right in the middle of me, some impermeable, rock-like substance that no one or nothing could break down.

"I think," I said, "we ought to report him to the Head. It was a disgusting thing to do and—it isn't hygienic."

The *Mens Sana in Corpore Sano* syndrome had come right to the fore.

The Captain of the School said firmly, "I cannot accept that motion until we've voted on the other ones," and suddenly I knew I'd been clever. By putting the idea of reporting to the Head into the minds of the others I'd made it impossible for them to vote for anything as dull as five hundred lines, or even the swagger stick.

It might, I thought quickly, have been the kind of thing my father did at board meetings. But for better reasons, of course.

I was quite right. The Captain and the Vice-Captain were the only ones who voted for the imposition, the swagger stick and the Housemaster. I and the other two prefects voted against them.

We came to the last motion on the agenda, and then something frightful happened. The Captain of the School said, "I know that this is quite irregular, that prefects' meetings cannot be interfered with by any member of the teaching staff, but Mr. Baker has particularly asked me if he might be allowed to put in a word."

My whole heart and stomach instantly rose into my mouth. I had the same terror of Baker as I'd had for the demon brothers at Crawley's, except that it was added to immeasurably by Baker being a master and therefore legally entitled to inflict fear. And inflict fear he did.

He was a tall, bony, awkward man with gingery hair and a wild blue eye, who was given to truly terrifying outbursts of rage. But he had another, even more powerful weapon. His right wrist. He'd broken it, years before, and now, when he felt another burst of fury coming on, he'd twist it fiercely and repeatedly, so that the injured bone clicked in a series of sharp reports.

We could hear the clicking coming at us round corners, and I could hear it outside the door of the classroom now.

I'd been so busy preparing for W. P. Toone I'd altogether forgotten that Baker was the offender's Housemaster. And now it seemed he was on the boy's side.

"I don't think we ought to let Baker in on this," I said. "It's got nothing to do with him. We can make up our own minds without him, can't we?"

"He asked me very specially if he could talk to us," the Captain said. "I think we really ought to let him."

All the others murmured their agreement. I think they were glad to know that Baker was coming to the meeting. He'd probably be able to take this terrible business off our hands.

"All right," I said. "But it won't make any difference."

And I knew it wouldn't. For some extraordinary reason I was prepared to fight even Baker in this matter. I, who'd never been aware of having any principles, was prepared to defend this one to the death. And even then I knew it was the wrong one.

He came in, clicking his wrist, with an air of pent-up fury. When he spoke, however, he was extremely courteous and correct.

He apologised for intruding on our meeting, and thanked us for our generous waiving of the rules. He then came to the matter in hand.

"For all kinds of reasons," he said, "I want you to leave this business to me. There are various domestic matters of a confidential nature which you cannot be aware of. But I promise you—" his temper suddenly cracked—"I promise you, if you leave him to me, I'll beat the little bastard to within an inch of his life."

He clicked the wrist five or six times, his blue eyes bloodshot, glaring at us in appeal. He found a small measure of calm.

"All that I ask," he said, "is that you don't report him to the Head. He's only been here for a couple of terms and you'll ruin his whole career."

Suddenly, I saw that the bloodshot, blue glare was fixed on me. "I know you're at the back of this," he yelled, without warning. "Christ knows why. I'm warning you, leave the poor little bugger alone. You're leaving next week. It's nothing to you. But just leave him alone!"

He stood alone in the middle of the classroom, clicking the wrist like a machine-gun, glaring at me with his wild eyes. Then he suddenly turned on his heel and walked out of the room, slamming the door savagely.

It was a foregone conclusion after that. The Captain and the Vice-Captain voted against the last motion, but I knew I had the others on my side. Baker had gone too far. Terrified as we were, we knew that he had no right to intimidate us with a performance as hysterical as that. I think we felt that the three of us had emerged as the only ones with any regard for calm and dignity, for law, order and reason.

At 6 o'clock that night the Captain of the School tapped on W. P. Toone's door, and the rest of us filed in behind him. The proceedings were disappointingly short, after all I'd been through.

The Captain said that 'So-and-So urinated in an unnecessary manner on the wall of the outside lavatory', and that the prefects' meeting had decided that it was 'its duty to report the matter to you, sir'.

W.P.T. thanked him with the gravest courtesy, and said that he would take steps to deal with it. Then we all filed out again. It was the smallest reward I'd ever received for anything. But there were, I was sorry to discover, still greater depths of ignominy to be touched.

At no time during this unpleasant business, which seemed to become more and more unpleasant by the minute, had I thought of the physical nature of the punishment that would be handed out to the offender. He seemed to be altogether disconnected from our proceedings, merely the starter button that had set them in motion. If I considered him at all it was probably to think that it would be all the same to him if he got five hundred lines or six strokes from W.P.T. or the Captain of the School.

What had not occurred to me was the possibility that he would receive no punishment at all. Nor did he.

After prayers in Big Hall the following morning W.P.T. said he wished to speak to us about a serious matter that had come to his attention.

It was a moment of high drama. I wondered if the handwriting expert was going to receive a public beating, and wished more passionately than ever that I'd never started it. I could see him, sitting up in the front row with the smaller boys, but could deduce nothing from the back of his little bullet head.

W.P.T. began to address us in gravely measured tones. He was brief in the extreme. He said that a member of the school had committed an offence againt decency which, while trivial in itself, might lead to far more serious self-indulgences were it allowed to go unchecked. He reminded us of the school motto—"a good, working principle for all of us, boys and adults alike." He then said that the offender had been dealt with 'by democratic process', from which—and I was certain he looked at me for an instant—he hoped that all those concerned 'would draw conclusions which would be of benefit to them in the future'.

That was the end of that. We filed out of Big Hall on our way to a breakfast which I was unable to touch. For the next few days, until the merciful release of the end of term, I slunk around the place trying to keep out of everyone's way. I felt as if

I'd been genuinely insane and now, rational again, had to endure the contempt of the witnesses of my madness.

From that day to this I've never had a job that put me in a position of authority over anyone. The only people I've ever given working orders to have been occasional charwomen, and mostly I've told them not to bother, that I'd do it myself. Perhaps I learnt it at Castle Park, but it seems to me that the exercise of power is a thoroughly dangerous business that tends to bring out the worst in everyone. Or, alternatively, that it brings out the best—if the nature of the person concerned is capable of giving it.

For either reason, I've always kept well away from the exercise of power and left those who like it to get on with it—dodging, or enjoying, as the case may be—the effects of their efforts on myself.

I didn't learn anything else that I can remember at Castle Park, but Castle Park had one more thing to do for me. It got me to Rossall, a public school on the bleak coast of Lancashire, a couple of miles north of Blackpool—a place where a healthy body was of much greater benefit than a healthy mind.

I got to Rossall in the same haphazard way that by now seemed to have become the fixed pattern of my education.

For some time my father had been talking at odd, despairing moments about what was going to happen after Castle Park and on one occasion—we must have been on holiday in England—went so far as to take his family to look over Charterhouse, his old school.

I don't remember a single instant of the visit, but I imagine the Lord enjoyed it, pointing out his name on various boards and recalling the dramatic events of his youth. For the rest of us, the visit to Charterhouse had only one outcome.

From then on, whenever we were faced with boredom or discomfort beyond endurance, we always said, "This is worse than Charterhouse."

A picnic to be suffered in the rain was worse than Charterhouse. So was one of the Lord's banking friends, talking too profoundly and too long. The Lord even used it himself from time to time, but we could see that he'd been wounded, and did so without pleasure.

It must have been the failure of Charterhouse that caused him to take the extraordinary step—though it seemed quite normal at the time—of asking me where I'd like to go to, after I left Castle Park, though he could have had no confidence of any kind in my knowledge of English public schools.

It seemed inevitable that it was going to be an English public school, though there were several alternatives in Ireland, because the Foreign Office, incredibly enough, appeared to be looming up in the Lord's mind as a career for his eldest son.

His brother Cecil, who was now in Cairo as a financial adviser to the Egyptian Government, had had some kind of Foreign Office connections. No doubt the Lord, continuing to detect in me no trace of professional or commercial ambition, was hoping once again that influence could launch me into some kind of job that I might eventually be able to do.

I told my father I'd like to go to Rossall. He asked me why, perhaps for the reason that he might not have heard of a public school so far to the north of Charterhouse.

I told him that there was a very nice boy at Castle Park, who was marvellous at games and cross-country running, and that he'd gone to Rossall, and that W. P. Toone had gone to Rossall, too, and that there seemed to be some sort of connection between the two schools. "There's a cupboard at Rossall," I said, "that all the Castle Park boys carve their names on. It sounds all right."

Some boys have their names put down at birth for Eton, Harrow and even Winchester. I went to Rossall because of the cupboard and the cross-country runner, and because W. P. Toone was probably helpful in easing me in, assisted—for his part—by the fact that my grandfather was Chairman of the Irish Senate.

One evening the Lord and I took a taxi right across Dublin to the North Wall, and the Liverpool boat. I had a new trunk and a new tuck-box and a new, heather-mixture cap.

Apart from school caps I'd never had a hat of any kind. The heather-mixture thing, chosen for me by my mother in Switzer's Men's Clothing Department, was a compromise between bare-headedness, which seemed too informal for so important a journey, and a brown trilby which she snatched off my head as soon as the assistant put it on.

It hung around the house for years afterwards, often doing good service for Marjorie in her impressions of intoxicated, golfing colonels, but I could scarcely bring myself to look at it. It brought back, with perfect clarity, the misery of that first trip to Rossall.

The journey itself was interminable, a matter of eight or nine hours from Dublin to Liverpool. Then we had a couple of hours wait for the train to Preston, where we'd have to change for Fleetwood and Rossall, so the Lord took a room with bath in an enormous Liverpool hotel.

I had a bath while he shaved and at one point I got soap in my eye. "I've got soap in my eye," I told my father. "What'll I do?" I felt absolutely helpless in the limbo of this huge Liverpool hotel. I seemed to have forgotten everything I'd ever known.

The Lord turned round from the shaving mirror, looking as helpless as I felt. Then he recovered himself. "Bathe it with a sponge," he said. "Put water on it."

Then he looked at me for a moment with such despair that I had to cry behind the protection of the sponge. What hope could there be for a son who couldn't even deal with soap in his eye?

The train journey to Preston went on for ever. After the gentle green fields of Ireland and the gracious Georgian houses of Dublin Lancashire looked like a stricken hell. Gigantic factories belching fire and smoke, and wizened, grimy, bow-legged people scurrying about them like ants.

The Lord and I looked out of the window in silence, as mile after mile of nineteenth-century industrialisation sped by. I don't think he'd ever been there himself, and was probably thinking of his elegant, intellectual life in a charming little house in London before the war.

The cross-country runner and the cupboard had long since been forgotten by both of us as rational reasons for my going to Rossall. We were in a foreign country that gave us no welcome of any kind.

Something happened at lunch in the Pullman that made it more foreign than ever.

The Lord asked the waiter for a bottle of stout for himself, and a cider for me.

The waiter said, angrily, "Gymis?"

Neither of us knew what he was talking about. It sounded like a foreign language, possibly Greek.

"No," my father said, "just a cider, and a bottle of stout."

The waiter clicked his tongue in exasperation and went away. He came back some time later with a bottle of stout and a bottle of cider. The Lord looked at the label on the cider. He grinned. "Gaymer's," he said. "Gymis."

I was only just able to grin back. England, and specially Lancashire, was not only a foreign country. It also had an incomprehensible language of its own.

When we changed at Preston, where there was an hour's wait for the Fleetwood train, the Lord bought me a magazine— *Popular Mechanics*—in which there was an article 'For the Advanced Model Maker' about how to build a scale model of a Red Label Bentley, using a biscuit tin for the bodywork. I read every word of the article, referring with care to the numbered diagrams, sitting on a bench on Preston platform in my heather-mixture cap, with the Lord beside me, smoking his pipe, trying to find his way through the *Liverpool Post*, after the comfortable familiarity of the *Irish Times*.

I wished my mother was there. She'd have had a passionate outburst about there being no point in people suffering for nothing, and we might have been hurrying back to Dublin, probably in a hired car.

Instead, we got into a small train, for Fleetwood, and were soon passing through a countryside even more desolate than that poisoned by the factories.

It was absolutely flat and covered as far as the eye could reach with grimy, white hens, broken-down hen houses and rusting wire netting. Not a blade of grass could be seen. The hens, thousands upon thousands of them, scratched about in dun-coloured mud.

I believe it was Poulton-le-Fylde, an area of Lancashire famous for its egg production. It looked like one of the more fearful parts of the moon.

Neither of us was prepared for it when we saw Rossall for the first time. It was unmistakably Rossall, a low-built tangle of red-brick buildings with the grey sea behind it, so that it seemed to be on the very edge of the beach. The railway line ran parallel to it for a quarter of a mile or so, so we had plenty of time to have a good look.

The Lord must have been as shocked as I was by the stern, almost military look of the place. He tried to make it better for me by making a joke.

"It looks a bit like a workhouse," he said, giving me one of his smiles with the corners of the mouth turned down.

It finished me off. I looked out of the other window until we got to Fleetwood, fighting with tears.

I don't remember any of the indoctrination process. I suppose we must have met the Housemaster, and someone must have showed us round, but all at once the Lord had gone, on his way back to Dublin, and I was sitting in a study the size of a broom cupboard, quite alone and reading *Popular Mechanics*.

There were some quite interesting bits in it about tricks with magnets and glasses of water. I became almost absorbed in *Popular Mechanics* for more than an hour, though I was listening at the same time to the steadily increasing uproar of other boys arriving, trunks being dropped, water-pipes banged and people running up and down stairs. Then the door burst open and someone came in and my real life was over, until I could go home to Dublin again.

Four years later, round about the same time in the evening, I was drinking a bottle of Bass in the buffet on Preston station in the company of a number of other fully grown men who'd also left Rossall for good.

We were singing, fortissimo :

"Lord dismiss us with Thy blessing,
Thanks for mercies past receive . . ."

As usual, the end-of-term hymn in the chapel the previous evening had been a moment of strong emotion, up till the last two lines, which I sung with as much cynicism as I could get into them.

"Those returning,
Make more faithful than before."

"And you can have it," I added, for the benefit of the friends on either side of me who were staying on.

At the same time I knew I hadn't made the best of yet another school, that once again a comparatively large part of my life had been spent at half speed.

Since then I've met a number of Old Boys from other public schools who have maintained into their sixties the friendships they made in the Lower Fifth. I even knew a man who ten years after he'd left Marlborough still went on walking tours in the Lake District with his former physics master.

All of them must have been completely and fully alive while they were at school. They must have felt, in their last year, that they'd begun to live adult lives, that they were already serving an intelligent apprenticeship to their chosen careers.

For me, it was all just a blur.

I remember that early on I was christened 'Lucy', not in derision but as the devious result of a paragraph in a local paper. A Dr. Campbell, oblivious to his own discomfort, had impaled his forefinger on a safety-pin stuck in a child's throat. I discussed the event a good deal, not because a namesake was involved, but because I couldn't see how he could have got enough purchase on the pin to shove it into his own finger without at the same time choking the child, whose name was Lucy.

In spite of my stammer I was beginning to find I could make people laugh by flights of fancy which seemed new to them. With names like Barraclough, Thorpe and Furness, and solid commercial backgrounds in Manchester, Liverpool and Preston, their humour was a good deal more rugged.

No doubt the nickname Lucy assisted me in overcoming boredom by almost continuous clowning around, though not all of the clowning was well received. "Daft" is a Lancashire word that doesn't always convey admiration.

While taking refuge and even finding pleasure in being daft, I still played a fairly commendable part in the life of my House.

I got my House Colours for rugger, cricket and hockey, the latter game being a fearful invention unique to Rossall. It was played on the beach, in the winter, with a hard rubber ball and instruments like heavy walking-sticks with flattened heads. The six forwards on either side lined up shoulder to shoulder, facing one another, and the referee dropped the ball into this scrum over our heads. The resulting clash of sticks against ankles puts my teeth on edge to this day.

I served in the O.T.C. for four years without earning a stripe, though this was probably owing to my inability to articulate an order without an interval of several seconds, during which anything could happen, particularly with a platoon at the double.

I can remember no single master who fired my imagination

or who gave me an enduring interest, though I found I could pass examinations, including the Higher Certificate, by writing down all the relevant facts in dozens of note-books, all beautifully written and carefully underlined. This process enabled me to remember them just long enough to complete the examination paper, and then they would vanish from my mind.

The friends I made—and I cannot remember one of their faces—were probably as heedless as I was of the privilege of being at a public school. We spent long hours in our study playing cricket, as silently as possible, with a tennis-ball and a ruler for a bat, breaking at least one window a term.

I can best judge the fairly low opinion in which we were held by the attitude of the cross-country runner from Castle Park.

He'd already been at Rossall for some time when I arrived, and was by now captain of nearly everything in sight. Members of the school teams, as opposed to house teams, were allowed to wear caps of considerable complexity, both in colour and in design. Charles had enough caps for every day of the week.

Although we were in the same House I scarcely saw him at all. I had an idea that he might like to keep an eye on me, seeing that he'd been entirely responsible for my emigration to Lancashire, but I soon saw that the division between the upper and lower classes was absolute. The monitors and the school Colours lived in studies at the far end of the passage in quite considerable luxury, as I observed while fagging for them, while the rest of us survived on the hot pipes in the hall. We all shared studies with one or two others, but they were so small that one of us had to move his chair before the door could be opened.

One evening I was engaged in discussion with some other boys, on the hot pipes, when Charles went by. I thought for a moment he was going to speak to me, but then he went on out into the square. A moment later he came back again, looking unusually serious, and beckoned me to follow him. I did so instantly, delighted by this sign of favour. Charles was waiting outside the door.

"Some of us," he said, without preliminary, "try not to talk like that and I think you ought to, too."

He walked quickly and stiffly away.

It took me a moment to realise that he was referring to the bad language which came as naturally to us as breathing.

It was another whiff of *Mens Sana*. I tried fairly conscientiously for several days to thin out the fouler expletives and then abandoned the task, for ever, as hopeless.

At the same time I hoped Charles hadn't got to hear about my other self-indulgence, which was a profound and romantic interest in a beautiful little boy called Brian, who had the most remarkable golden skin. Golden skin was at a premium at Rossall, where the savage weather conditions turned most of us puce or blue.

On Sunday afternoons Brian, a wary child, used to go for long walks by himself in the sandhills, and for a whole term I pursued him with chocolate bars and similar favours without, however, catching up with him. I don't, I must admit, know what would have happened if I had, but in all probability we would have been saved from sin by the howling north-east winds and sleet that seemed to be a permanent feature of the Lancashire coast.

Years later, when I was doing a story in Belfast for the *Sunday Dispatch*, I met an extremely handsome and well set-up vicar. It was Brian, no doubt expiating a subconscious sense of guilt.

This was my only venture into homosexuality, as my true interest lay in an astonishingly pretty Irish maid called Molly, who waited on the top table in the dining hall. Molly had jet-black hair cut in a bob, a creamy skin and the sapphire blue eyes that sometimes go with this colouring in Irish girls. Molly must also have been almost entirely devoid of commonsense in expending these advantages on serving minced liver in a school in Lancashire, but for three or four terms we used to stare at one another with exhausting intensity through a round window in a service door while the Headmaster was saying Grace. The affair advanced no further. Matron looked after all the maids so carefully that she was reported to lock them up in cages between meals.

Probably the warmest physical contact that anyone ever achieved at Rossall came from the tradition of linking, because we walked everywhere arm in arm with one or two other boys.

Even this minor pleasure, however, was hedged about by a number of restrictions. I don't think first term boys were allowed to link, and as far as I can remember linking was frowned upon with people younger or older than oneself. But one thing I am certain about. To link with someone in another House, unless one was a school monitor or a school Colour, was as glaring an offence as going to bed with them. It did happen, however, from time to time with the more daring and raffish boys, and provided a scandal to be talked about for several days. As far as I could tell there were no homosexual tendencies in linking. The restrictions upon it were purely those of a rigid and conventional society, in which protocol was everything.

On one occasion Charles, who was Captain of the First XV, came up behind me linked with the Captain of the First Eleven, and impelled by some sudden burst of generosity put his arm through mine. The three of us, arm in arm, walked right across the square together and all the way to the gym. I was so staggered I had the greatest difficulty in keeping in step. It never happened again.

The other big event in my career at Rossall was having prayers said in Chapel "for our school-mate, Patrick Campbell, who is now lying dangerously ill".

They were said, it seemed, only just in time.

Some weeks before I'd been put into the day-room of the sanitorium with an all-time record of thirteen boils, most of them on my back, to wait for the doctor to come and attack them. There was another boy there when I arrived, sitting slumped in a chair in misery as acute as my own. He said he didn't know what was the matter with him. He just felt hot. Certainly he was bright red in the face. We played desultory card games together for the whole of that afternoon, until the school doctor arrived about six, instantly to diagnose scarlet fever in the other boy.

He scarcely looked at my boils. "Get them both," he told Matron, "into the Isolation Hospital. The other one's certain to catch it, too."

It was a fearful sentence, like being sent to Devil's Island.

The Isolation Hospital was a place of dread for everyone. A gaunt, red-brick building, it stood on the very edge of the beach, well away from the school itself, battling for survival against the wind and the sand that blew against it from the surrounding dunes. It was scarcely ever used. The wind seemed to guard Rossall against infectious diseases.

Within a week of going into the Isolation Hospital I had scarlet fever, a temperature of 104, two more boils—bringing that total up to fifteen—and an abcess on the side of my neck that turned my whole head into the shape of a soccer ball. A full house, indeed.

I was semi-conscious for days and nights on end. The only thing I can remember of this agony was the sound of the nurses' feet as they scrunched across the sand that lay on the bare boards of the ward. No sooner did they sweep out the sand than more blew in again. It was a hard winter in every way.

One evening I opened my eyes and saw my mother, in a white coat, sitting beside my bed. I had a faint memory that they'd told me she was coming, but the news seemed so certain a guarantee of my approaching death that I'd decided not to believe it.

She sat beside me for what felt like weeks. She lived in a hotel in the fish-ridden town of Fleetwood and took a tram up to the school every day. The white coat they'd given her was to guard against infection, a precaution for which the proprietor of the hotel would, no doubt, have been grateful, if he'd been told about it.

A surgeon arrived to lance the abcess. The scarlet fever died down and every inch of skin peeled off my body. My mother succeeded in removing the sole of one foot in one piece. She pinned it on to a sheet of cardboard and we were fascinated by the delicacy of its construction.

One day she said, "I peeped in through the window of your study this morning. I've never in all my life seen dirtier lace curtains."

I said, "I never noticed them. I didn't know we had any."

She said, "And there's only one picture on the walls—that bulldog in the sailor's hat."

"It was there when I arrived," I told her. "It fell off and I stuck it on again with condensed milk."

We both started to laugh and went on laughing.

The prayers for my recovery had worked.

Early in the morning, a few days later, I tottered down the stairs of the Isolation Hospital with a nurse on either side and my mother bringing up the rear. They put me into the back of a hired car, my mother got in beside me, and we set off to drive all the way to Liverpool, and the boat.

My dream about the car from Preston had almost come true.

I was fearfully sick on the boat, and when we arrived at the

North Wall, in Dublin, the following morning, my mother told me for the first time that I was going to my grandfather's house, and not to our own.

"It'll only be for a couple of weeks," she said. "The doctor thinks you might still be a bit infectious, and he doesn't want Biddy or Michael to catch it."

While it was an improvement on the Isolation Hospital it wasn't the best of news.

My grandfather lived in a huge house in Milltown, on the outskirts of Dublin, in style which was high enough to include half a dozen servants and a butler called Beale. He'd renamed it Glenavy, after his new title.

My mother, Biddy and I had stayed there once before for some weeks after our own house was burnt down by the I.R.A., and I had no very happy memories of the place. It was guarded at that time by police and all night long I'd listened to the sound of heavy feet on the gravel outside my window. I had a constant fear that it was the I.R.A. all over again.

The Old Lord, himself, was not much of a one for comforting small boys.

He was extremely good-looking, in a most distinguished and autocratic way, with silvery white hair and an elegantly drooping white moustache. We used to go there for occasional lunches on Sundays, times of severe trial for everyone.

My mother used to say, "Every time I look round that awful drawing-room and the huge marble mantelpieces and the rubbishy pictures I can't believe that anyone could have so little taste."

My grandmother was a much shadowier figure than the Old Lord. Once a fortnight or so she would take Biddy and me to lunch in the restaurant of the Grafton Street Cinema in Dublin, giving us lobster salads and all the most expensive food. Then we'd see the film and the chauffeur would drive us home.

But her life was centred entirely around a group she used to call 'the ladies'. The ladies were all refined and aristocratic Protestant matrons, and they came to Glenavy to play bridge. There were often as many as four tables in the 'awful' drawing-room, with Beale making his stately way among them with silver trays and expensive china.

It couldn't have been more different from my own gay and carefree home, but it was better—as I've already said—than the Isolation Hospital on that freezing beach in Lancashire.

In fact, of course, the Old Lord and my grandmother were much more spirited characters than they ever gave me reason to suppose.

The Old Lord, during the last years of his life, spent quite a lot of time and money on the tables in Monte Carlo, and on an attractive Spanish girl who numbered tennis among her accomplishments.

After he died my grandmother moved to London, where she proved to be the terror of no less than fourteen South Kensington hotels in less than a year.

I used to have regular lunches with her, trying to combat her belief that the waiters were all 'as black as your hat', despite the fact that there were nearly always a couple of raw-boned, ginger-haired lads from Glasgow among them. She died in her fifteenth hotel, after making an outraged complaint to the manager that 'little soldiers on horseback' were galloping about all over her eiderdown.

My mother smuggled me into my grandfather's large and opulent house by a side door, and installed me in a small upstairs bedroom. She went back to our own house that night. The discomfort of the hotel in Fleetwood was as nothing to her, in comparison with the rigours of Beale, the 'ladies', too many parlour maids and bridge.

I don't remember having too much to do with them myself, but I do remember the morning when my mother came into the room with a look on her face of gleeful but guilty joy.

"I've just been talking to the doctor," she said, "and he doesn't think you ought to go back to Rossall next term. He says you're very run-down."

It was a moment before I could take it in, and then I threw back the bed clothes and, looking like a human skeleton, did a wild dance of triumph, leaping up and down and waving my arms. My mother joined in, dancing round the bed herself, adding subdued Indian war whoops to my own cries of delight.

Like myself, she probably felt that Rossall—or any similar kind of school—was merely something that had to be endured, something that wasn't of any real importance. Both of us, as usual, were certain that 'it would all come right in the end'.

In a kind of way, it did. Having missed a term seemed to have made no difference. I cannot imagine I did any work at home, but before leaving Rossall I managed to pass the Higher School Certificate by the usual method of writing everything down in exercise books and then reading them through a couple of times. I remember a history paper in which we were invited to 'discuss' various matters. I discussed them at a length which must have been great enough to conceal the scarcity of fact, because I got an astonishing 80 per cent. The Latin paper was based largely upon the works of Tacitus. A brilliant feat of memory here earned me something like 85 per cent. Three months later, when I went up to Oxford and had to deal with Pass Moderations, I was delighted to find that I'd come face to face with Tacitus again. This time, to my surprise and irritation, I found that the examiner was able to grant me only seven marks out of a hundred.

It's probably fair to say that every shred of the knowledge revealed in my Higher Certificate papers had passed from my mind before the papers were even collected, never mind marked.

A week before I left Rossall for the last time I was given my Second Eleven School Colours. This entitled me, for the first time in four years, to wear a cap different to the ordinary house one. It was sky-blue with white hoops, and I borrowed it from an athlete who had a number of others. It also entitled me to link with other School Colours who were not in my House, but with only a week to go I didn't bother.

My career at Rossall was drawing peacefully to its close. I hadn't won a single prize. There was no revered or remembered master. I had made neither a lasting friendship, nor an enduring enemy. The only sporting trophy was the Second Eleven cricket cap, which was probably bestowed out of a sense of charity, more than anything else. And the only connection I maintain with my old school is none of my doing.

I get occasional letters from Old Rossallians that begin, "I'm sure you'll remember me from good old Ross . . ."

Their names are entirely unfamiliar. Their faces have faded utterly from my memory. And the only reason they remember me is because they've seen me on television.

Rossall gave me nothing that I can remember because it simply couldn't compete with my home. That was where everything happened. That's where the positive and exciting talk was. That's where the writers and the actors and the other interesting people were.

No schoolmaster could have competed with my parents, and especially my mother, in forming what I've come to regard defensively as my mind.

My mother held passionate opinions about everyone and everything, and particularly about everyone. She would find vitality and imagination—to her the two most desirable characteristics—in people that I thought were dull, until she assured me that they weren't. And then the Lord, surfacing briefly from his detective story, would intervene to say that he'd rather talk to the lavatory attendant at Harcourt Street station than to the person in question. Sometimes people that I liked were dismissed by my mother as 'rather rubbishy', or by the Lord as 'maniacal ego-maniacs'. You certainly had to keep your wits about you at our house. But all in all it was the most stimulating of atmospheres in which to grow up.

The house was constantly open to celebrities of every kind, and the adolescents were allowed to shout their heads off as loudly as anyone else.

There was one summer holiday in a hotel in Kerry when Shaw and his wife arrived. My parents had known them in London before the war. Shaw was writing *St. Joan*, but came on several picnics with us in the afternoons. I listened with absorbed attention and no understanding whatever to tremendous metaphysical and theological arguments between Shaw and the Lord, and was relieved when my mother gave Shaw her seal of approval.

"Shaw's all right," she said, and presented me with an omnibus volume of all his plays, including the prefaces, which I read at the age of thirteen or fourteen far into the night.

I thought *Candida* was the most exciting thing I'd ever read. "It's as good as a detective story," I told my mother, though nearly all my earlier reading had been confined to motor-cycling magazines and the adventures of Buffalo Bill.

I don't know if I would have read Shaw quite so avidly if I hadn't seen him in the flesh. On the other hand, though I did once hide D. H. Lawrence's hat, I was only three at the time, so that quite a number of years went by before I got round to reading him.

The hiding of Lawrence's hat took place when we were living in London during the first world war. It was a time when my father and mother provided food, shelter and comfort for quite a large number of literary figures like Middleton Murry, Katherine Mansfield and the Lawrences who, apparently, often used our house as an arena for their more savage battles.

It was after one of these that I, joining in the general mood of censure, said, "And I hided his hat", but I cannot claim to remember even what Lawrence looked like. None the less, the literary aura of those days has always continued to cling to me, so much so that unthinking people have come to believe that on our return to Dublin I became friends with such celebrities as Lady Gregory, George Moore and W. B. Yeats, despite the fact that I would have been seven or eight years of age at the time and a great deal more interested in Hornby trains than in the Abbey Theatre. But I do remember the house in which we lived, when we came back to Ireland.

It was called Clonard, and it stood in its own grounds on the outskirts of Dublin. Admittedly, there were a number of other houses, many of them bigger than ours, in the same road, but once I went in through the gate I always had the feeling of living in the country.

There was a gate lodge where Cook, the gardener, lived with his wife, and a drive leading to a big sweep of gravel in front of the house. There was a tennis court and a small field between us and the road. In the middle of the field was a weeping willow.

A flight of steps led up to the front door and then there was a big circular hall, with a long passage at right angles to it, with the bedrooms leading off it.

The house was made of red brick and apart from the basement it was all on one level, but it always seemed to me to be of substantial size.

A big conservatory led off the dining-room. From the balcony at the back we went down a flight of iron steps into the garden, which must have been a couple of acres in size. Beyond it was a field in which the Lord had had a small lake made, with an island in the middle of it and several home-made canoes.

It was a marvellously happy house to me, with room for

everyone to enjoy themselves in as they wanted to. We played croquet on the front lawn at night by the light of the head-lamps of cars. The Lord and I had a game called Beezers, a kind of coarse golf. We drove off from the hall-door steps with tennis balls, round the weeping willow, back past the side of the house, up through the back garden and out into the field with the lake in it, where we holed out into a bucket. We would then tee-up again, trying to lash our tennis balls high over the hedge back into the garden, hack our way through the vegetables, past the other side of the house, round the willow again and finally from the range of fifty yards or so try to hole out through the front door into the hall. We counted every stroke with meticulous care, working away side by side through the long grass counting, "Seventy-eight—seventy-nine—eighty—" until the dramatic finale when one of us slotted it through the front door with a great cry of "Beezer!"

I went back to look at Clonard the other day, some thirty years after we'd left it. All at once I wanted to see how big the willow had grown, and whether the spiky monkey-puzzle tree that was so painful to beezer into was still there.

I couldn't find the house. What had been almost open country was now an enormous housing estate, hundreds of neat little villas with tiny gardens. I thought that Clonard must have been demolished. Then I turned into a side road that had never been there before—and I saw it. A shabby, little, red-brick bungalow standing empty and uncared-for in the middle of dozens of brand-new villas. The willow had gone and the field and the tennis-court. There were new houses all over the back garden and more where the field and the lake had been.

Clonard had shrunk to the size of a match-box. I sat in the car for a long time looking at it, trying to remember what it had been, trying to remember what now seemed to be the magical things that had happened there.

I remembered coming home from school one afternoon and hearing someone in the sitting-room singing in the most powerful voice I'd ever heard. I opened the door and saw a huge black man standing by the piano, with my mother in her usual desperate concentration bending over the keyboard. It was Paul Robeson and he was singing 'Ole Man River' as loudly and triumphantly as though for a whole cheering concert hall.

I remembered interviewing Prince Chavchavadze for the *Irish Times*, after he'd given a piano recital in Dublin, and having dinner with him in the Dolphin Hotel and gathering up more and more people and bringing him back to Clonard round about midnight. He sat down at our small, upright piano and began to touch the keys very gently and softly, but he couldn't resist it. In a moment he was giving his recital all over again, with such passion that the little piano almost seemed to leap off the ground.

When he was leaving we found a note on the hall table. It was from my mother. "WHO was the Master Hand??" she had written.

The Master Hand wrote underneath it, "Forgive me for keeping you awake. Chavchavadze."

It was impossible to believe that the shabby, little, red-brick bungalow had ever been so alive with music. Then I remembered the night that Michael MacLiammoir and Hilton Edwardes had come out to discuss the finances of the Gate Theatre with the Lord and Hilton becoming more and more impassioned about the mystique of the theatre and Michael quietly leaving the room to make a dramatic re-entry some time later heavily made-up with my mother's cosmetics, his head draped in a chiffon scarf, his body enveloped in a bed-sheet.

He had become Sara Bernhardt, including the wooden leg and the most exquisite of French accents. He laid himself on the sofa and for half an hour was the Lady of the Camelias in her death throes, the most profane Sara of all time.

I started the car and turned it round in the new road. The match-box had become unbearably small.

Chapter Four

IN the same way as the credit for my going to Rossall can be laid at the door of Charles, the all-round athlete, I owed my entry into Pembroke College, Oxford, to the good offices of my tennis-playing uncle, Cecil.

Like all the other forward steps in my education this one seemed to be dictated much more by chance than by any master plan.

On one of his irregular and tentative explorations into my future the Lord asked me, while I was still at Rossall, if I'd thought about going to a university. "Perhaps," he said, "you'd like to try Trinity? Or, if you were going on with this Foreign Office idea, Oxford or Cambridge might be more useful. Of course, we'd have to do something about your stammer."

I saw that things had taken a serious turn. The stammer was mentioned only when the Lord had become re-convinced that he would have to support me, as a non-wage earner, for the rest of his life. It happened three or four times a year.

I said I didn't much care for the idea of Trinity. "I find Dublin's a bit too small," I said, though I hadn't actually tried to fill it. "I suppose it'll have to be Oxford or Cambridge. I think I like the feel of Oxford better."

He was good enough not to ask me how I'd come to form this opinion. To him, any decision on my part was more than welcome. Nor did he advance any further into the Foreign Office plan. I don't think he had a clear idea of the contribution I might be able to make to international diplomacy, and at no time had I given it even a second's thought. The Foreign Office for him was a shadowy and faintly comforting possibility, well away in the background.

"If you like the idea of Oxford," he said, "I'm sure Cecil can do something about getting you in."

Cecil was my father's younger brother, and the Old Lord's pride and joy. He was extraordinarily handsome, hawk-nosed and blue-eyed with jet-black, wavy hair. Cecil was a tennis-player who'd been in the final of the Men's Singles at Wimble-

don on a number of occasions, though the number seemed to
vary from time to time. Like my father, he was a very funny
and imaginative story-teller, with a tendency to toy with the
facts.

Every year, for Wimbledon, Cecil would have his tailor make
him a white, lamb's-wool overcoat, to be slung round his
shoulders when he came on to the court and then tossed to the
ground for the ball-boys or the umpire or even his opponent to
pick up. Cecil was well aware of his magnificent appearance and
accepted every attention as his natural right.

After Wimbledon he would come to Dublin with a troupe of
international stars for the Irish Championships, which are
played at the Fitzwilliam Club, and the Old Lord would give
glittering tennis parties on the court at Glenavy, which was
scarcely ever used at any other time of the year.

I never attended any of them, even in the capacity of ball-
boy, because Cecil was always punctilious in keeping his poor
relations in Ireland separated from his cosmopolitan London
friends. Neither he nor the Old Lord could overlook the fact that
my mother's family were 'in trade', even if it was sports goods
rather more than haberdashery.

They could, of course, overlook the strong probability that my
grandfather's grandfather had been a policeman in the village of
Glenavy, in the North of Ireland, and it was from this connection with the law that my grandfather had become a K.C. and
Lord Chancellor of Ireland. Also, when he became the first
Baron he took his title from Glenavy more because he liked the
sound of it than because of landed estates in the area. I doubt, in
fact, if he'd ever been in the village in his life.

The most that Cecil had done for me, his only nephew, up till
now had been to give me one of his racquets, after Wimbledon.
It was too heavy for me, and probably too heavy for Cecil, too,
but it was an exceedingly beautiful instrument.

He was now, however, going to get me into Pembroke College, Oxford, through some indefinable connection with the
Vice-Chancellor of the University, who was also the Master of
Pembroke. It was probably only of a social nature, but it
worked. All concerned were no doubt grateful for my contribution to the deal, in passing the Higher Certificate, but Cecil's
natural radiance would certainly have swung it without my help.

I only met him, in London, a few more times. By now he was

living permanently in Cairo, working for the Egyptian Government and for various business concerns. He'd been made a baronet. He was now the Honourable Sir Cecil Campbell, and looked every inch of it. Even in London he was attended by his Egyptian servant, Fahmy, who wore a tarbush and a double-breasted livery with gold buttons.

I had lunch with Cecil once in the Hyde Park Hotel shortly before the war. He'd come to England for what he described as 'a couple of weeks of fresh air at Eastbourne', but during the course of the meal he disclosed a secondary purpose. He had now married for the second time but was still without an heir. He said he thought that he and I ought 'to get together a bit', as he'd just made a will making me his sole beneficiary.

"Quite a substantial sum," Cecil said, seriously. "Something in the neighbourhood of ninety-seven thousand pounds."

I found it difficult to believe. In the first place there was Cecil's well-known ability for dickering with the truth—one in which I shared, almost to a fault, myself—and secondly his reputation was much more for spending, on himself, rather than saving, for posterity. Also, I didn't see how we could 'get together a bit' when he spent almost all his time in Cairo.

Ninety seven thousand pounds sounded, however, like a very handsome sum. If only half of it was there, it would be more than welcome.

I never saw Cecil again. Some years after the war he shot himself, in mysterious circumstances, in Cairo, and his third wife scooped the pool. But not, I'm glad to say, all of it.

She came to London, after Cecil's death, and asked me to dine with her.

During the course of dinner she pressed something into my hand. It was a pair of onyx cuff-links, each link joined to the other by a thin gold chain. One of the chains was broken.

"I know," she said, "Cecil would like you to have them."

It was a sharp drop from ninety-seven thousand pounds.

But, at least, Cecil, while he was alive, gave me this other gift —the gift of a half-open door into Pembroke. I regret to say that I never managed to open it any wider. Oxford, like *Mens Sana in Corpore Sano*, proved to be much too big for me.

I arrived there with the remnants of the rugger kit that I'd used at Rossall, including a pair of boots. I knew so little about

Oxford I thought that games might still be compulsory, as they'd been at Rossall.

The boots came to light the first afternoon at Pembroke, when I was unpacking. My scout, a venal-looking old man of lacklustre disposition, picked them up. "You a rugger man, then, sir?" he asked me, brightening a little.

"Not really," I said. "I just thought perhaps I'd have to play."

He gave me a puzzled, sour look, and put the boots away in a cupboard.

By a coincidence which was going to affect the whole of my life at Oxford my first visitor that afternoon was the secretary of the College rugger club, a large young man of earnest demeanour.

"I don't know if you're a rugger man," he said, "but I'd be delighted if you'd care to join the rugger club. With your height," he said shrewdly, "you'd be pretty useful in the line-out."

Something in my face seemed to suggest to him that he'd failed to strike oil.

"Of course," he said, "you don't have to. Perhaps you play cricket?"

Suddenly, I perceived I didn't have to play rugger, or anything else. I was grown-up. I was free to choose.

"I'm sorry," I told the large young man, "I'm getting too old for rugger. It's too much like hard work."

"Oh, well," he said resignedly, putting away his membership form, "I suppose that's that."

During the next few days the secretary of the cricket club called on me, and I turned him down. He was followed by the secretary of the hockey club and half a dozen others, including the secretary of the music society. I turned them all down. The last one was the secretary of the boat club, a huge, ginger-haired youth who looked not unlike my tormentor at Crawley's prep school.

"I'm told," he said, a stern disciplinarian, "you're not joining anything. It's pretty unusual, you know. In fact, it's a damn bad show."

"I just don't feel like it," I told him. "I might join something later on."

He couldn't believe it. "What are you going to do in the meantime?" he wanted to know.

It was a much better question than I realised. By refusing, out of idleness, obstinacy and probably fear to join anything, I'd cut myself off from the life of Pembroke and, indeed, from the life of the whole University. But there was one thing I did join, and it was disastrous.

Up to Pembroke, at the same time as myself, went two young men from Dublin. Strangely enough, I'd never met either of them before, though our tastes and backgrounds were approximately the same. We joined one another, defensively, against the sophisticated young Englishmen around us, and the three of us sank together.

It was, I had to note, the first time I'd ever rebelled against authority and it was—as it so often is—the drink that did it.

We drank beer, with an occasional glass of sherry if anyone had any, and we drank enough to promote enterprises like tipping buckets of coal down the Junior Dean's staircase, or shooting air-gun pellets from a top-floor window into people going into the Chapel. We created pandemonium in cinemas. We patronised a restaurant several nights a week which was run by an elderly Swiss couple and filled our pockets to bursting with their knives and forks.

One night, after looping lavatory paper all round the walls of someone's rooms, we set fire to it and doused the flames with soda siphons, while sheltering under umbrellas. On the way back to my rooms I fell over the first-floor banisters of my staircase on to the flag stones below and only grazed my knee.

It was a sad time, and it became sadder still when all three of us failed Pass Moderations, an entrance exam which tried to do little more than to discover whether we could read and write. This was when I found that my knowledge of Tacitus had declined by 78 per cent in a matter of weeks.

We went down after the first term making various conscience-stricken resolutions to do better in the next. Though we had been inseparable in Pembroke we split up as soon as we got home to Dublin, and didn't see one another until we went up again next term. Not even true friendship bound us together.

We made a little more effort next term. Sean joined the rowing club, Pat toyed—I think—with a little football, and I began to play golf. It was no great contribution to the social and educational life of the college, particularly in my case, because I played golf not at Southfields, which was the University course, but at the much less distinguished North Oxford club. And I played golf, nearly every afternoon, with a shy and pretty undergraduette from one of the women's colleges. Her christian name was May and she was a very nice girl. She was much too nice to tell me what we both knew—that we were idly and feebly wasting our time.

During those afternoons at North Oxford she might have been working—she was intelligent and industrious—and I might, at least, while no great hand at the game, have been putting myself in line for a golf Blue. But, knowing I wasn't good enough, I didn't even try. I taught May how to play golf instead, though she was only slightly more inaccurate than myself.

Sean, Pat and I were, however, working a little harder this term, at any rate in the mornings, when we attended occasional lectures, always sitting at the back and trying to amuse ourselves as best we could.

We now had a goal to aim at, for Sean had come up with a Morris Cowley two-seater only to find that he wasn't allowed to use it at the University until he was through Pass Moderations. All three of us worked with some determination that term, and all three of us failed P. Mods again.

This was, in part, due to friendships which had arisen between us and three girls—of good family—who worked in an establishment called the Chelsea Tea Rooms. They were, as can be imagined, much in demand, but they used to come to parties in our rooms which came to an end, by college regulations, at 9 p.m. There was no precise division of the three girls among us. We seemed to change partners about once a week, and during the afternoons, I was still playing golf with May. I'd also taken to wearing a black shirt, while keeping well away from the Oxford branch of the British Union of Fascists, which were beginning to become active in the University.

I also endured long admonitions in my rooms from a youth in gold-rimmed glasses who was recruiting for Moral Rearmament, who appeared to find in me the ingredients of a promising novice.

I didn't know what I was doing at all.

At home in Dublin the Lord was becoming more and more concerned about my future and, after a minor motor accident, went so far as to give me a formal lecture, becoming a conventionally stern parent for the very first and the very last time.

I was going out to play tennis when he intercepted me in the hall. "Come in here a minute," he said. "I want to talk to you."

I said I couldn't, that friends were waiting for me down the road.

"It won't take long," he said. I'd never seen him looking so stern, or so sad.

It was not a memorable address. He was too unhappy to be angry, and I think he was sorry that he'd chosen this particular moment. It was a Sunday afternoon and he was wearing his tattered gardening clothes, while I sat opposite him in white flannels and a red, white and blue Old Rossallian blazer.

Neither of us looked like people ready to buckle-to to the serious business of earning a living, but that was the main theme of the Lord's address.

"I'm not criticising you," he began. "You must understand that. And I'm not asking you to give up any of your pleasures. I love playing games myself. But you must really begin to think about what you're going to do for a living. I've only got what I earn and if anything happened to me I don't know what you'd all do for money."

I felt frozen, and bored. I'd heard all this business about approaching bankruptcy so often before.

I closed my ears and my heart and my mind, a process of combating criticism, however helpful and affectionate, that was going to become increasingly familiar later on.

It was the same thing as my regarding anger as a waste of time. It was a lovely afternoon. A moment before I'd been rushing off to play tennis, and now everything had stopped.

I sat there, aggressively silent, looking my father straight in the eye. I could think of nothing whatever to say.

"It's getting to be a very competitive world," my father went on. "You've got to have some kind of background of knowledge, some sort of diploma, if you're going to get a job that'll give you enough to live on."

It seemed to be so self-evident I could only imagine that it gave him pleasure to trot out all this old stuff. I couldn't think of any reply to it, except to mutter from time to time, "Yes, of course. Yes, I can well see that."

"I'm honestly not criticising you," my father went on, "but you don't really seem to be trying to do anything yourself. One of the bank directors said he'd seen you with the car in the ditch and he said, 'I see your young hopeful's been at it again.' "

The poor Lord grinned, trying to ease his own hurt.

So that was where he'd heard about the accident. "It was nothing," I said. "This madman came shooting out of a side road and pushed me into the ditch. The car's perfectly all right. I'll touch up the paintwork myself. You don't have to bother about that."

This stung the Lord almost to anger. "It's your whole attitude," he said. "You don't really seem to care about anything. If only you'd tell me what you want to do I'm sure I can help you. I know a lot of people in Dublin. They'd be only too glad to do something for—"

He paused. I thought he wanted to say—"for Lord Glenavy's son"—emphasising, without immodesty, the respect in which he was held.

He changed it to—"for you."

I relented, became a little more generous. "That's very kind of you," I said. "But it's very difficult," I went on, "to know what sort of thing I ought to do."

I shifted the blame. "I never really seem to have been trained for anything," I said. "At least, you were a lawyer, to begin with."

He let me get away with it. "I know how hard it is for you," he said. "But if you had an inclination towards doing any kind of job I'm sure I could get you started." He grinned again. "Have you ever thought about it at all?" he said.

I couldn't let him think I had no ambition of any kind. "Well," I said, "I've been thinking for some time I'd like to be a writer."

I was frightened to go on. At long last I'd produced a suggestion for my own future, but it was underhand. I told my father I'd like to be a writer because he had known Shaw and Lawrence, Middleton Murry and Robert Lynd, and because he'd written a play himself. It would surely please him, and relieve me of his concern. But it seemed to be a fearful commitment. I felt I'd have to begin to learn how to be a writer the very next day.

The Lord wasn't as pleased as I thought he'd be. "Writing's a precarious profession," he said. "It would be years before you were earning a decent screw."

I thought he sounded like his own father, using an old-fashioned expression like 'a decent screw'. I thought it proved he was out of touch with the modern world of newspapers, books and magazines.

"I've met some very interesting people at Oxford," I said, telling him a lie he couldn't disprove. "One of them's already written a novel and two more are going to join the *Daily Express* as soon as they go down." I had a sudden inspiration. "Wasn't the Old Lord a great friend of Beaverbrook's?" I said. "There might be an opening there."

"I don't think you'd be cut out for that sort of world," my father said, trying urgently to damp down the idea before it took too firm a hold on me. "You'd never be able to do any reporting. I mean, you couldn't use the telephone with your stammer."

"It wouldn't have to be a reporting job," I said. "There are all kinds of other things, like articles and so on."

I had a moment of conviction that I knew was completely fictitious. "I just know," I said, "that some kind of writing is the only thing I want to do."

The Lord looked deeply troubled, almost as though he felt he was worse off than ever.

"It might be a useful sideline," he said. "But in the meantime you really ought to think seriously about the Foreign Office idea."

I couldn't believe we'd got back to the Foreign Office again, when I'd gone out of my way, for the first time, to make a definite proposal for my future.

"I'll do that, of course," I said. "But in the meantime, when I get back to Oxford I'll check up on the Beaverbrook thing with these two chaps who are going to join him."

At that moment, though I'd invented them, I could see them and hear them talking to me. "They tell me," I said to my father, "that the Beaver's always looking for—for likely lads."

I found for the first time that I was able to grin myself. Nearly all the earlier clouds had been thrust away.

"I'd better get along now," I said, getting to my feet and picking up my racquet. "I want to try out my new spinning service with loop and kick-back."

The Lord and I had always had elaborate descriptions of various strokes on the golf-course and the tennis-court. I thought this was a good time to give him one, now.

He grinned faintly. "You'd better do that," he said. But he had one last appeal. "You'll take things a bit easier, won't you?"

he said. "I mean, cars and too many parties and things like that. The world's a pretty tough place."

It was, for him. As for me, I skidded out of the gate in a shower of gravel and roared off down the road to my tennis-party, singing aloud because a fairly serious crisis in my life had been dexterously smudged and finally blotted out. It was still a lovely day.

The only thing I can remember of the next term at Oxford was an interview with the Junior Dean. He was round, pink and plump with a young face but very little hair. He looked to me to be very much like a monk who had severed his connection with the world, to be imprisoned in Oxford for life.

He had some pained words to say. He said that in his experience some 'men' took longer than others to settle into the kind of life most beneficial to themselves, and to the University, and that it seemed to him—he had no wish to give offence—that I was one of them. He made a glancing reference to 'somewhat unfortunate companions', but felt he had no doubt he was doing them an injustice. He permitted himself a small smile. The Irish, he said, had always had a reputation for being a little rebellious.

I looked straight back at him, in my usual aggressive silence. I was coming to the conclusion that people enjoyed giving advice, that it gave them a feeling of comfortable superiority. I let the Junior Dean feel superior. There was no way of stopping him. Once again, receiving advice, I found I had nothing to say.

He went on for some time, speaking of the riches, both social and educational, that Oxford had to offer, of the privilege of being *in statu pupillari* at Pembroke which, while being one of the smaller colleges, had an honourable record of service to the University. Many young men, he said, unable for various reasons to pursue their further education at Pembroke, would be deeply envious of my good fortune—a good fortune, however, of which I seemed to be unaware.

I could have done it for him, word for word. As usual, I felt I was listening to self-evident truths which had been rolled out by parents and teachers since the beginning of time. I knew they were all very well in their way, but they had no relevance to me and to my special situation, whatever that might be.

I had to qualify it by 'whatever that might be' because, being confused about it, I'd never tried to explain it to anyone, and it was only by talking that I could find out what I was talking about.

This attempt at self-analysis, while listening at the same time to the sound advice of the Junior Dean, wearied me into the familiar sensation of the beginning of general anaesthesia—my eyes closing, my face setting, the world getting farther and farther away.

The Junior Dean brought me out of it by asking me a question, a question that people seemed to be asking with increasing frequency. He asked me what I wanted to 'do'.

In desperation, I was about to launch out into the matter of writing when the Junior Dean—fortunately, perhaps—made himself clear. He meant what subject or subjects did I wish to study for my degree?

I was beginning to get a feeling of being hunted. The questions about my future were becoming more and more precise. And this was a particularly awkward one because, so far as I could remember, it had not come up before.

I was astonished, in fact, to find that I'd come to Oxford with no declared purpose in mind. It seemed I could become anything I wanted or, at least, try for a degree in any subject that might be available. A geologist, a physicist, a Mus. Bach. or even a classical scholar.

I had a moment of terror in which I seemed to have had no past of any kind. There seemed to have been no discussion, no preparation for this moment of decision—a decision that was clearly going to change my whole life. Then I remembered the Foreign Office. For the first time I welcomed it with open arms.

"Modern Languages," I told the Junior Dean. "My father wants me to go into the Foreign Office, and I think it's a pretty good idea."

For a moment I was on the verge of elaborating the good qualities of the idea, in relation to my own potential, and then found the ground was rather too bare.

"My uncle's in it," I said.

The Junior Dean was too surprised to examine this latter qualification. "The Foreign Office!" he said. He leant forward across his desk. "How many languages do you have, then?" he asked.

"Well," I said, "French and a little— Just French, really," I told him. "I got a credit for French in the Higher Cert."

"I see," said the Junior Dean.

Despite the fragility of the structure he was working upon, he decided to lay another burden upon it.

"I'm going to come to a decision with you," he said. "It's rather an unusual one. In fact, I cannot remember it happening before. You still haven't got P. Mods, but rather than waste any further time I suggest that you study for it and for your degree at the same time."

He permitted himself a quizzical, academic smile. "I cannot venture to think," he said, "what will happen if you continue to fail P. Mods into your second year, while advancing with some promise towards taking a degree in Modern Languages, but we shall have to see."

He consulted a file on his desk. "Miss Rhys will be your tutor," he said. "I suggest you call upon her without delay. There is her address."

It was like being given a one-way ticket to Australia. The die was finally cast. I was being dragged forward, bound hand and foot, towards a place behind a desk in the Foreign Office, and I hadn't an idea in the world what the Foreign Office did.

I called on Miss Rhys the following day, cycling out to one of the red-brick villas in North Oxford. It was in the same direction as the golf-club where May and I had spent so many idle hours. I sincerely hoped that the intervention of Miss Rhys wasn't going to be bring about an end of that side of my life at Oxford. It was the only one that had given me any real pleasure, so far.

I have only the faintest memory of my tutor, Miss Rhys. For all I know her name might have been 'Reece'. I never saw it written down.

I believe I can recall a large Welsh lady, dressed in black, but this impression might have been created by the gloom of her sitting-room.

She said the Junior Dean had spoken to her on the phone and explained the circumstances. She then had a mild burst of irritation. "Do get this Mod. thing out of the way," she said. "It's perfectly absurd that a person of your education cannot pass it."

"Yes, Miss Rhys," I said.

She gave me a leather-bound volume. "Translate some of this for me," she snapped. "I want to see what you can do."

I began to open the book.

"Not now!" she cried. "Come back some time next week."

She returned briskly to the papers on her desk. I let myself out of the front door.

I opened the book when I got back to my rooms and saw, with the sensation of someone who has had a practical joke played upon them by a total stranger, that it contained pages of poetry in a language which at first I didn't recognise but slowly realised must be French. But it was a kind of French I'd never seen before. I turned back to the title page and learnt that the work in hand had been written in the sixteenth century by someone I'd never heard of. It looked as though Chaucer had been having a go at the French language.

I put it away. Some kind of appeal would have to be made to Miss Rhys or Reece next week, some suggestion that it might be better for me to begin with some rather more modern author, and work back to the earlier ones, but in the meantime Miss Rhys or Reece had given me a piece of advice which, for the first time in my life, I felt had been intelligently presented, a positive spur to action.

Miss Rhys had wasted no time on sententious counsel or abstract exhortation. She'd more or less said, "Stop arsing about and get on with it." She'd made a direct approach to an almost non-existent pride in my intellectual capabilities. And, furthermore, she'd frightened me severely.

I got Pass Moderations that term, if only just. And with it, a licence to drive Sean's motor-car. It meant the end of my career at Oxford.

At the beginning of this fourth term Sean, Pat and I—even our names seemed to be excessively Irish—moved out of college into digs round the corner.

Despite the fact that it was an incredibly grimy little house in a narrow alley-way facing north, so that artificial light was needed all the time, it felt like the beginning of a new and somehow more promising life. Each of us had a bedroom to ourselves, and a communal sitting-room. It almost seemed as if we might be able to work here, without the distractions of college. It looked as though we could make a real, fresh start.

Then the landlord had a little chat with us. He was a big, dyspeptic looking man with a few strands of black hair plastered across the top of his lard-like head, and was probably a retired publican.

He came into the sitting-room without knocking, on the evening we moved in.

"I got something to say to you gents," he announced. "I heard all about you from the Head Porter."

It was a bad beginning. The Head Porter, a genial character called Ponsonby, was one of the few friends we had among the college authorities. He'd once spent a holiday in Dublin and as a result contracted what he called 'a soft spot for the wild Irish'.

Whatever Ponsonby had told this lump of a landlord could only have been in our favour. When we'd air-gunned the Chapel-goers Ponsonby had shaken each of us, privately, by the hand.

"And what did our good friend Mr. Ponsonby tell you, then?" said Sean. He had a sharp, unpredictable temper that often alarmed me.

"Never you mind," said the landlord, altogether unintimidated. "My missus's a sick woman, and we don't want any of your larks in here. This is a respectable house and that's what it's going to be."

We put the respectability of the house to the test that very night. We dined in the George Restaurant, to let the Swiss couple know that their knives and forks were once again in danger, and went back to another college with some people we met. We got back to our new home at twenty past twelve, or twenty minutes after the regulation hour, to find that the chain had been put across the door.

Sean's temper cracked and he shouted abuse through the gap while in the street outside Pat and I sang 'The Rose of Tralee'.

The landlord came down in his dressing-gown and released the chain. He didn't speak a single word. Next morning the three of us were summoned to attend upon the Junior Dean.

This time he didn't look like a plump, pink monk at all. There were no wry, academic smiles. He was the loud harsh voice of authority, and he meant every word he said.

He said that any further infringements of the regulations would be punished by gating, and if after that they continued, all three of us would be sent down.

When we got back to our digs we sat silently for a while in the dark sitting-room, none of us liking the other two very much. Sean suddenly said, "Let's go out to a pub. Let's get out of this bloody gaol."

I drove the car. We travelled all over Oxfordshire, drinking pints of beer in numberless pubs. It wasn't a successful celebration. I told Sean he shouldn't have shouted at the sodding landlord. Sean got involved in a long, jealous quarrel with Pat about the people we'd met in the George, and who'd dragged us away to the other end of the town, making us late.

We slept that afternoon in a field, while the pubs were shut, and then had a couple more. We were friends again, as we drove back to Oxford, and had actually formulated a plan for work. Shortly after 6 p.m., swerving away from a bus, I drove straight into the Martyr's Memorial, in the middle of the city. The car seemed to try to climb the steps. The door on my side burst open and I shot out, to skid along the tarmac on the seat of my trousers.

I don't remember anything that happened after that, but it must have been shock rather more than serious injury that obliterated the rest of the evening because I woke up in my own bed the following morning, instead of in hospital or a cell.

I felt in worse shape than I'd been at any time since the scarlet fever crisis in the Isolation Hospital. From the stunned and racking hangover I judged we must have had a lot more to drink after the accident, probably whiskey, by the cauterised state of my throat. Then I became aware that my bottom was on fire. I felt it gently. It was covered with some hard, tacky substance that could only be blood.

I crawled out of bed with my bottom blazing. Every bone in my body seemed to have been stretched and twisted during the night. I arranged the horrible walnut mirror on the bamboo dressing-table to the best advantage and peered at my bottom through the gloom in which the bedroom was perpetually enveloped. It was corrugated, and black with blood.

I turned on the light, to make a closer examination, and found that it wasn't blood. It was tar. Tar from the road had been driven into the very pores of my skin. I was marked for life, on the bottom, with a six-inch circle of tar.

Then a new fear assailed me. Unless I could get it off quickly the tar was going to give me blood-poisoning, probably leading to cancer.

I put a towel round my waist, holding it away from the tar, and inched my way along the passage to the bathroom. The door was locked. I beat on it. Either Pat or Sean was being sick inside.

I beat on the door again, shouting to be let in, and suddenly the landlord was standing behind me.

"That'll be all of that," he said savagely. "You made enough trouble already."

I turned round in agony. "I'm badly hurt," I said. "I've got to bathe my—my back."

"Ablutions," he said, "is provided in college." Then he said, with extraordinary venom, "Don't think you're going to get away with any of this."

So something else, even more awful if possible, had happened. Perhaps we'd smashed up his piano, or set his sofa on fire. But all that would have to wait. The tar had begun to eat into my very tissues. I had to get it off.

I put on a dressing-gown, crept out of the house and round the corner to Pembroke. There seemed to be no one about. It was probably very early in the morning. Then out of the gates of Pembroke, looking like a small, chunky galleon in full sail, came the Junior Dean, in his mortar-board and long gown.

I'd forgotten all about him. I jumped backwards round the corner into the lane and waited, holding on to the wall, until the sound of his footsteps disappeared in the direction of Christchurch. Then I flew through the gates of the college, heedless of the tar, wanting only to reach the safety of the bathrooms.

Twenty minutes later I was standing on one leg in a bath of lukewarm water, still trying to scrape off the tar with a sponge. There was a firm but polite knocking on the door.

"Are you there, sir?" a voice said. I'd never heard it before. "I'd just like a word with you, if you don't mind. It's the police."

The landlord, no doubt choosing his moment with care, had betrayed me again.

I put a towel round my waist, opened the door, and in came a plain clothes policeman. He wore a mackintosh and a brown trilby hat and he was—God bless him—a kindly and elderly man.

He said he just wanted to make a few routine enquiries. Then, seeing my stricken condition, he gave a sympathetic grin. I didn't have to worry about the police, he said. The college authorities had taken up the matter and they'd deal with any further developments, if there were going to be any.

It was a microscopic crumb of comfort.

Then he said, "Your two friends, as you probably know, got off with a few bruises. We just wanted to check up on your injuries, if any."

I had to tell him, he looked so fatherly and kind. "I got a lot of tar shoved into my bum off the road," I said. "I can't get it off."

I turned round, lowered the towel an inch or two, and showed him the upper edge of the patch of tar. He leant forward, and whistled softly in surprise. "Strewth," he said, "I never saw anything like that before." He became concerned. "Perhaps surgical spirit or something like that would do it," he suggested. "I'd take it along to the doc, if I was you."

I didn't. I worked away at the patch of tar myself for the next couple of weeks, reducing its dimensions a millimetre at a time. There was plenty of opportunity for this solitary pursuit because after another interview with the Junior Dean—one which has faded from my mind in its entirety—the three of us were gated for the rest of the term. That was, we had to be in our digs, the front door of which was locked, every evening by nine o'clock, or be sent down.

Surprisingly enough, it turned out to be an intolerable imprisonment. There wasn't time to go to a cinema after dinner, and we had to leave the George Restaurant before the more boisterous and enjoyable part of the evening began. On the few occasions when we went to a party in another college we had to confess to the juvenile disgrace of being gated, and leave early, before the more amusing guests arrived.

It should certainly have provided an excellent opportunity for working, but Sean and I, at least, had decided we'd had enough of Oxford. We'd stick it out until the end of term and then we'd quietly retire.

Pat had begun to withdraw from us, to stay in his bedroom in the evening. We could hear the rustle of books and papers and judged that he was working, studying law. This he must have been doing because years later I met him in El Vino's in Fleet Street as a fully fledged barrister, wearing a black Homburg hat and an English accent that was as fine as any I'd ever heard. He greeted me apprehensively. He'd risen far above the good old days.

So, during my last term at Oxford, I played a lot of golf with May and did really nothing else. Even Miss Rhys had passed out of my life, after I'd received no reply to my courteous note returning her volume of poetry, with the suggestion that I might begin with some more contemporary author. No doubt she'd talked again to the Junior Dean on the telephone, and both had decided it was better to let sleeping dogs lie.

On the last night of the term Sean and Pat and I had a final dinner in the George. As we left we emptied our pockets of all the cutlery we'd collected during the evening and gave it back to the Swiss couple, assuring them we had no further need of it.

We left Oxford round about midnight in Sean's car, now shakily repaired. On my insistence we left a crate of a dozen bottles of Guinesses's stout on Miss Rhys's doorstep in North Oxford, with a brief note of thanks for her forbearance. I meant it, too. For a brief moment she'd given me the feeling that it might have been possible to pull myself together, and work for a degree.

The only other thing that Oxford had done for me was to leave me with a round, white scar, quite large, just below my right hip-bone.

Before Oxford, the years I'd spent being educated had passed in a kind of mildly demanding and not unpleasant dream.

I'd managed to pass exams, thanks to a retentive memory, and had forgotten nearly everything a few weeks later.

I had totally disgraced neither myself nor anyone else. But the entire process of schooling had left no aftermath of any kind.

Oxford was different. A sense of shame and waste still lingers over the four terms I spent there, made all the keener by the knowledge that so many other people had derived so much benefit, both in learning and social pleasures, from a way of life that I couldn't come to grips with at all.

And there was another thing. Almost everyone else I met had a clear goal before them—a Blue or a degree—and worked for it in a way that made my caperings seem just plain silly.

I've never liked looking plain silly. And when I feel I've been plain silly my agile mind is always ready to provide me with adequate compensation.

It did so now, at the age of eighteen, when I went down from Oxford for the last time.

It was plain I was never going to be able to compete with all these embryo lawyers, scientists, historians and mathematicians. They had a capacity for work that could be looked upon as mechanical. In fact, it was all they could do.

Though I couldn't imagine how I was going to earn a living I knew it would all come right in the end. I didn't have to go through the drudgery of learning anything by rote. I'd be able to get a job by luck. Some future employer would see the very quality in me that he was looking for—some unique quality I couldn't even guess at myself. But once he let me know what it was I'd be able to play up to it so successfully that he'd get something even better than he'd bargained for.

Even at eighteen, however, this kind of self-assurance was not too solidly based. It didn't trouble me unduly, though. Through the mists and uncertainties surrounding my future I could always see one steady, abiding light—the certainty that the Lord, in the person of my father, would provide.

Chapter Five

MY belief in the Lord's capacity to provide was justified. It wasn't until the comparatively mature age of thirty-two that I achieved complete financial independence.

It was, however, through no fault of the Lord's that it took me so long to earn my own living.

About a fortnight before leaving Oxford I'd written to tell him that I would not be going back.

"Oxford," I wrote—and I felt I was doing something helpful at last—"is no place for me. Everyone seems to be so juvenile and the discipline is worse than school. I honestly don't think I ought to stay on here any longer. I'm only wasting my time and your money."

As usual, however, I had no suggestion to make about what I should do next. I had no need to, though.

On the very evening I arrived in Dublin I found that the Lord had made a personal and entirely arbitrary decision about my future for the very first time. He had arranged for me to serve a period of apprenticeship in Munich on the business side of the German electrical firm of Siemens-Shukert.

The fact that he'd been able to do this in two weeks was a clear measure of the way in which his anxiety about my future had come to a head, or perhaps he'd had the idea in his mind for some time, as soon as he guessed that Oxford was going to fail.

Some years before, Siemens-Shukert had built on the River Shannon, at Arnacrusha, a hydro-electric scheme that was to provide the whole of Southern Ireland with power. The Lord, working for the Ministry of Industry and Commerce, had done a great deal to smooth the negotiations between Siemens and the Irish Government. Probably, one letter from him to Siemens had got me the job.

I must have taken the alarming news fairly well. At least, I'd been presented with a fait accompli that allowed of no argument or decision on my part.

The Lord, expecting opposition or at least a certain amount of defensive complaint, went off into one of his rare surges of enthusiasm. It was as though he had discovered, finally and for the last time, the ultimate secret of playing a bunker shot out of heavy sand.

Everything had been arranged down to the very last detail. I'd begin in the branch office in Munich, to find out which particular niche in the business suited me best, and then go on to Siemensstadt, almost a town on its own, in Berlin. Through a friend in Dublin, who knew Munich well, he'd even found me accommodation with an elderly baroness, who was looking forward to my arrival.

But—and this was the bit that pleased me most—I would not be going to Germany immediately. First of all, the whole family would spend a month's holiday at the Oatlands Park Hotel, near Weybridge, and from there I'd go up to London every morning by Green Line bus to have speech training for my stammer from a colleague of Lionel Logue, the man who'd done so much for the Duke of York, who was later to become George VI. Then, with my stammer cured or, at least, coming under control, they'd go back to Dublin and I'd stay in London for another couple of months, doing a crash course in German at the Berlitz School in Oxford Street. The Lord had even booked me a room, for an indefinite period, at the Prince of Wales Hotel in South Kensington. My grandmother had stayed there for some weeks, and found it quite comfortable.

"It all sounds a terribly good idea, Lordship," I said. "Thank you very much indeed."

Then the Lord, as he always did when he got excited about something, told me all about it, in a different order, all over again.

The holiday in Oatlands Park, was not, however, a complete success. It was a beautiful summer and I soon began to complain about the nuisance of having to catch the bus from outside the gates of the hotel and make my way to Harley Street and the colleague of Lionel Logue, only getting back in time for a late lunch.

I don't remember anything of the speech correction methods employed by Logue's colleague, but it couldn't have been his fault. I was thinking of the swimming-pool and the tennis courts and the nine-hole golf course at Oatlands Park, and certainly didn't give him nearly enough of my attention.

When the Lord asked me—all his old anxieties were coming back again—how I was getting on, I told him I didn't find the man very sympathetic, and his methods seemed to be too slow.

One day, after lunch, the Lord wanted to know what, exactly, these methods were? Perhaps I had some exercises to do, like reading aloud? He could hear me, in the afternoons. He'd do anything he could to help.

I said I was doing some special breathing exercises in my room at night, but I was sure that reading aloud would be useful. Then, to get away from an uncomfortable situation, I told him I had to go and play tennis. I ran down the steps of the terrace on which we were sitting, saw the pretty Italian girl I was going to play with, put on an additional burst of speed and leapt over a low hedge. Half way across I saw the back netting of the tennis court on the other side. I'd forgotten about it. I put out my right hand to save myself and impaled it on a six-inch iron bolt protruding from one of the uprights. I had time to see the bolt pushing out the skin on the back of my hand and then I fainted, falling into the hedge so deeply that my father was still trying to pull me out of it when I came to.

The Lord's grand plan had suffered a reverse from which it only partially recovered.

The doctor put six stitches in the palm of my hand, and put me to bed. I was suffering, he said, from a considerable degree of shock. He also feared that several bones had been broken in the hand and suggested an X-ray as soon as possible. The result of this unexpected development was that I had a new appointment, every second day, in Harley Street, with a physio-therapist who gave me treatment for my hand.

By chance, his consulting rooms were almost opposite those of the colleague of Lionel Logue, but I never saw him again. As I told the Lord—and my mother backed me up—I couldn't possibly endure the two treatments at the same time. The arm in the sling and the stoically borne pain must have gone some way to illustrate the truth of this.

The last few days at Oatlands Park were enveloped in tension and gloom. Once again—and as ever—my parents didn't quarrel in front of me, but they must have had some bitter arguments about what was to happen next.

My mother must have been determined to take me back to Dublin with her, at least until my hand had healed. I don't think she'd ever believed in the Siemens-Shukert idea. It was just another of the Lord's wilder plans, like diverting a stream and turning half the back garden into a boating lake. But this one was more serious, in that it threatened me with probable physical discomfort and certain loneliness.

The Lord, however, refused to change his mind. It was going to be the Prince of Wales Hotel, and the rest of the programme as planned. He knew only too well what happened every time I got back to Dublin. I clung to it like a leech.

Once, I overheard him say, "He'll be perfectly all right. My mother can look after him. She only lives round the corner."

My mother said, "She can't look after herself." We'd already heard from Archie Robinson about the 'black as your hat' delusion.

It made no difference. The Prince of Wales Hotel it was going to be.

The whole family had breakfast together on the last morning in the large and noisy dining-room at Oatlands Park.

My brother Michael, who was eight, after inspecting the Lord's gloomy appearance for some time, suddenly said in a clear voice, "Mummy, why can't our Daddy be jolly and jokey like the other daddies?"

I knew only too well, but I laughed aloud with my mother and my sister.

That evening, they left me at the Prince of Wales Hotel while they went on to catch the Irish Mail at Euston.

I removed the sling—my hand was already very much better —and unpacked, but it didn't make the anonymous hotel room look any more comfortable, or the prospects for my stay in London any more pleasant.

I scarcely knew London at all. There had been some quick trips from Oxford in Sean's car, and the Green Line bus to Harley Street, but I didn't know where the hotel was in relation to Piccadilly Circus or even Oxford Street, where I'd soon have to find the Berlitz School.

I thought of going out by myself—it was a bright summer's evening—and having a look round. Then I remembered Peter, a wild, frog-eyed young Englishman who'd often appeared in Dublin, staying with friends of mine. He'd always made me laugh, so much so that I'd found myself copying something of his convoluted and exotic style. He lived in Kensington. It was round about dinner-time. He might be at home, where he lived with his mother and two pretty sisters. It was just the sort of family warmth I needed.

I found the number in the telephone book and rang him up. His mother answered. I explained who I was, apologised for ringing in the middle of their dinner, and asked if I could speak to him.

In a strange, mocking kind of voice she said that Peter wasn't there, but if it was urgent she could tell me where to find him.

I began to say that it wasn't really important, but she interrupted to tell me that I'd find him in the Gloucester Arms in Gloucester Road.

"He'll be in the chair just inside the door in the saloon bar," she said. An edge was coming into her voice. "He's always there," she added. She bade me goodnight and put down the phone.

I knew I should leave him alone. Someone who lived in the saloon bar of the Gloucester Arms was exactly the kind of person I ought to keep away from—if I was going to gain a working knowledge of German in a couple of months.

I didn't hesitate. I took a taxi to the Gloucester Arms, making a note of the turnings so that I'd be able to walk there next time, if it wasn't too far away.

It wasn't nearly far enough. Within a week I was one of the regulars, morning and evening, adopting without too much trouble Peter's habit of scarcely ever paying for a drink. All we wanted, he explained, was our entrance fee of $4\frac{1}{2}$d. for half of bitter. From then on it was up to us to be sufficiently entertaining for the others not to notice, or not to mind, when we failed to pay our round.

This was an economic necessity. The Lord had given me an allowance, which was to look after everything, of £3 10s. a week, and Peter never seemed to have any money at all.

Probably, if I hadn't found him I'd have run into even worse company, looking for laughter and entertainment and the fairly wild and undoubtedly irresponsible way of living that I was coming to look upon as the natural one. From time to time he made efforts to find a job that never got much further than the door of the Gloucester, but I had a much better salve for my conscience. Three or four times a week I took a bus to the Berlitz School in Oxford Street, preparing for my business career. I didn't talk about it very much to Peter. He had an imitation of a German professor giving a lecture on electro-magnetism that was a masterpiece, and reduced the whole Siemens project to nonsense.

However, I persisted with the Berlitz School, being lucky in my teacher there. He was a young and intelligent German Jew who quickly saw that my stammer made it almost impossible for me to speak German, so he made me write it instead. I obtained a good grasp of German grammar, while remaining almost unable to reply to his formal greetings every morning. In my letters to my mother I included a number of German phrases, to show the Lord how well I was doing, and posted the letters on my way round to the Gloucester.

The only other duty I attended to, about once a fortnight, was lunch with my grandmother, almost always in a new hotel. Her habit of treating the manager and the whole of his staff as though they were her personal servants led to disturbances which kept her constantly on the move. The 'black as your hat' business was mercifully beginning to die down, but was being replaced by fearful animosities against the other guests—all old ladies like herself—which were expressed in a clear and carrying voice.

My chief purpose in attending these agonising lunch parties was to get her to give a good account of me, in case she was writing to the Lord, but it was almost impossible to distract her attention from her private feuds. Sometimes, however, she would give me a pound, slipping it into my hand over the lunch table with piercing instructions not to let 'the queer old things in the corner' see what we were doing.

As usual, my mother must have guessed at the semi-dissolute kind of life I was leading. I'd mentioned Peter casually in my letters, and she'd met him in Dublin. Suddenly, I received a letter from Sylvia Lynd, the wife of Robert Lynd, who wrote beautifully wise and funny essays in the *New Statesman* under the pen-name of 'Y.Y.' Both my parents had known the Lynds for years.

Sylvia said my mother had told her I was living in London, and that she'd be delighted if I could could come to one of her Thursday evening suppers. "It won't be anything very grand," she wrote. "Just a few friends." They lived in Hampstead, in Keats Grove.

The first time I went there the 'few friends' were Priestley, Norman Collins and his wife and Rose Macaulay. It felt splendid to be sitting round the dining-table with them, listening to talk about books and the theatre, and even more splendid to be able to tell a much less distinguished gathering all about it the following morning in the Gloucester Arms.

I went to Keats Grove fairly regularly after that. Robert had a passion for rugby football, but wasn't allowed to talk about it very much. He'd draw me on one side after supper, putting a bottle of whisky between us with one of his meaningful winks, and we'd finish it together, while he ranged over the Varsity match and Ireland's chances at Lansdowne Road.

It was marvellous for me to have found a home not unlike my own in Dublin. Then, one evening, someone began to talk about Germany and Hitler and the National Socialist Party. I'd read about Hitler in the newspapers and found the pictures of rallies and street fights exciting and interesting, as though they'd been floods or earthquakes, but with no greater significance.

I was surprised by the Lynds and their guests. What surprised me was the intensity of their loathing for every aspect of Nazism.

There had always been a certain amount of political talk at home in Dublin, but it amounted in the main to derisive and amusing abuse of de Valera and his Fianna Fail party. This was quite different. The Lynds and their friends were deeply concerned. The Nazis had already begun burning books in the streets. To the Lynds this kind of thing wasn't just an escapade by mindless hooligans. It was an attack upon humanity itself.

Even Robert joined in. He said, in his soft, gentle voice, "This is going to be the foulest thing that's ever happened to the world," and it was all the more frightening coming from him, who normally just sat back in his corner, listening to the arguments that ranged about him with his gentle, abstracted smile.

Suddenly, I wondered if Hitler would be a way of escape from Siemens-Shukert. I wrote to my mother the next morning, telling her about the evening at the Lynds, and what Robert had said.

"Everyone here," I told her, "is very worried indeed about what's going to happen in Germany. They're talking about revolution and civil war and the fearful things Hitler's going to do to the Jews. I suppose Siemens is still a good idea?"

It was my father who answered. He said he was pretty certain that there was nothing for me to worry about. Conditions in Germany were quite stable. Furthermore, he thought the time had come for me to make a start on my new career. He suggested I come home to Dublin for a few days, in case there were clothes or other things I wanted to collect, and then leave for Munich. "I'm sure," he added, "your German must be quite adequate by now."

My mother had a going-away present for me. "It'll probably be fearfully cold in the winter," she said, "so I got you the biggest one Switzers had."

It was a camel-hair overcoat or, rather, an overcoat made of material that looked like camel-hair.

It was the smartest garment I'd ever worn. It almost consoled me for having to walk aboard the mail boat at Dun Laoghaire, and to lean over the rail and wave goodbye to my parents and my sister and my little brother, and to the safety of Dublin, too.

I was still wrapped in the new overcoat when I woke up in a second-class carriage some mornings later to find that the immense train, which I'd boarded in Boulogne, had come to a halt at a station that provided the only sign of human habitation for what looked like hundreds of miles.

It sat in the middle of an endless plain that was white with snow to the horizon. I'd never seen so much snow in my life. I believe the station was Augsburg. For the first time the realisation came to me that I was in a country that was going to bear no resemblance of any kind to England or Ireland, the only two I'd known. I was alone in Germany. Even if I'd been able to articulate the words I scarcely spoke a word of German. And if the Frau Baronin wasn't at the station to meet me God alone knew what would become of me.

I sat bolt upright for the remaining, interminable hours of the journey, looking out at the snow and wondering how to tell a taxi-driver to take me to the Irish Consulate—always supposing there was one in Munich. I didn't know the German word for consulate and couldn't decide if Irish was *Irische* or *Irländische*.

My dictionary was in my school trunk at the back of the train.

I was waiting outside the luggage van for the trunk and my golf-clubs to be unloaded when I saw a very frail little old lady in a shabby black coat and hat coming down the platform towards me.

In the way that one always knows these things I knew it was the Frau Baronin, even if it wasn't the kind of Baronin I'd been expecting. I'd formed a picture of a robust, jolly woman, fallen upon hard times, but running a boarding-house with brisk and cheerful efficiency.

This little old lady looked neither brisk nor cheerful. Indeed, she looked to be only just alive.

For a moment I thought I must have made a mistake, but there she was, looking up at me fearfully as I towered over her, and saying, "Herr Kempel?"

"Jawohl," I said.

She said something which I didn't understand. I smiled, and with some difficulty put a sentence together in German, asking her how she'd recognised me.

She deciphered my meaning, after a moment, and pointed at my sleeve. "Your coat," she said.

She became briefly involved with a porter. In that time I realised that the Lord must have written to her, as soon as my mother had bought the coat, telling her to look out for it. He'd thought of everything. Then I realised he must have written to her in English.

The porter had found my trunk and golf-clubs, which were heavily labelled.

I said to the Frau Baronin, following up the letter idea, "You speak English, then?"

She was startled. "Kein Wort," she said.

Not a word.

So someone must have translated the letter for her. And I'd have to speak German all the time.

She was pointing apprehensively at my golf-bag. The leather hood concealed the clubs. It might have been anything.

"What is it?" the Frau Baronin asked me.

"Golf-kloobs," I said, hoping it was the same in German.

She shook her head helplessly. Golf-kloobs meant nothing to her whatsoever.

In silence we got into a very old, horse-drawn cab. The driver, wearing an extraordinary coat that touched the ground, put my luggage on the box beside him, and slowly we trundled out of the station yard.

Dirty snow filled the gutters of the city. It was colder than anything I'd ever known, a fearful Arctic cold that made it painful to breathe.

The Frau Baronin made some polite remark. I didn't understand it. I again said, "Jawohl." She looked at me, almost in despair, shrugged her tiny, invisible shoulders, and went back to looking out of the window again.

Several times, as we jogged along through back streets that ran through very tall, grimy buildings, I formulated a remark about the weather, but decided not to say it. I was afraid of stammering. There'd be time enough, I thought, for the Frau Baronin to find out about that.

We left the city farther and farther behind, gradually becoming enveloped in a kind of wasteland—a wide and derelict open space with enormous concrete blocks of flats standing about everywhere, unhampered by plan or design. A few old women, muffled to the ears, plodded along narrow paths in the snow.

The Frau Baronin and I exchanged no word.

The silence became so oppressive I knew I had to say something. A particularly stark and fortress-like block, with every window shuttered, loomed up ahead of us. I thought it was probably a barracks or an outsize police station—neither function surely making it popular in the neighbourhood.

I tried to please the Frau Baronin by asking her, "Was ist das Ungeheuer?"

'Ungeheuer'—monster—was one of the words I'd looked up in the Berlitz School. It was a word I used often in English, and hoped it would brighten up my German.

The Frau Baronin turned upon me a look so injured that I knew what the barracks was before she spoke.

"Das Gasthaus," she said.

It was, indeed, the guest house or, more accurately, the block of flats in which she lived and in which I was just about to join her.

"Verzeihen Sie mich," I said. Though 'Pardon me' wasn't really enough, in the circumstances.

In some strange way we settled down together in comparative peace, though it was more like an endless, grey and uneventful dream in which there was scarcely any division between sleeping and waking.

We got up very early, round about six o'clock, while it was still pitch-dark outside, and had breakfast—bread and jam and a cup of some thin, synthetic coffee.

After breakfast I went back to my room while the Frau Baronin cleaned the rest of the flat, polishing her few pieces of furniture until they shone like glass.

At nine o'clock I put on my nearly camel-hair overcoat—it had the luxuriance of sable in those Spartan, glittering little rooms— and walked half a mile across a frozen common, slipping and slithering on the grimy, granite-hard ice, to another giant block of flats in which lived Fräulein Müller, a niece of the Frau Baronin.

It had been arranged that she would give me German lessons, at five shillings an hour. It was the Frau Baronin's idea. We didn't talk to one another much, but the little I had to say she clearly thought could be more fluently put.

Fräulein Müller was about twenty-five. She had very thick, coarse black hair that sprang out around her head, restrained here and there with ornamental combs. She had a black and lively eye, but she was very shy.

Fräulein Müller was a hunchback. Her chin almost touched her hard, high little bosom, in the thick red jumper she'd knitted for herself.

She spoke some English. It was she who had translated my father's letter about the overcoat. She teased me a little about my stammer, but in a good-humoured way. We were both afflicted. We had quite a lot of fun.

The Frau Baronin and I had lunch at midday, usually sausages or a small meat pie. Then she retired to her own room until five o'clock.

I did some home-work for Fräulein Müller or with great difficulty read one of the paperback romances that seemed to be the Frau Baronin's only self-indulgence, apart from the cakes.

Sports Day at Crawley's, when I won the 220 yards Under Eleven.
The Lord, Biddy and Grandmother Glenavy.

The Lord.

The next one.

Chief Petty Officer Campbell and his first wife, Sylvia Willoughby Lee.

She went out at five to buy them—large and elaborate pastries filled with synthetic cream and a thin jam. We ate them at six. It was the last meal of the day. I was very hungry, all the time.

After supper she cleared the table and washed everything up with meticulous care, after closing the kitchen door. I went on sitting at the table, because there was nowhere else. Before smoking my pipe I spread a sheet of newspaper over the table in front of me, and two more on the rug under my chair. The Frau Baronin had done this several times herself, until I began to save her the trouble. Sometimes I forgot the ashtray—a brass bowl as big as a soup tureen—which lived on the sideboard. She'd put it in front of me, with ostentatious care, and sit watching like a hawk for stray embers until I knocked out my pipe into the tureen. Then she'd take it into the kitchen, wash and polish it and put it back on the sideboard, where it sat waiting for me until the following evening.

There was never so much as a bottle of lager in the flat. The Frau Baronin was a life-long and dedicated teetotaller.

Sometimes she talked about her husband, and of the house they'd had in East Prussia. It was small, but everything in it was of the best quality. Then he'd been killed at Verdun, and that was the end of everything to her. The sideboard was the only piece of furniture she'd been able to save. All the rest had been sold.

"It's been very hard since the war," she'd always say, and look me straight in the face. "You couldn't understand."

She was saying I couldn't understand what it was like to have lost a war and a husband and a home and everything that made life worth living. But I could understand a little of it, just by looking at her. Then I remembered Robert saying, "Nazism is going to be the foulest thing that's ever happened to the world," and saw that there was no hope for the Frau Baronin anywhere.

One evening she came home from her cake-buying expedition with a smiling Burmese youth no bigger than herself. She introduced us without even attempting to pronounce his name.

She explained that he, too, lodged in the block, on the fourth floor under the care of her friend, Frau Schiller.

The Burmese youth smiled and nodded. He seemed to understand German.

The Frau Baronin went on to say that he'd bought two tickets, one for Frau Schiller, for a gala presentation of 'Der Fliegender Holländer' at the State Opera House this very evening, but now Frau Schiller had colic and would be unable to go. Would I care to buy the ticket, and go with him?

"It would be good," she added, "because your German is better than his."

The Burmese youth smiled and nodded again. He said, "Komm, komm."

I went.

In the tram, he chattered away happily—he was the happiest person I'd seen in weeks—in a language that must have been German, because I recognised a word here and there, but his accent made it impossible for me to understand him.

After a while he shook his head, laughing, as though he'd over-indulged himself in frivolous conversation, opened his brief-case and took out a large, paperbacked volume which turned out to be the score of 'Der Fliegender Holländer'.

I had no difficulty in identifying it, because my companion opened it at the title page, placing the score between us so that we could go through it together, during the long tram-ride that lay ahead.

I said, "No, thank you", and made a circle of my forefinger and thumb to indicate that I was unable to see without glasses. I'd never worn glasses but could think of no other way of avoid-ing having to go through 'Der Fliegender Holländer' note by note.

The Burmese youth nodded his understanding and sympathy, and fell to the task himself, becoming totally absorbed. He hummed extracts to himself in a very high voice, as the tram clattered along.

It didn't look promising, for my first evening out since I'd arrived in Munich weeks before. I began to consider the possi-bilities of selling my ticket outside the theatre and seeing what the night-life of the city looked like while the Burmese student got on with his work inside. I rejected the plan, however. I didn't know where to go and I was certain that my absence would be reported to the Frau Baronin, who would have a number of injured ques-tions to ask which I wouldn't be able to answer.

It was, beyond doubt, a gala performance. It took us a long

time to push our way through the crowds outside the Opera House, hundreds of whom were still queueing to buy tickets. Huge Mercedes drew up and disgorged the high society of Munich. For the first time for what felt like years I saw women in evening dress.

My companion, however, had no time to stand and stare. Like a small, determined ferret he wove his way through the masses of opera lovers in the foyer, which was as large as a railway station. The house was only beginning to fill up as we took our seats, high under the immensely ornate dome. From here the stage, which was later to accommodate a ship in full sail, looked to have the dimensions of a Punch and Judy show.

The overture, when it was eventually presented to us, seemed to me to be a whole night's entertainment in itself, both in length and volume. It was followed by the first act of 'Der Fliegender Holländer', which aroused my interest for several minutes in that I'd never seen so many people on a stage at the same time. But I had no knowledge of the plot or of the music. I just sat slumped in my hard and narrow little seat, wishing to God the whole thing would come to an end.

Beside me, my companion followed every note of the score. From time to time he cried out indignantly, or in commendation, as the orchestra thundered and the singers roared. As the curtain came down on the first act he produced a large packet of sandwiches from his brief-case, and a bottle of milk, and fell to. From time to time he offered me a white-toothed and ecstatic smile, but no sandwiches.

I got to my feet. Everyone else in our row had a picnic of some kind or another on their knees. I fought my way out to the aisle and after wandering up and down endless corridors and stair-cases found myself in the foyer again. It was as crowded as it had been before. I joined a queue, judging by its mixed composition that it mightn't be for the Gents, and after ten minutes or so reached a bar lined six deep with people clamouring for food and drink.

I'd just got an elbow to it when bells began to ring, throwing everyone into a fever of agitation, shoving food into their mouths and swallowing the last of their beers. I waited patiently. Even if I'd known how to get back to my seat I wouldn't have bothered. I'd seen enough of the Flying Dutchman for one night.

I ordered my first drink for more than a month as the last of the opera lovers rushed out of the bar. The barmaid was in a hurry to serve me, for fear I'd miss a moment of the second act. I told her she could take it easy, that I wasn't going back. I clutched my leg, biting my lower lip. "Cramp," I said, "I can't sit down."

The Flying Dutchman had probably put to sea by the time I limped, stiff-legged, over to a large velvet sofa in a corner of the bar, taking with me a tray with several bottles of beer and a plate of meat pies and sausages. While the Flying Dutchman roamed the oceans of the world I got drunk on the velvet sofa on a combination of beer and Danziger Goldwasser, lolling back in a state of sodden bliss.

I'd been away from the flesh-pots too long, even those provided by the Munich Opera House.

I got home in a taxi, long after midnight, making no attempt to find my Burmese friend. In her room, the Frau Baronin stirred uneasily, but did not appear.

Next morning, I didn't even hear her six o'clock knocking on the door. I woke at eight, wondering where I was, knowing only that the previous night must have involved the Gloucester Arms. When I remembered what had happened I sprang out of bed, opened my door a fraction and called, "Guten Morgan, Frau Baronin". There was no answer. She'd gone out, and I knew where she'd gone to. Checking with her friend, Frau Schiller, on the fourth floor.

I'd just finished dressing, when she came back, looking hurt and anxious and frightened all at the same time. She said at once, "What happened to you last night?"

I'd been put in her charge, and she'd failed in her duty. Something terrible had happened, for which she would be answerable to my father.

I began to tell her how I'd lost my way, getting back to my seat after the end of Act I, and was about to say I'd been lucky in finding an empty seat in another part of the house, when she gave a sudden, startled sniff. She gave me a look of pure terror. The aftermath of the Danziger Goldwasser had just got through to her.

Instinctively, she clasped her little hands together. She closed her eyes and rocked herself backwards and forwards. "Mein Gott, mein Gott," she moaned.

That was the end of the good old days.

When I came back from my lesson with Fräulein Müller the Frau Baronin informed me, distantly, that she had rung the offices of Siemens-Shukert and with some difficulty had managed to speak to a Herr Bronski who, it appeared, had been waiting for me to get in touch with him for some time. He was prepared to give me an appointment at eight-thirty the following morning.

It was a relief, in a way. The whole Siemens project had been becoming more and more shadowy in my mind.

I hadn't referred to it in my letters home, though I'd once considered telling the Lord that I'd spoken to the office and they'd advised me to do some more work on my German, before joining them. I'd decided against it, however, not knowing how close the liaison was between them and the Lord.

But now the Frau Baronin had done it for me. The sole responsibility of looking after an obviously dissolute young foreigner had proved too much for her.

At eight-thirty the following morning—I'd arrived at eight—I entered the offices of Siemens-Shukert and asked for Herr Bronski.

He came down to meet me himself, an intelligent and business-like young man. He wore a dark suit and seemed a little taken aback by my camel-hair overcoat, which he examined with some care as we shook hands.

I followed him into his office. He offered me a cigarette, as we sat down, and suddenly launched out into a flood of German of which I understood only an occasional word. Once, he said, "Spurlos verschwunden"—disappeared without a trace—and laughed loudly. He seemed to be talking about my failure, for weeks past, to put in an appearance. From the way that he kept glancing at my coat I judged he thought he'd got a rich, cosmopolitan playboy on his hands.

I told him, haltingly, that I'd thought it was better to keep on with my German lessons, before coming to see him, but I'd been finding the language very difficult to learn.

In perfect English, with a slight American accent, Herr Bronski said, "You can say that again." He laughed and then asked, with genuine curiosity, "But where have you been?"

I told him what I'd been doing, and the excitement of speaking English again went to my head. I exaggerated, wildly, the horrors of the Frau Baronin's flat. I told him about the cakes and the horrible coffee that took the place of dinner. I parodied our stilted evening conversations. I told him about Fräulein Müller and made some indelicate assessments of her sex-life. I was beginning to get to work on the Burmese student and the fearful tedium of the Fliegender Holländer when Herr Bronski looked at his watch.

His smile had been becoming progressively less and less amused, and now he interrupted me with asperity. He said he was sorry to learn that my first impressions of Germany had been so unfavourable. Germany, he pointed out, was a poor country which had not yet fully recovered from the effects of the last war and was not, therefore, likely to provide me with the kind of entertainments to which I was obviously accustomed. He said he hoped I would not find my work in the office too boring, got up and suddenly snapped, "Kommen Sie mit—"

I followed him down a dark passage, trying to find a way of telling him I'd only been joking, but it was much too late. The only people I'd spoken to for weeks had been the Frau Baronin and Fräulein Müller. They'd given me no clue to the temper of the German people. It was going to bear a lot of watching, if I wasn't to make the same mistake all over again.

We entered a small, untidy office where four elderly clerks were making entries in ledgers. In the middle of one wall was an empty desk that was smaller than the others. I didn't look at it. I knew I'd be occupying it soon enough.

Herr Bronski conferred in a low voice with the eldest of the clerks, gave me a brief nod at the end of it, and left the room. He hadn't introduced me, so the old man had to do it for himself.

"Herr Pabst," he said, and bowed and clicked his heels. I shook his hand. I'd only seen the heel-clicking done before in films.

"Herr Campbell," I said. Then I tried to say, "Es freut mich—", that I was glad to meet him, but I couldn't articulate the word 'freut'. I struggled with it for a while, with grotesque facial contortions, and had to give it up.

Herr Pabst looked at me in astonishment. One of the other clerks burst out laughing. As usual, I said, "Pardon me."

Herr Pabst made a disordered gesture, trying to find something to hold on to, to give him help, and translated it into a finger pointing towards the empty desk.

"Danke vielmals," I said excessively, but I had to show them I could speak.

I sat down at the desk. There was nothing on it. After a moment of indecision Herr Pabst went back to his own, picked up his pen and submerged himself in his ledger.

An eternity went by. The clerk who had laughed glanced at me occasionally out of the corner of his eye. He was a liverish-looking old man with a red nose, and a Nazi pin in his buttonhole. He was looking forward to some unexpected fun in the future.

Suddenly, Herr Pabst, my only ally, got up and left the room.

Another age went by. The red-nosed man said something under his breath. The other two bent more deeply over their ledgers, as though they hadn't heard, though their shoulders were shaking.

Herr Pabst, my saviour, came back again carrying a very large sheet of squared paper and something that looked like an instruction manual. He was much more relaxed. He'd found something for me to do.

The task he'd found for me was to draw on the squared paper a diagram of the whole Siemens organisation, branching out like a family tree from Carl von Siemens at the top. The whole thing was already laid out in the handbook, but with only one branch —as it were—per page. Herr Pabst felt it would give me a clear, over-all picture of the constitution of the firm if I put them all together.

He gave me some coloured inks, a pen and a ruler, and returned to his own work.

There was no point in the task. Many of the departments had technical names I wouldn't have understood in English. I didn't know what our department was called, or where it fitted in. I began by printing CARL VON SIEMENS neatly across the top of the page in red ink.

By midday, when Herr Pabst announced that it was lunchtime, I'd got a couple of inches farther down the page with the names of the board of management. I put my chart face downwards, with the handbook on top of it, and followed Herr Pabst to the canteen in the basement. The lunch was large and coarse and filling. When we all filed out again I lost Herr Pabst and my other three colleagues, but found my way back to our office.

They came in shortly afterwards, each carrying a paper bag. The paper bag contained at least three rich-looking pastries. They ate them slowly, with relish, while they read their morning papers. I got on with my chart. Ten minutes later we were all back at work again.

At five-thirty p.m. they closed their ledgers, and reached for their coats and hats. Herr Pabst paused for a moment beside my desk to say that he'd see me in the morning, confirming something I'd been wondering about. I couldn't believe that my business career had begun. The launching had been too haphazard, too informal. But it seemed that I was in. Every morning, at eight-thirty a.m., I'd have to arrive at the office and sit there until five-thirty, and if I didn't turn up I'd probably get the sack.

I felt no elation, no stirring of ambition. I went hurrying back to the Frau Baronin, as though I were going home.

Two weeks later I moved into a pleasant, sunny bed-sitting-room overlooking a park. I cannot remember how this happened. Probably someone in the office found it for me. It was only a couple of minutes away. Nor can I remember saying goodbye to the Frau Baronin or to Fräulein Müller I merely drifted out of their lives as inconsequentially as I had drifted in.

Herr Pabst was now giving me some real work to do, on the order forms from the project engineers on some hydro-electric scheme in Yugoslavia. They sent us long lists of materials required, and we had to make out the prices from our catalogues. I was even eating three cakes after lunch every day.

In the evenings I ate a cheap meal in the café next door and went home to read the English papers, and to play my mandolin, an instrument I'd left in my trunk during my stay with the Frau Baronin.

Instead of using a plectrum and disturbing the other lodgers, I played the mandolin with a corner torn off a cigarette packet, which made it softer, so that the ashtrays and the wastepaper basket were continuously filled with small, eroded triangles of thin cardboard.

One evening the landlady made a point of calling on me. She was a lively, raffish woman with dyed black hair who'd told me early on, with a significance that escaped me, that her house was 'sturm-frei'. I found out from Herr Pabst that it meant that the landlady had no objection if I wanted to have girls in my room. I was as embarrassed as Herr Pabst.

Now, however, she had something to ask me. She said she was dying of curiosity, that she simply had to know where all these little pieces of paper were coming from.

I told her I used them for picking my teeth.

She looked at me for a long time, shrugged her shoulders resignedly and left the room. A young foreigner with a rich-looking coat who didn't want to avail himself of the 'sturm-frei' privilege, and who picked his teeth with pieces of cardboard was beyond her comprehension, and interest.

Apart from the mandolin the only other amusement I dared to find for myself was playing golf, a short tram-ride from the centre of the city, on a nine-hole course where a good deal of gravel was distributed among the thin grass on the fairways. I played every Saturday and Sunday, making up a fourball with three thick-set Japanese businessmen whose German was as incomprehensible to me as mine evidently was to them.

In the beginning I'd played with some young Germans who, despite their Mercedes and winter sports sun-tans, were only novices at the game, while I was beginning to play rather well, even on the gravel-strewn fairways. I used to give them quite a bit of instruction, in particular to a remarkably pretty, long-legged girl called Hansi.

After a while, they began to ask me to play with them less and less frequently, until one day I heard Hansi say, "Oh God, not the Hauptmeister," when someone suggested I should join them.

After that I played with the Japanese.

Once again, as at the Frau Baronin's, I retired into a waking dream, poring over the catalogues in the office all day and playing my mandolin at night, sitting in the window-seat overlooking the park, waiting for the dream to come to an end and for something else to begin.

Something else began one morning when I was walking to the office. I turned a corner and found a small and strangely glum crowd standing round the windows of a department store. I looked over their heads and saw that the windows had been smashed to pieces. Daubed in red paint all over the front of the store were the words "Juden heraus!" In the ruined windows were a number of Brownshirts, laughing boisterously as they trampled crockery into the floor with their jackboots.

I caught the eye of an elderly man with a briefcase, a business-man on his way to work. He was very white. He looked as if he was going to be sick.

Every day, after that, something of the same kind seemed to happen. In the evenings, there'd be quick scuffles in the street and an old man would be left bleeding in the gutter, while the laughter and the jackboots died away in the distance.

One night, I was attacked myself. For once, I'd gone out to a beer-cellar and got rather drunk. It was a Saturday night, and the process had probably begun at the golf-club.

I was weaving along a dark street and suddenly began to do the goose-step. Then, in time with the tramping of my feet, I started to sing the Nazi anthem, the Horst Wessel Lied.

Something very heavy hit me on the shoulder, swinging me round. Two Brownshirts had appeared behind me. They were ready for action, the straps of their caps under their chins.

The bigger one asked me what I thought I was doing, a for-eigner singing the Horst Wessel Lied?

I said it was only a joke.

The bigger one said it wasn't a joke. Without warning, the smaller one reached up and pulled the knot of my tie so tightly round my neck I could scarcely breathe.

"Remember that, next time," he said. Shoulder to shoulder they tramped away.

I couldn't loosen my tie. I thought I was going to die. When I got home and found a scissors my face was dark-purple in the mirror over the basin. I couldn't get the scissors between my neck and the tie. I cut it off with a razor-blade and half-fainted on the bed, drawing in whistling lungfuls of air.

I made a funny story of it in a letter to my mother. Ten days or so later I got an anxious one from her. She wondered if I was all right. She hadn't heard from me for almost a month.

I realised my letter had never got there. It had been opened, and put into a dossier against me.

I became genuinely frightened. They must know I was working for Siemens-Shukert. Perhaps they thought I was a spy.

I wrote a very careful letter to the Lord, saying that for various reasons which he might be able to guess at I thought I'd come to the end of my time in Munich. Perhaps he'd read something about it in the *Irish Times*? Perhaps I ought to come back to Dublin?

That one got there. The Lord wrote back to say that he fully understood, and agreed that the time had now come for me to move to Berlin. He appreciated the difficulties of working in Munich, but was sure that in Berlin I'd find things a good deal more comfortable.

He suggested that I leave at once.

It felt like the most heartless betrayal. But then he couldn't have known about the tie business, and my genuine fear, and there seemed to be no way in which I could let him know about these things.

I got Herr Bronski to write to Siemensstadt, to let them know I was coming, and left a week later. I arrived in Berlin to find the city delirious with cheering crowds and massed bands and blazing Swastika banners.

Hitler had become Reichskanzler that very day.

It seems incredible now, but with the whole of Germany afire I once again managed to settle down into the same kind of soporific, half-alive life I'd lived in Munich.

I went out to Siemensstadt every morning in the tram, added up figures in a desultory way in the office and got home by seven o'clock, to have a quick dinner in the next-door café and go to bed, to read the *Continental Daily Mail*.

I'd found a dingy room in Charlottenburg, where the landlady was even older and more beaten than the Frau Baronin. Once, seeing a picture of Hitler in my paper, her face was suddenly illuminated and she said, "This man is God."

"Oh no, he isn't," I said savagely. "He's just a filthy nuisance."

She glared at me with pride and hatred and contempt.

"Filthy" was a word that was beginning to take deeper and deeper root in my mind. For the first time in my life I was beginning to feel for other people, for the old men left bleeding in the streets, for the elderly couples sobbing in one another's arms as they looked at the ruins of their little shops. And everywhere daubed the unspeakable arrogance of 'Juden heraus'.

In the office 'Heil Hitler' had become the standard greeting.

The office boy, delivering order forms, gave the salute at the door when he came in and again before he left.

The head of my department was a tall, very good-looking young man called Peter Genrich. He, too, seemed disturbed by the way things were going. He seemed to agree with me when I spoke about the brutal cruelties I saw every day in the streets.

One Saturday morning the door of our office burst open with a crash and there on the threshold was a terrifying figure in the black uniform and skull and crossbones of the S.S.

It was Peter Genrich. I shall never forget the genial grin he gave me as he roared out the greeting, 'Heil Hitler!'

He'd merely been biding his time.

One afternoon, in the lavatory, an old man with a gentle face and white hair who worked in the same office approached me with his finger to his lips. He peered into the three cubicles and then quickly up and down the corridor outside. He locked the door and, almost crying, begged me in a whisper to be more careful in the office, to watch my words. "You must not make jokes about the movement," he said. "It isn't safe."

I said I couldn't help it. The whole thing was so filthy I couldn't hold my tongue.

He begged me again to be more careful. Then suddenly he broke down, sobbing into his hands. "I know," he said. "I know." He put his hands tightly over his ears, to shut out everything.

"We're all destroyed!" he cried.

The feeling of filth became stronger and stronger, the leaden fear that the whole of Europe was going to be drowned in a sea of brutality and squalor beyond imagination.

To this day I remain pretty well unmoved by politics. I'm uncluttered by civic conscience. But when something happens today, as it often does, that has the flavour of Berlin, in 1933, I'm very liable to describe it as 'filthy'. It's the nearest I can get to making a protest on behalf of humanity.

My mother, as ever, must have guessed that I was getting more and more lonely, and more and more frightened. My letters to her were regularly impounded, but she tried to make up for it by writing to me at least twice a week. Also, she got other people to write to me. One of them was Alan Duncan.

Alan still lived in Paris. He said he'd love to see me, if I was ever passing through.

I thought about it for two days. Then I went to Peter Genrich and told him I was resigning from Siemens, that I'd been offered a job in Dublin that was too good to miss.

He was surprisingly kind about it. Out of his S.S. uniform he was a very nice man.

He said he was sorry to hear that I was going. The management were very pleased with the progress I was making, and were looking forward to using me in their offices in London in the near future.

I said I'd made up my mind to take the Dublin job.

"That's it, then," he said, with a smile, and gave me a chit for the cashier. It was for 400 marks, about £30!

I was astonished. I said, "But I'm not supposed to get paid. I'm only learning the job."

"You've earned it," Peter Genrich said. "Goodbye and good luck."

It was the first money I'd ever earned. And almost immediately it was taken away from me. As the cashier paid me he warned me, with every appearance of satisfaction, that as a foreigner I would be unable to take it out of the country.

I had just enough money of my own for the ticket to Paris. That night I had dinner by myself in Horcher's, then one of the most expensive restaurants in the world. I got rid of the rest of the marks on a Tyrolean hat and a meerschaum pipe, and left for Paris with 45 pfennigs in my pocket.

Perhaps I should have told Peter Genrich I was going to Paris. There was really no need for me to invent the non-existent job in Dublin, but I felt I had to give him a solid reason for leaving Siemens, one that he could believe. It wasn't enough to tell him, of all people, that I was running away.

Alan Duncan and I hadn't seen one another for years.

I spent the whole journey from Berlin trying to re-create his appearance, wondering at the same time—with mounting anxiety—whether he'd remember me. I'd been at Castle Park the last time we'd met, a schoolboy in shorts.

I walked down the lurching corridor of the train to the lavatory, to look at myself in the long mirror. Apart from the remnants of the camel-hair coat, I couldn't see much difference. I said aloud, to my reflection, contriving an appearance of humble sincerity, "Please God, let Alan be there."

Alan was there, the long grey hair flowing out from beneath his beret, the cigarette in the corner of his mouth, the bundle of newspapers under his arm. I couldn't imagine why I'd found it hard to remember him. I rushed up to him and said, "You got my postcard then!"

I suddenly saw that he wasn't very pleased to see me.

"I did," Alan said. Then he grinned, but it was an anxious one. "I hope to God you've got some money," he said. "I haven't got a tosser."

I said I was terribly sorry but at the moment I had 45 pfennigs, but I'd written to the Lord and money was on the way.

Alan groaned, almost aloud. "Belinda has some," he said, speaking of his wife, "but it'll be a job to get her to lend you any."

I saw that the lack of money was Alan's main preoccupation, and I found out why an hour later, when the taxi left us outside the Café Mathieu, at the top of the Boulevard St. Michel.

Alan told the taxi-driver to wait, while he had what looked like a painful discussion with a large woman dressed in black, sitting behind a cash register at a high desk. He came back with enough money for the taxi.

"I told her," he said, with his slightly lop-sided grin, "your father was a rich Irish baron, and we'd soon be rolling in it."

Alan paid the taxi and shot back into the café. He was already seated in a corner when I joined him, dragging my trunk. There was a pile of saucers in front of him. I guessed immediately they'd been left over from the morning session, and not yet paid for.

A waiter gave Alan a glass of beer and laid another saucer, with care, on top of the heap. Alan looked up. "Would you," he asked me hesitantly, "like some lemonade, or something?"

"I'd much rather have a glass of beer."

"Thank God," said Alan, with immense relief. "I was afraid you weren't old enough to drink."

Belinda arranged everything for me. She found me a room in a tiny hotel nearby, and lent me enough to pay them a week's rent in advance, and some more for my own living expenses.

"Don't spend it all in the Mathieu," she said, trying to make a joke of it. "They get enough of our money already."

In the next three or four months they got a great deal of mine. It was the Gloucester Arms all over again. Alan and I met at the same table every morning round about eleven. The saucers mounted steadily while he read all the newspapers, on their long sticks, and I stared at the passers-by.

I'd told the Lord that I'd come to Paris to learn French. "With French and German," I said, "I'll surely be a good commercial proposition." But, as usual, I was unable to add in what capacity.

In the next three months I learnt scarcely a word of French, speaking English to Alan all the time in the Mathieu. When I ordered two more beers it often came out, through force of habit, in German.

When I wasn't sitting in the Mathieu I walked for miles through Paris, astonished—after the hardness of Berlin—by its romantic beauty. After Berlin, indeed, Paris should have been a taste of Paradise, but it wasn't.

The February riots of 1934 were looming up. Moorish cavalry were encamped outside the Chambre des Deputies, their camp fires glaring frighteningly at night. There were police charges in the streets, with dignified old men with white spade beards running as briskly as the shouting students. There seemed to be no peace anywhere.

Then I got a letter from my mother. She'd been making a Cook's tour of art galleries all over Europe, by herself, and would be in Paris in a week.

I wrote to her in Florence, arranging to meet her in the Mathieu at six o'clock the following Wednesday evening.

I was in bed with an American girl, after lunch on that Wednesday, when my mother walked into my room in the Hotel de l'Opéra, two hours earlier than I'd been expecting her.

I'd pulled the curtains. The room was dark. She stood in the door for a moment or two. Perhaps she was wondering if I was alone, and then she saw I wasn't. She closed the door gently behind her as she went away.

We met in the Mathieu at six. Alan and Belinda were there, too, and we had a gay reunion. Towards the end of it my mother leant over to me privately and put her hand on the sleeve of my coat, the imitation camel-hair.

"I've never seen anything so threadbare," she said, much more concerned than accusatory, but laughing at the same time.

"It's done a lot of hard work," I said.

My mother said, "I think you'd better come home. You're as thin as your coat."

We left Paris the following morning in a big De Havilland biplane held together with a maze of wire struts. I'd never been in an aeroplane before, and I was going home to Ireland. It should have been an occasion for high rejoicing, but it wasn't. Because the Lord was waiting in Dublin and there was nothing I was going to be able to say to him. This was a worse failure than Oxford.

He surprised me, not for the first time. It had happened before, when I'd been expecting gloom and the injured look, that he'd turned out to be happy and cheerful, making jokes, and planning some new move as though its success were assured.

This was one of those occasions, and this time it seemed to me he'd had the best idea yet.

He must have been working on it, probably since I'd arrived in Paris, because something that looked almost like a steady job had been prepared for me to step into.

Bertie Smyllie, the Editor of the *Irish Times*, was ready to try me out as a regular contributor to the paper.

The Lord was at pains to explain that my experiences in Berlin and Paris would certainly be of benefit to the *Irish Times*, but I had no difficulty in guessing that Smyllie, as an old friend of the family, had been talked into trying to do something for me.

Robert Maire Smyllie was one of the figures of Dublin, in more ways than one. He was of average height, but must have weighed eighteen stone. He had a small, button nose and wore large sombrero-like hats. He'd sung comic songs with my mother at musical evenings in the Dublin Arts Club and gravely sought my father's advice before writing a weighty leading article on the subject of finance.

I went to see him, having up till now got no closer to him than greeting him respectfully in the street, and was surprised to find that for a man of his distinction he was strangely shy.

He enquired after my mother, whom he hadn't seen for a long time, and then said, "Your father tells me you want to try your hand at journalism."

I began to say that it was the one thing I'd always wanted to do, but he cut me short, not believing it himself.

"There's no real job for you here," he said. "Everything's full up. But, look, go out to the Zoo and write me something about it. Say, a thousand words."

It was the end of the interview. It had been so short and so inconsequent that I realised that my prospects of employment with the *Irish Times* were not as rosy as the Lord had led me—and probably himself—to believe. But I went to the Zoo and I wrote the thousand words, making them as funny as I could. I delivered them to Smyllie in his office. He pointed silently to a tray on his desk, and returned to his typewriter. I went home, not knowing what to think, or what to hope for.

Next morning, the piece about the Zoo appeared in its entirety, filling a whole column of the paper.

It was the Lord who showed it to me. He came into the dining-room while I was having breakfast, and gave me the paper, as he usually did. But this time he said, "There's a bit by you in there. You got the chimpanzee with the straw in its mouth exactly. Very good writing."

He left the room immediately, to give me the chance to read my piece alone—and over and over again.

For him, it was the first gleam of hope I'd given him that one day I'd be able to earn my own living.

As for me, I knew that I'd found my profession at last. At that moment I was much too excited to realise that I'd stumbled into the only job that required no degrees, no diplomas, no training and no specialized knowledge of any kind.

In that way, journalism might have been designed for my special benefit.

Chapter Six

OR so I thought, until I went back to see Smyllie again later that day.

He made no mention of the piece about the Zoo. He only wanted to know if I could type, and seemed relieved to hear that I couldn't.

"I wouldn't be able to take you on here," he said, "unless you can type, and do shorthand."

He knew he was making a job for me, and it was on his conscience.

I said I could teach myself typing and shorthand, that I was sure it wouldn't take very long.

"Art is long," said Smyllie, using one of his favourite aphorisms, "but life is shuddering shorter than you think. You'd better go to Skerries College."

I'd heard of Skerries College, a place where little girls went to learn to be typists. It seemed to be no place for a newspaperman, but Smyllie was already talking to the college on the phone.

He put down the receiver. "It's the middle of the term," he told me, "but they'll let you into the beginners' class. Starting tomorrow."

It looked like the end of the interview, and he still hadn't said anything about my Zoo column.

I said, "I hope the bit about the Zoo was all right."

Smyllie drew his typewriter purposefully towards him. "It was in the paper, wasn't it?" he said.

My father's influence had gone as far as it was going to.

It was up to me, now, to learn shorthand and typing, and to present myself humbly, when I'd done so, in case the Editor might be able to give me a job.

I spent every morning for the next six weeks sitting at the back of a class filled with fifteen and sixteen year old girls. My presence convulsed them. When the instructress paused at my desk to see how I was getting on every head in the room turned to watch. Smothered giggles broke out like escaping gas.

Dublin is a small town. Frequently I'd meet some of my class-mates in the streets, and the giggling would break out all over again.

It was a low period. After the first three weeks I saw that the effort of learning shorthand was going to be beyond me. The girls were already far ahead of me, seeming to find no difficulty in remembering the grammalogues that vanished from my mind as soon as I'd learnt them. But the typing was almost a pleasure. Before the end of the term I was able to touch-type at a fair speed, without looking at the key-board. I left Skerries College at the end of the six weeks and went back to see Smyllie, to tell him that I was now fully equipt and ready to go.

He didn't believe me. To test my shorthand he gave me a piece of dictation, slowly and clearly, and almost immediately I was twenty or thirty words behind.

He stopped and looked at me impatiently. "Mr. Campbell," he said, "we have not been doing our shuddering home-work. I suppose you can type?"

I told him my typing was rather good and that I'd just bought a typewriter. "It's called a Bluebird," I said.

He looked at me again, trying not to laugh. "Well, take your shuddering Bluebird round to the Rotary lunch at the Gresham and get it to write not more than two hundred words," said the Editor of the *Irish Times*, giving me my first official marking as a reporter.

Those Rotary lunches were the only kind of straight reporting I was ever going to do in my thirty-odd years on newspapers, thanks to my failure to learn shorthand. I'm deeply indebted to my lack of it. It probably saved me from a life-time of hard work.

Not that the Rotary lunches were all that easy. They took place in the ballroom of the Gresham Hotel, and were attended by a couple of hundred Dublin businessmen. After lunch, which was eaten in about twenty minutes, they were addressed by a captain of industry on the problems of his own particular field.

The only thing I had to do was to get his name right, the gist of his message and the names of some of the people at the top table. The only thing I remember about those Rotary lunches was that they always wound up with *Charlotte Russe*.

I spent the rest of the time hanging about the News Room, trying to keep out of the way.

A sheet of paper used to be pinned to the bulletin board every day with the reporters' names and their markings. My name appeared at the bottom of it, but except for the Rotary lunches the Chief Reporter never gave me anything to do. It was clear that he regarded Lord Glenavy's son as surplus to any requirements he might have.

Two or three weeks went by before I even got on to the payroll, and then it seemed to happen by chance.

I met Smyllie one evening in a pub on the other side of Westmoreland Street. It was his habit always to surround himself so deeply with courtiers and accolytes that no one from the office could get near him, to ask him to make even minor decisions about the next day's paper, but this time he was alone, drinking his large brandy and dry ginger.

I said, in the established formula, "Good evening, Mr. Smyllie, sir."

For a moment he looked hunted, and then he said, "Tell the curate to give you a bottle of stout and bring it over here."

I did so, and sat down at his table. Without warning, he said, "What are you doing?"

I told him, though he must have known already, about the Rotary lunches.

"Are they paying you anything?" he wanted to know, again knowing quite well they weren't. I said they weren't.

"I'll do something about it," Smyllie said. "And you'd better go and see Alec. He's probably got a couple of Diary paragraphs you can do." He broke off, in visible relief, to welcome three of his cronies, drawing them round him like a blanket.

I'd have done anything for him at that moment, a sense of devotion that was only slightly tempered by the discovery the following Friday that I was to get £2 a week.

From then on I began to get more and more jobs to do. I became the expert, for a couple of weeks in the Irishman's Diary, on King's Ale—beer brewed to celebrate Edward VII's visit to Dublin. A number of bottles had survived and a large correspondence developed until Smyllie suddenly decided he never wanted to hear about King's shuddering Ale again, and put me on to writing a small feature called 'The Courts Day by Day'.

I'd never been inside a magistrate's court before. I was shocked by the misery of the victims, and by the emotionless way in which justice was dealt out.

Smyllie, as usual, made no comment on the feature, but other people did. My father reported praise from some of the directors of the Bank. Sarah Purser, Dublin's leading literary and artistic hostess, told my mother, "Your son is educating us all."

For the first time I felt I was being 'a writer'. It was exciting to know that I could interest other people in things that shocked or amused or interested me.

It was also good to know that the Lord's business associates were being entertained by the stuff I was writing. It fed a growing belief on my part that I'd always been destined to be a writer, and had been only kept away from it by family obtuseness. On several occasions, indeed, I went so far as to air this view—albeit obliquely—in the home circle, driving the Lord still more deeply into his detective story.

He must have been reflecting that the rising star of the *Irish Times* was being paid £2 a week, while living comfortably at home. Furthermore, until the day of his death, he regarded journalism as an extremely precarious way of earning a living, one that could come to an end at any time. I'm surprised, now, that he was able to keep silent as I dispensed my news and views.

Then I received a new promotion, to the true inner life of the *Irish Times*, writing the fourth, mildly humorous leading article, working in the Editorial Room at night.

There were four of us—Bertie Smyllie, Alec Newman, Bill Fleming and I, with the Editor sealed off by a head-high wooden partition.

We got in round about nine o'clock and searched through the English and Irish papers of that day for leader subjects. Some time after ten Smyllie would fling his huge bulk through the door and go to ground in his cubby-hole, muttering curses and imprecations against everyone and everything. For an hour or so, then, there would be the clatter of four typewriters as each of us wrote our leader. From time to time wordless snortings and trumpetings from behind the Editor's partition convulsed the rest of us, so that we had to put our hands over our mouths to avoid a rebuke.

The rest of the night, until the first edition came out some time before 1 a.m., was spent in reading proofs of our leaders and of the other main features of the paper. We'd usually finish up with a gloriously funny game of dominoes, that had a private language of its own, and I'd get home about three o'clock in the morning, to have a large supper and go to bed, until my mother woke me with lunch on a tray.

It was an extraordinary, monastic kind of life in which we scarcely spoke to anyone except one another, but it gave me the opportunity to learn a great deal from Bertie Smyllie.

For the first time someone outside my family circle was having an effect upon my life, and particularly upon the profession into which I'd drifted so much by chance.

The first leader I wrote was about the unsavoury condition of Dublin taxis, and Bertie took it to pieces word by word. It was, in fact, quite a difficult exercise in journalism, being five hundred words in length, all in a single paragraph. Even if one did manage to have a thought it was not easy to keep it going without the breather that a new paragraph can give, so I hit upon the device of beginning an occasional sentence with 'And' or 'But'.

Bertie crossed out the ands and the buts with roars of pain and outrage. "Never, never begin a sentence with a shuddering preposition!" he cried. "A preposition has never initiated a sentence and never will."

A split infinitive drove him to bang both fists on the desk. "To actually justify!" he snarled. "To actually justify. Listen to it. It turns the stomach. If you must—'actually to justify'—but what's 'actually' doing there anyway. It's superfluous. It's even otiose. The graces of style, Mr. Campbell. The graces of style."

'The graces of style' became my watchword. I found that it was possible to write in such a way that every sentence had a balance of its own, so that no word or syllable was too long or too short to break its flow. I also learnt the value of breaking the flow on purpose, to underline a joke. I even tried using the semi-colon, one of the most unwieldy of the punctuation marks, until checked by the Editor.

"The semi-colon, Mr. Campbell," he said, "is the prerogative of the senior practitioner. It requires exceedingly delicate handling. You're showering the shuddering things all over the place. Desist!"

It was always a surprise, and a pleasure, to find that he read my leaders with such care—not for their content, which was usually frivolous in the extreme, but to ensure that they had our old friend grace of style. He was a wonderful teacher. His exaggerated outbursts of fury made it seem that an offence against the graces of style was a catastrophe of the first magnitude. He made me try harder to do something properly than anyone before or since . . .

And—rebelliously beginning with a preposition—as I write that sentence I hear the voice rise ominously above the partition, "Mr. Campbell, sir."

"Yes, Mr. Smyllie, sir?"

"I've just stepped in something horrible."

"I'm sorry to hear that, Mr. Smyllie, sir."

"It has risen over the top of my boot. 'He made me try harder to do something properly than anyone before or since.' It breaks my jaw to read it, Mr. Campbell. It fragments my mind. Should we make it, 'He made me try harder to do something properly than anyone before or since had or has done to try to make me try harder to do something properly?' Does this emendation do anything for the greater illumination of our minds? It does not. A sentence must flow as smoothly as milk from the Great Tit of the Shuddering Sacred Cow of Cahirciveen. Milk it, Mr. Campbell, sir. Milk."

The voice rises to a thunderous roar. "Nemo me impune lacessit! And give my kind regards to your Uncle Dick!"

I shall try to provoke his splendid and enormous ghost no further.

Thank you, Mr. Smyllie, sir. My very best thanks.

In addition to being a leader writer I soon became not only the Film Critic, but also the Literary Editor as well.

Bertie said, "I do not heap these honours upon you, Mr. Campbell, because you are worthy of them. You've got no education whatever, but at least you've got some rudimentary taste—which is more than can be said for a lot of the other gowjers under my command."

In fact, there was no honour to be won from these new posts. They merely involved me in a great deal of running about.

Until then, the film criticism in the paper had seldom been more than paraphrases of the publicity hand-outs. I, on the other hand, actually went to see the films. As there were no morning showings for the benefit of the Press I often saw four films,

between 2.30 p.m. and 9, or as much of them as I could manage
before rushing into the office to write my leader.

As Literary Editor it was my job to hand out books for
review—and to try to keep the detective stories away from the
rapacious maw of the Editor.

"Mr. Campbell, sir."

"Yes, Mr. Smyllie, sir?"

"Bloods."

"But only four have come in, sir, this week."

"Bloods, Mr. Campbell. Bloods."

"But, sir, by my calculations I'm still waiting for reviews, from
your good self, of seventeen recent publications in this field."

"Yours not to reason why, Mr. Campbell. Bloods."

In the year that I was Literary Editor he never reviewed a
single one.

Besides keeping the Bloods away from the Editor, and trying
to preserve for myself some of the more expensive publications for
re-sale to booksellers, I wrote a weekly column for the Book Page
of a vaguely literary nature, and also laid it out.

It was a purely formal make-up, with three photographs a
week. Sometimes I put one of the pictures on top and the other
two on the same line underneath it, and sometimes reversed the
process. Occasionally they ran diagonally down the page. But
making up the Book Page did mean I had to learn something
about type and, even more important, how to cut the work of the
reviewers all of whom wrote at enormous length, hoping to
advance into the guinea bracket from the normal rate of 10s. 6d.

I also had to supervise the making up of the page on the stone,
the clamping of the type itself into a large steel frame. However
hard I cut the reviews one or more of them were always several
lines too long.

Mr. Murphy, the Foreman Printer, would remove the offend-
ing slugs and, holding them between finger and thumb, perform
the astonishing feat of reading the type aloud, this being all the
more astonishing to me in view of the fact that each letter was
reversed, as though seen in a looking glass.

"While one continues to be impressed by Mr. O'Connor's deep
insight into humanity," Murphy would read, "one rather hopes
he will turn his hand to a less metaphysical subject next time."

He would look at me over the top of his small, steel-rimmed
glasses.

The Port Control marching past Eamonn de Valera, on the steps of the G.P.O., in commemoration of the Easter Rising.

Part of the garden and the back of Clonard. The bedroom where I copied out Dostoievsky is on the right of the balcony.

"Piss?"

"Piss indeed, Mr. Murphy."

"Kill it?"

"Kill it."

"Right."

Sometimes the last paragraph couldn't be removed without destroying whatever sense the review might have had. I would then try to cut other lines on the galley-proof, but Mr. Murphy nearly always beat me to it.

Reading the type upside down and back to front he'd remove an adjective which caused a line to turn.

"Her remarkable grasp of dialogue is a real
    joy."

Mr. Murphy took out the word 'real', so that we'd saved a line.

It was as close as I ever got to the practical side of the production of a newspaper. When I ceased to be Literary Editor I never saw a Linotype machine ever again.

I ceased to be Literary Editor because I became Our Parliamentary Sketch Writer, the most burdensome task that had yet fallen upon me.

It was bad enough while I was working at night. Once a month we got Saturday and Sunday off, but for the other three weeks Saturday was the only night that was free for social pleasures.

This led to some of the most agonising Sunday night hangovers I've ever known.

I'd get home from the paper round about three o'clock on Saturday morning and get up again at eight, to go and play golf at Greystones, twenty-five miles down the coast.

By this time I'd bought a car—a bull-nosed Morris Cowley—using £40 of the £3,000 which I'd inherited from the Old Lord, at twenty-one. Until then my father and Archie Robinson had guarded this treasure as grimly as if it was their own. When I pointed out the miseries of riding a bicycle three miles up-hill in the winter on my way home from the *Irish Times*, and suggested I might buy a small, cheap car with my inheritance, the Lord said, "You can't afford the petrol or the insurance or the road-tax on what they're paying you."

Both of us knew who was going to pay for all three. I got the

car. So that every Saturday morning, after three or four hours'
sleep, I'd drive down to Greystones and play two rounds of golf
in hail, rain or snow. I'd get back to Dublin round about seven
that evening, often to go dog-racing but always to finish up at a
party that went on until four or five the following morning. I'd
get up again at eight, to drive back to Greystones for another
two rounds of golf, subsequently to arrive at the office at nine
o'clock that night armed with a bottle of milk of magnesia,
unable to drink a drop of anything else.

Smyllie—despite his large brandies and dry gingers there was
a powerful Puritan streak in him—silently disapproved of the
excesses that caused me to present myself on Sunday evenings
red-eyed and green in the face. He'd take one look at me, on a
specially bad night, and dismiss me with a grim, "Goodnight,
Mr. Campbell." From then on he excluded me from his
conversation.

But this business of becoming Our Parliamentary Sketch
Writer cut me off from everything.

The Dail sat from 3.30 p.m. until 10.30 three times a week.
This meant I had to sit in the Press Gallery for seven hours,
rushing out to the pub in Molesworth Street for an occasional
pint of stout, but they were always excursions that were full of
dread.

The Dail Sketch was intended to pick out the high-lights of
the day, a light and amusing account in support of the factual
piece written by Our Political Correspondent. I don't remember
who he was but I do remember that he thought I'd got the
softer end of the assignment. "Any old thing'll do for your old
guff," he used to say.

I'd point out that he could stay at home in bed until nine
o'clock at night, and then write his bit from the official shorthand report, but I had to be there all the time, waiting for
something interesting to blow up.

Those interminable hours in the Press Gallery were more
agonising even than the empty boredom of Siemens-Shukert.
There might be a lively argument at the very beginning, at
Question Time, that would give me my piece for the day. Not
being able to use a typewriter in the Gallery, I'd write the 1,000
words in longhand, and then sit there until 10.30 that night
hoping to God that nothing else would happen that Smyllie

would obviously want me to write about. Sometimes it did and I ignored it, with the inevitable result.

"Mr. Campbell?"

"Yes, Mr. Smyllie, sir?"

"Eternal vigilance is the price of—?"

"Of safety, sir?"

"Precisely, Mr. Campbell. You've got it exactly right."

When I did change my mind, and tear up the piece I'd written, I'd rush into the office at 10.45 with a couple of sheets of disordered notes, and try to write my 1,000 words with Mr. Murphy standing silently and accusingly over me. When I'd finished them the Editor would probably want Bloods, so that I'd stay on for the game of dominoes and get home at the usual three a.m.

It meant that twelve hours of my life were being devoted to the *Irish Times* on three days of each week, and it gave me a horror of office work—of 'having to go' whether you wanted to or not—that was to have a considerable influence on my later career.

The Dail Sketches, on the other hand, became one of the leading features of the paper.

The *Irish Times* was—and is—a stoutly Protestant paper in a predominantly Catholic country. I came from a Protestant home wherein Catholicism, and all its words and works, was the subject of constant derision.

Bad Irish art was dismissed by my mother with the inevitable, "But what else would you expect from the tenement Catholic mind?" My father, only half in jest, used to deliver great rolling denunciations based upon, "The bottomless squalor of Roman Catholic superstition—" and conclude with a string of Hail Mary's in the genteel accents of a Dublin Civil Servant.

I'm sure that both of them had a genuine intellectual aversion to Irish Catholicism, and after listening to them for twenty-odd years so had I.

Soon after I began to write the Dail Sketch there was a General Election, and de Valera and his Fianna Fail party came to power. Whereas the former Prime Minister, William Cosgrave, and his Fine Gael group, were well disposed towards the British Government and even contained some Protestants among their number, de Valera and Fianna Fail were republican and Catholic to a man.

I had no political knowledge by which I could assess the validity of the policies of Fianna Fail, but many of the Fianna Fail Deputies were sitting ducks for a sharp Protestant pen.

Dublin has always been a town for vitriolic comment. It's done almost always without real malice. The pleasure lies in finding the exact phrase, the precise analysis that will lay bare the very soul of the subject under review.

At the funeral of Sir William Orpen, who had painted several portraits of my mother and was her great friend, Oliver St. John Gogarty, the Dublin writer and wit, laid his supple tongue upon the deceased.

As they lowered Orpen's coffin into the grave Gogarty said to my mother, "Our painter never got under the skin until he got under the ground."

My mother told me afterwards, "I nearly struck him with my handbag but then I thought in a fearful way it might almost be true."

I began to write about the Fianna Fail Government in the same spirit of probing derision, scoring a fairly considerable coup early on.

One of the Fianna Fail Deputies, a huge old farmer given to wild outbursts of incoherent rage, got to his feet one afternoon and spoke for the best part of half an hour in Irish, a language which perhaps twenty per cent of the Dail might have understood. He was listened to, even by the Opposition, in comparatively respectful silence. The Irish language is sacred in Ireland, where few people speak it. Jeering at its archaic convolutions is a certain method of losing votes.

At the end of the half-hour the old man paused, looked round the Dail with disgust, and said, "And now I'll talk to yez in the tongue of the Sthranger."

"At de laast maytin' uf de Dubbullun Corpuraychun," he began—and gave me a pure and lovely idea.

I reported the whole of his speech phonetically, with the brief introduction : "Deputy C——— addressed the Dail yesterday in what he called, 'The tongue of the Sthranger.' Sthrange it was, indeed."

Even Smyllie laughed out loud. "You'll be getting us all shot," he said.

Next day, when I took my usual seat in the right-hand corner of the Press Gallery, the old man glared up at me. He half rose in his seat and shot a look at the Speaker. It looked as though he was about to raise a Point of Order, even a complaint about a breach of privilege.

I smiled down at him, politely interested, and poised a pencil over my notebook. He grunted in fury and sat down again.

I was thrilled, a real feeling of excitement. All the hours of agonising boredom were suddenly worth while. For the first time I'd appreciated the power of the Press.

Some of the brighter and more ambitious members of the Dail began to appreciate it, too, particularly on the Fine Gael side. It became a habit with them, after a specially sharp passage of invective at the expense of the Government, to glance up to see if I'd got it.

I invented an expression to show that I had—a slightly cynical half-smile, and a casual jotting made in my notebook.

It was the first taste of power I'd ever had. It was warming and relaxing. It was very good indeed.

The Dail Sketches became more and more impertinent, and less and less respectful of the dignity of government. Then, one Saturday morning, when I was shaving before going off to play golf, the Lord came into the bathroom wearing a look so profoundly melancholic that I knew some bad news must be on the way.

"The Dail Sketch," he began. "Some of your bits are very good and funny but—but you're putting a lot of people's back up."

I said, immediately, "That's the sort of feature it's supposed to be."

"It doesn't have to be offensive," the Lord said. Looking out into the garden, from the bathroom window, he gave me one of his addresses on the subject of Catholics and Protestants, based upon his conviction that the Catholic business world of Dublin was working day and night to do the Protestants down. He mentioned several directorships he was holding on to by the skin of his teeth. Then, feeling that the situation was being, perhaps, over-dramatised, he grinned and said, "And your Dail stuff isn't making it any easier for me."

In a town as small as Dublin this was probably, in some part, true. And it was also true that some of the Dail Sketches had been gratuitously offensive, concentrating too much on the personal peculiarities of the people I was writing about.

On the other hand my attitude towards politics and politicians had been formed almost entirely by the Lord's outspoken derision at home.

I began to feel that Dublin was getting too small. Derision was the only method I had of making my Dail pieces lively and readable. I found it alarming to think that people were getting annoyed. There might be a libel action. If I'd been writing out of personal conviction a libel action might have provided a stimulating fight, but in fact I had no principles to defend.

I turned against Dublin more and more in the following weeks. I'd had brief affairs with nearly all the girls in my own circle, and no more seemed to be available. The long sessions in the Press Gallery and the burden of working at night were becoming more and more intolerable. I started to think about London, Lord Beaverbrook and the *Daily Express*, and the William Hickey column in particular.

It was then being written by Tom Driberg, though I didn't know this at the time. It seemed to have exactly the wry, ironic attitude that I looked upon as my own style. I saw myself beginning as a regular contributor to William Hickey and then—it could easily happen—taking over the whole column myself.

From time to time I'd interviewed visiting celebrities, getting next to them through the password of the *Irish Times*. How much more interesting it would be, I thought, to work for the *Daily Express*, and how many more world-famous doors would be opened to me.

I had no doubt of my ability to write the Hickey column, as so many people had told me that my contributions to the *Irish Times* were the only readable things in the paper. I realised that this might possibly be through lack of competition, but was certain at the same time that my kind of journalism must have a high market value.

Any of the national dailies in London would have done me, but Beaverbrook, through my grandfather, was the only Press Lord to whom I had an entrée. I asked my father to write to him, about the possibilities of a job.

Beaverbrook wrote back to say that he was always interested in young journalists, and had held my grandfather in high esteem. He would be glad to see me the next time I was in London.

I wrote to tell him I was coming at once. Then I told my

father I was leaving the *Irish Times*. He pointed out that Beaverbrook probably had no job for me, that the competition in Fleet Street was tougher than anything I could imagine. Wouldn't it be better if I took a week's holiday from the *Irish Times*, saw Beaverbrook and then I could come back to Dublin if he had no specific offer to make?

I said I was certain I could get a job out of Beaverbrook. Privately, I felt I was almost working for the *Daily Express* already.

Then I told Smyllie I was going.

He was very angry. "God damn it!" he shouted. "I teach you young bastards how to be newspapermen, and then you go flying off to London the first chance you get."

Then he calmed down. He was a generous man. "All right," he said. "Go." But there was still bitterness in his voice when he said, "And I hope it keeps fine for you."

Chapter Seven

FOR several weeks, in the bed-sitting-room I'd found in Hallam Street, behind Broadcasting House, everything was fine indeed.

I had a marvellous sense of freedom in being liberated from the Press Gallery in the Dail, and from working in the mouldering *Irish Times* office all night.

I had a couple of hundred pounds in a bank in Piccadilly, the result of another dip into my legacy. "It's just for running expenses," I'd told the Lord, "until I get going."

There was an astonishingly attractive and sophisticated red-haired maid called Barbara in my digs, and Peter was still there in the Gloucester Arms, though my visits weren't as regular as they had been before. I found him, in fact, not quite as amusing now. After all, while he'd been sitting in the Gloucester I'd been in Berlin for the arrival of Hitler, in Paris for the February riots and for three years I'd been on the *Irish Times*.

He had a new circle of friends, however, one of whom was a very pretty girl, blonde and slender and gentle, called Faith.

After Dublin, London was enormously exciting, sparkling and alive. I was able for it now, in a way I never had before, with my Continental travels behind me and my success on the *Irish Times*.

When I felt I'd settled in I wrote to Beaverbrook, giving him my address and telephone number, saying that I was ready to call on him at any time.

As the days went by and there was no reply I supposed he must be out of the country, probably in Canada or the West Indies. I was well pleased. With the best will in the world I couldn't go to work until he came back. In the meantime there was money in the bank, and Faith, and the beautiful anonymity of London where, unlike Dublin, no one knew or cared what you were doing. I had a splendid time, for nearly a month, and then a letter arrived, from the *Daily Express*, from one of Lord Beaverbrook's secretaries.

It informed me that I'd been hired, at seven guineas a week, and that Lord Beaverbrook would like me to call on him at Stornoway House the following morning so that we might discuss how best I could serve the cause of Express Newspapers.

I was so delighted—seven guineas was almost twice what I'd been getting from the *Irish Times*—that I didn't even pause to wonder about this curious method of hiring me, sight unseen.

It seemed to be quite natural that Beaverbrook should take me on, on the strength of my *Irish Times* reputation, and wish me to call on him at his private house, to discuss my future with the *Daily Express*.

I went over to the Gloucester Arms, in a taxi, soon after it opened, to tell Peter the good news, a particularly gratifying expedition in view of the fact that he himself continued to be apparently unemployable.

We drank at the Gloucester until it closed and then we plunged into a tour of the afternoon clubs in Soho. Three or four hours later I lost him, but met two friends from Dublin, with whom I had dinner. We spent the rest of the night in a club in Gerard Street, called Smokey Joe's, and the earlier part of the morning in the Dublin friends' hotel room.

I got back to Hallam Street as the grey, winter dawn was coming up, round about 8 a.m., and climbed the stairs to my room on the top floor with some difficulty. When I opened the door the phone was ringing. I picked it up automatically, too drunk and too exhausted even to wonder who it could be at this hour.

"This," said a nasal voice, "is Lord Beaverbrook. Where are you?"

It wouldn't be true to say that I was instantly sobered, but my mind certainly started to work more quickly than it could have done a moment before.

"I'm just getting up, sir," I said. "I'm afraid I've got a very heavy cold."

"Ha," Beaverbrook said. Then he had a note of warning. "Unless" he said, "we can garner the crops more swiftly we may no longer find ourselves among the labourers in the field." He paused, and added, "I want you here—now," and put down the telephone.

It was at the top of the list of the worst shocks I'd ever had. I started to try to shave and to change my shirt, all at the same time.

Looking back on my introduction to Lord Beaverbrook, I realise that the way in which it was done might have been for the purpose of testing my mettle. The hiring, sight unseen, to promote a feeling of elation. He'd certainly achieved that. Then the dawn telephone call, to indicate that my appointment was stern and earnest. That had been made clear, too.

It also, of course, gave him the opportunity to deliver the rolling injunction about garnering the crops more swiftly—one that was given all the more force by the fact that I hadn't as yet even joined the labourers in his field.

I thought I remembered an undercurrent of suppressed laughter when he said it. It sounded as if it might be fun to work for him. I was very sorry indeed I wasn't in better shape to take him on.

Ten minutes later I found a taxi in Great Portland Street. Though it was a cold, grey winter's morning I opened both windows as far as they would go, thinking about the rumours of Beaverbrook's Presbyterianism and how it would certainly promote, at 8.30 in the morning, a powerful aversion from the smell of drink.

The hurried shave had left me with a number of small cuts around the chin. They were all bleeding. I also had the sense of doom that tells the experienced drinker that he is, in the next hour, going to be sick.

As the taxi drove down Regent Street I rehearsed a number of openings, bearing upon this apprehension.

"May I use your convenience, Lord Beaverbrook? I've got food poisoning."

But I'd already told him I had a heavy cold.

Perhaps if I stopped the taxi and used the public one in Piccadilly? But I was already late.

I sat on the edge of the seat in the taxi, shivering, with the bitter wind blowing in upon me, knowing there was nothing I could do to improve my situation. I could only wait helplessly for whatever was going to happen next.

The taxi turned right at St. James's Palace, drove along a narrow street and stopped at a large mansion on the edge of Green Park.

Stornoway House was demolished during the Blitz, but in 1938 it was a very desirable residence indeed.

I rang the bell. After a while I heard feet clumping along what sounded like bare boards inside. The door was opened by a butler-like person in a black coat and striped trousers. He invited me in.

"Lord Beaverbrook," he said, "would like you to wait for a few moments." He indicated a window-seat in the panelled hall, and disappeared through a large door on the right.

I sat down on the window-seat. There seemed to be moving, creaking wood-panelling everywhere. A beautiful staircase of polished, light wood swept up in an elegant curve to the first floor.

I thought of all the powerful people to whom this great hall must be familiar. I could see Cabinet Ministers coming to dinner, international stars, great ladies and millionaires.

Smokey Joe's cellar had never seemed dingier. I wished to God I'd gone to bed at seven o'clock the previous night.

The butler-like person reappeared and, holding open the door, said, "Lord Beaverbrook will see you now."

I walked into a large room, lined with book shelves. There were french windows into a small garden and the Green Park beyond.

For a moment I couldn't find Lord Beaverbrook and then I saw him, a small figure with a big head enveloped in a huge armchair with his back to the light. There was a table beside him covered with telephones and other instruments.

"Good morning," said Lord Beaverbrook. "How are you?"

I noticed again the curious emphasis he put on certain words. 'How are you?' was almost barked, demanding a specific, detailed reply.

I told him, faintly, about the cold. He hadn't asked me to sit down.

"And what did you do," he asked, "for that excellent newspaper, the *Irish Times*?"

I'd got as far as leader-writing when there was a tap on the door and a young man came in. I discovered later he was Arthur Forbes, a feature writer on the *Sunday Express* and a son of the Earl of Granard.

"Arthur," said Lord Beaverbrook, "take an airplane—today. Go to Moscow. Tell me what they are thinking and saying there."

Arthur said, "Yes, sir," and left the room.

It was difficult to see Beaverbrook's face, with the light behind him, but I was sure I could catch a trace of the famous impish grin. It had been a useful interlude to show a new recruit what life was like in the Beaverbrook empire.

"You have written leading articles?"

"Yes, sir."

"Write me a leading article now."

I was trying to find some method of telling him what kind of leaders I'd written, but the only one I could remember had been about a one-eyed Bosnian shepherd who'd derailed a train with his wooden leg. At that moment, however, the butler-like person came back into the room carrying a wide strap made of webbing.

I couldn't believe it. Was this some form of indoctrination ceremony? Was I going to be beaten before writing my leader? Beaverbrook was taking off his coat!

Then I saw he was dismissing me with a wave of his hand.

"When will I bring it back, sir?" I said.

"Write it here," said Beaverbrook. "Outside. Now."

At the door I saw that the butler was fastening the strap round Beaverbrook's chest. It was too intimate a moment, like spying on someone in their own bathroom. I closed the door behind me and sat down on the window-seat again.

A second later I realised I had neither paper nor pen, nor— even if I'd had them—had I anything to write on. Nor had I anything to write about. The latter discovery was the most alarming of all.

I got to my feet. The whole, huge hall creaked as I walked across the polished boards. I knocked on the door of Beaverbrook's study.

After an interval of several seconds it was opened by the butler. With the same feeling of peering into someone's bathroom I saw Beaverbrook hunched in his chair, gasping for breath, holding the strap tightly round his chest.

"I'm very sorry, sir," I said, as quickly as I could, "but I haven't any paper—or a pencil."

Beaverbrook sat up, releasing the strap. Suddenly I guessed he must have asthma and the strap was a way of finding relief.

He looked at me for a long moment. I still couldn't see his face clearly, but I sensed a look of incredulity.

"Albert," said Lord Beaverbrook, "kindly supply this young man with the tools of his trade."

Albert gave me three thin sheets of typing paper and a thick red pencil. At the door I remembered the other matter.

"What would you like me to write a leader about, sir?" I said.

Beaverbrook paused in the act of re-tightening the strap. "Why," he said in a surprised voice, "the situation. Go do it now."

A quarter of an hour must have gone by on the window-seat before I could even begin.

During my study of William Hickey in the *Express* I'd occasionally allowed my eye to pass over the leader column, but hadn't really been able to read it. It seemed to me to be the worst kind of portentous tub-thumping, a horrible blend of Biblical exhortation and American journalese.

I picked up the thick red pencil and tried to reproduce some of it now, balancing the three sheets of typing paper on my knee.

I was trembling with cold and last night's drink. My eyes were half-closed with a headache that seemed to come from a knitting-needle that had been driven through my head from ear to ear. But even under those circumstances I still couldn't believe that Beaverbrook was serious in expecting me to write a leader with a red pencil, and three sheets of typing paper on my knee.

I didn't try very hard. I wrote: "The warmongers, the prophets of doom, make their voices heard in the land.

" 'Woe, woe,' they cry. 'The power-crazed despots of Europe are on the march.'

"This newspaper believes them to be mistaken.

"And for why?

"Because this newspaper believes that Signor Mussolini's ill-timed attempt to woo the Swastika will come to naught."

And I'd come to naught, too, at the same time as Signor Mussolini.

I looked at what I'd written. In several places the red pencil had gone right through the flimsy paper. I knew I couldn't write another word.

Albert came out of the study, carrying the strap. At least that operation was over. "Is he free?" I said.

Albert inclined his head. "I believe so, sir."

I knocked on Lord Beaverbrook's door.

"Come."

He was on the telephone, but motioned to me to come in. I heard him say, "That is not the way the *Daily Express* is thinking. Goodbye to you." He replaced the receiver, and held out his hand for my leader.

I wanted to tell him that leader-writing was not exactly my forte, that I'd probably be more useful to William Hickey, but he was already reading the first page. He held it up by one corner, so that he had to slant his head to one side. After a moment he let the sheet of paper flutter to the floor, where it joined a lot of others which had been discarded by the same method.

"Young man," he said, "you have something to learn. Go to my newspaper, the *Daily Express*, where they will teach it to you. Good day to you."

Albert let me out. His face was expressionless. He'd seen a lot of young men come—and go—before.

It was shortly after nine o'clock in the morning. From my experience of the *Irish Times* I thought that nothing would be stirring at the *Express* until at least eleven. I went home to Hallam Street and had a bath and changed my clothes.

Once again I cursed Smokey Joe's, and the chance that had led me in there. I'd liked Lord Beaverbrook. He was obviously as odd, original and eccentric as Bertie Smyllie, even if it was in a much more ruthless way. And he did seem to have a genuine interest in young newspapermen.

I had a serious attack of remorse about the way in which I'd presented myself to him. I clenched my teeth and whistled through them when I remembered the nonsense I'd written about Signor Mussolini and the Swastika. But at least I was still on the payroll. I could try again, even if it wasn't very clear what my duties were to be on the *Daily Express*.

Beaverbrook had said, "Go to my newspaper and they will teach you." But did anyone on the *Express* know I was coming and if so, who?

I took a bus down to Fleet Street, and arrived at the office at about 11.30. There was a bust of Beaverbrook in the foyer, a pervasive presence, and a couple of uniformed commissionaires behind the reception desk—a much more impressive entrance

than the *Irish Times*, where the front office was always clut-
tered with elderly charwomen searching the Situations Vacant
columns in the newspapers chained to the high reading desks.

A young man in a very smart, striped suit sprang out of a taxi
and ran up the stairs, probably with some hot news for William
Hickey.

I asked one of the commissionaires if anyone was expecting a
Mr. Campbell. He checked through a list and shook his head. I
said I'd just come from Lord Beaverbrook, that I was going to
join the paper.

The commissionaire nodded his head, this time, looking as
resigned as Albert. He suggested I should enquire in the News
Room, and got a boy to take me up.

I remember no more of my first day on the *Daily Express*. I
must have been given a desk, because I didn't get home until six
or seven o'clock that night, but I'd be surprised to learn that
anyone had given me anything to do. In those days one joined a
newspaper by osmosis. One went there every day and sat around
and slowly one was absorbed into the system—or not.

It was different, of course, in the case of reporters, trained
men with shorthand. They were given minor markings immediately, probably in some magistrate's court, but for someone
with no more than a vague ambition to contribute to the gossip
column the period of indoctrination was shadowy indeed.

I became friends with a charming little man called John Redfern, who seemed to specialise in ecclesiastical matters. Our desks
were side by side and we passed much of the day in general
conversation. He called me 'Dr. Johnson' and I called him, out
of respect for his interest in religion, 'Your Grace'.

After about a week, in which I'd written one leader column
and seen an entirely different one appear in the paper, I received
a telephone call from Lord Beaverbrook.

It was John who told me that the Beaver was on the phone,
in one of the callboxes in the News Room. The voice was only
too familiar.

"Where are you?" it said. "I want you at my house—now."

I took a taxi to Stornoway House and sprang in the moment
Albert opened the door. He seemed taken aback. I explained
that Lord Beaverbrook wanted to see me urgently, that he'd just
rung me at the office.

"His Lordship," said Albert in his stately way, "is at his villa in the South of France." His face cracked for a moment. "If I were you, sir," he said, "I should be careful about the telephone. It's not always reliable."

Then I remembered that almost everyone in the News Room was an expert at imitating Beaverbrook's distinctive voice and equally unmistakable style of speech. But which one of them was it?

I had no difficulty in finding out. John was at his desk when I got back. "Good news from headquarters, Doctor?" he asked gravely. "Off to the Hebrides again?"

He'd simply dialled the number of the call-box beside my desk from the one with its back to it, given me the receiver and nipped back into the first one, to become Lord Beaverbrook in person. He did it on several subsequent occasions, getting other reporters to do the Beaverbrook imitation while he stood, concerned, by my side, so that every time I got a Beaverbrook call I had to run round all the call-boxes in the News Room, to see if it was genuine.

John regarded these activities with gentle sympathy. "The rush and bustle of Fleet Street is wearing you out, Doctor," he said once. "Why not send Boswell along to Euston to get a couple of tickets back to the *Irish Times*?"

In fact, he was perfectly right. In a month I'd made no impact of any kind on the *Express*. I'd had a talk, lasting two minutes, with the Editor, Arthur Christiensen, who had time to ask me what I was doing and how I'd got on to the paper, but he became enveloped in some other crisis before I could reply.

Also, another leader-writer, Hector MacNeil, had been taken on to the leader-writer team and was writing leaders which were appearing in the paper, making my sporadic services to this group even less necessary than before.

It looked as though I was going to have to do something myself to further my career, like turning in an exclusive story or writing a publishable feature, but here there was an insuperable barrier—what were they going to be about?

Fortunately, Lord Beaverbrook struck again, with a new working schedule. He wanted me to write an individual report on the quality, politics, news coverage and quantity of advertising in no less than 150 provincial papers, a task for which I was fitted no way whatever. It was an alarming assignment because

Left to right: The author, Michael, my mother, the Old Lord, Biddy. (Back row) Cecil's wife Lavender, Cecil and the Lord.

At Rockbrook. Cherry, the author holding on to Brigid, my mother, Susan and Sally.

it seemed that he was thinking of buying half a dozen or so of them, and was relying on me to weed out the ones of no value.

The whole bundle of 150 papers appeared mysteriously on my desk one morning, bound with rope.

"Ah, Doctor," said John Redfern, when he saw it, "so we are making a start on our dictionary at last."

I was tied to that enormous bundle of newspapers for what felt like weeks. I devised a system of headings, like : Appearance, Size, Political Affiliations, Atmosphere, etc., but after looking at the dossiers on the first twelve I had to admit that they meant nothing even to me.

'Appearance—Rather Untidy : Atmosphere—None' seemed to be of no assistance to anyone. Furthermore, towards the middle of the pile I was beginning to run into some very curious publications indeed—very curious, that was, in the context of newspapers that Lord Beaverbrook might wish to buy.

Tiger Tim suddenly appeared, and *The Nursing World*, and all manner of other sheets that could not be looked upon as newspapers in the loosest sense of the word.

John Redfern was tremendously interested in this new development. "The political affiliations of *Tiger Tim*?" he said. "My dear Doctor, a knotty problem indeed." He looked at me with such concern that I saw, in a flash, what had happened. He'd been inserting all this stuff into the pile himself.

The idea caught on. Quite a lot of the people in the News Room began to make contributions of their own, so that the heap increased daily in size. It wasn't easy for me to keep on laughing, least of all when I found myself making a report on the *Daily Express* itself, which someone had concealed inside the front and back pages of the *Liverpool Post*.

Then I received another summons to Stornoway House, in the form of a memo left on my desk. It was impossible to check its authenticity, so that I was wary when Albert opened the door. He set my fears at rest immediately, however, by saying, "You're all right—he's here."

Even in comparison with the previous one the new assignment seemed to be impossible, though it began on a note of hope.

"I want you to write me a series of articles," Lord Beaverbrook said. "We must make propaganda for the Empire Crusade."

"Yes, sir," I said, briskly and efficiently.

"The people must be told about the British Crown Colonies,"

Lord Beaverbrook went on, and then he delivered a fearful side-swipe which took me entirely unawares.

"Where are they?" he asked. "And how many are they in number?"

I thought quickly of Canada and Australia, but guessed they weren't Colonies in the true sense of the word.

"I'm not sure, sir," I said.

"Make sure, young man," said Lord Beaverbrook. "We shall call this propaganda—'Great Deeds that Won Our Crown Colonies'. Go to it." As usual, he didn't specify in what way.

Back in the office, I had an anxious consultation with John Redfern. He immediately supplied Tasmania, Pago Pago and the Isle of Man as the first three Crown Colonies that came readily to mind, but then took pity on me. "If I were you," he said, "I'd nip along to the Reading Room of the British Museum, and take Boswell with you to do the work."

I spent the next two months in the Reading Room, where a kindly old librarian unearthed fourteen Crown Colonies for me, with their appropriate bibliographies. I wrote fourteen articles of more than 2,000 words apiece. The title of only one of them still lingers in my mind. It was, 'Sir Stamford Raffles and the Taking of Singapore'.

During this immense task I heard from Lord Beaverbrook only once, in the form of another memo. He wanted to know how much money had been spent upon each Crown Colony, from the date of its foundation.

Stunned by this new blow, I took a day off from the Reading Room and spent it being shovelled around from department to department in the Office of the Crown Colonies, in Whitehall. I finished up in the library there, where I presented my request to a young man who was reading, I noticed, *The Well of Lone-liness*, by Radclyffe Hall.

"My Christ," he said, "it's absolutely impossible."

I took his word for it, and abandoned that side of the enterprise. Lord Beaverbrook never mentioned it again nor did he, I believe, ever read 'Great Deeds that Won Our Crown Colonies'.

I delivered the completed opus to him one day at Stornoway House and he took it, as usual, by the top corner, holding it not without difficulty between finger and thumb. He glanced at the first page—I'd put Sir Stamford Raffles on top, believing it to be the best one—and then allowed the whole lot to fall to the floor.

It seemed that he'd had another idea for me. "Go to the *Evening Standard*," he said. "It is a fine newspaper. I have made Mr. Frank Owen the editor. You will learn much from him."

This was the best news I'd heard yet. The *Daily Express* was clearly much too big and vigorous for me. The *Evening Standard* felt much cosier. I read 'The Londoner's Diary' every night. It was much less sharp and distinctive than William Hickey. I felt sure I could contribute to it regularly.

I presented myself at the *Standard* office in Shoe Lane. This even felt better than the roar and rush of Fleet Street. I asked to see the Editor, and was shown to the door of his office by a messenger-boy.

I knocked and went in. A large man was about to put his hat on a hat-rack just inside the door.

"Good morning, Mr. Owen," I said. "Lord Beaverbrook has just sent me down here to work for you. I hope that's all right."

"I hope it'll be all right, too," the man said. "I'm Percy Cudlipp, and I'm just leaving for the *Daily Herald*."

He took his hat off the rack—I'd mistakenly reversed his intention—put it on his head and left the room.

Frank Owen took over the editorship that afternoon.

The *Evening Standard*, while it didn't overburden me with work, was indeed a great deal pleasanter than the *Express*.

There was a very nice and sympathetic man with one arm called Tudor Jenkins, who regularly gave me books to review and, furthermore, actually invited me to contribute to the series of short stories that ran in the paper every day. I wrote half a dozen or so and was paid seven guineas each for them, so that my salary was doubled in the week they appeared.

Only once, however, was I given a reporting job to do—a trip to Bosham, on the south coast. Bosham, it appeared, was being invaded by the sea, and the foundations of its ancient church were being threatened.

I passed the morning looking round the church with the vicar, and the lunch-break getting drunk with some elderly fishermen in a pub.

I wrote 1,000 words, 300 of which appeared in the *Standard* under the byline, 'By a Special Correspondent', but at least the sub-editor had left in my description of one of the fishermen. "Straight and true as a Roman sword," I wrote, no doubt subjecting him to a good deal of rough badinage from his fellows, if they ever read the piece.

It didn't inspire Frank Owen, however, or anyone else to send the Special Correspondent on further outside assignments and once again I sank into the doldrums of hanging round the office, trying to keep out of the way, only to be rescued yet again by Lord Beaverbrook.

It only occurs to me now that he must have kept quite a close eye on my activities, that he must have tried fairly hard to turn me into a useful member of his organisation, showing considerable thoughtfulness for a Press Lord of his dynamic temperament.

It was certainly my own fault that he was unsuccessful, though some of the blame might also have been ascribed to the extraordinary things he found for me to do.

This next task was the most extraordinary one of all.

One morning he sent for me and in the small garden of Stornoway House he said, without warning, "This man Churchill is the enemy of the British Empire."

I was so astonished, and alarmed, that I stepped backwards into a wet flowerbed, covering my shoe with mud.

"This man Churchill," Beaverbrook went on, in fine oratorical vein, "is a warmonger. He is turning the thoughts of the peoples of the British Empire to war. He must be stopped. Go get him."

I still had one foot in the flowerbed, too surprised to move.

"But how, sir?" I said. "How could I . . . get . . . Mr. Churchill?"

"We shall record his sayings," said Beaverbrook. "We shall make a dossier of his public trumpetings about war. Do it now."

I got my foot out of the flowerbed and was trying to scrape off the mud on the concrete path, when Beaverbrook became aware of what had happened.

He looked down at my shoes and grinned happily.

"I see," he said, "you're in it already."

He was still chuckling when he disappeared through the french windows into his study.

I worked on the Churchill dossier for several weeks, making notes about warmongering from the cuttings in the *Evening*

Standard library and reading minutely every newspaper report of a Churchill speech.

From what I'd seen in Berlin it seemed to me that Churchill was talking solid sense, but on the other hand the front page of the *Daily Express* was telling us constantly that there would be no war this year.

I added a new warmongering item, however, to the dossier several times a week and took them to Stornoway House with a note of the time, date and place in which they were delivered. Not a word of the great anti-Churchill campaign, that I can remember, ever appeared in the *Daily Express*, but suddenly— it always happened suddenly with Beaverbrook—I had a new job to do. A series of articles, to be published in the *Evening Standard*, entitled 'Defenders of London'—an account of the fighter squadrons and their personalities that the R.A.F. was hurriedly training for the defence of the city.

One of the part-time fighter pilots was Beaverbrook's son, Max, an elegant and dashing young man whom I'd occasionally seen around the office. I interviewed him briefly about his squadron and the other people in it. In fact, I didn't care for this 'Defenders of London' assignment at all.

All the young men I wrote about were preparing cheerfully and efficiently to go to war. Many of them were wealthy, yet all of them had unhesitatingly joined up to learn the dangerous business of flying fighter planes in their spare time.

I still couldn't believe that war was really coming, but if it did I knew, though I didn't say it even to myself, what I was going to do. I was going to run home to Ireland.

This secret knowledge caused me to write about the defenders of London in such fulsome terms that someone cut and re-wrote whole paragraphs of the subsequent articles before they appeared in the *Evening Standard*. It was the first time I'd suffered editing of this kind. It was lowering in the extreme after the *Irish Times*, where scarcely a word was ever changed.

I began to feel that I was in a foreign country, that the people of Britain were making private preparations for a war in which I had no part. If a war was going to come I felt I ought to be in Ireland, for Ireland sooner or later would surely be in it, too.

My conscience was working hard to smooth over the impending flight.

Then something happened that made my return to Ireland seem the only sensible thing to do.

I was in Stornoway House one morning when Beaverbrook suddenly said, "I am going to Waterloo. Come with me."

Instantly, I changed all my plans about going home to Ireland. If he wanted me to come with him to Waterloo it might just possibly mean that I was going to spend the weekend with him at Cherkley, his country house in Surrey. A weekend at Cherkley meant that I'd been admitted to the inner circle. Perhaps, in spite of 'No war this year', he wanted to make me a war correspondent, either for the *Standard* or the *Express*.

I liked the idea of being a war correspondent. It was just dangerous enough, and I wouldn't have to do any fighting.

I followed Lord Beaverbrook into his slightly old-fashioned Rolls-Royce, and Albert tucked the fur rug around his legs. I was wondering what to do about things like pyjamas and tooth-brushes, but guessed they'd be supplied at Cherkeley as a matter of course.

As we drove down the Mall Beaverbrook began to talk about my grandfather.

"Your grandfather," Beaverbrook said, "was a powerful advo-cate. Carson thought highly of him, and so did I. You must be proud of him, indeed."

I wanted to do something better than obsequious agreement. If I was going to Cherkley I wanted to show him I had a mind of my own.

I remembered something my mother had said about the Old Lord, after a particularly stiff and boring lunch party at Glen-avy. It was something like, "I don't think he can see how awful that drawing-room is. He simply hasn't got any aesthetic appreciation."

I said to Lord Beaverbrook, "My grandfather might have been a clever lawyer, but he simply didn't have any aesthetic appreciation."

Beaverbrook turned right round in his seat, to look at me in astonishment. "Ha," he said, and addressed no further word to me until we got to Waterloo.

As the car stopped he threw off the rug and jumped out the moment the chauffeur opened the door. He said nothing to me at all. I tried to follow him, but got tangled up in the rug. By the time I got out of the car he'd disappeared among the crowds in the station.

I went after him in a half-hearted way and then gave it up. When I got back to the forecourt the Rolls had gone.

I went back to Hallam Street by bus.

I'll never know what had been in his mind. Perhaps he merely wanted someone to talk to on his way to Waterloo.

At any rate, one thing was certain. He'd changed his mind, if he had any plans to make me a war correspondent. When I called on the cashier, the following Friday, for my seven guinea pay packet I found there was nothing there.

"Nothing for you, sir, at all," said the cashier. He looked a little uneasy, as though he knew something that I didn't.

I told Tudor Jenkins what had happened. He was very kind. "I'm afraid that's it," he said.

I thought of all the time I'd wasted in the last year. I was back again where I'd started, after Oxford, out of work and unemployable—back again on my father's bounty.

"It's a hell of a way to do it," I said. "He could at least have told me himself."

Tudor Jenkins gave me a smile of genuine sympathy. "It sometimes happens like that," he said, "around here."

I got very drunk indeed in the Gloucester Arms that night.

I made up my mind to go back to Dublin. London was getting ready for war. Gas masks had been issued. Trenches were being dug in Hyde Park. Something quite appalling was on the way.

But before I went home I decided to accept Denise's invitation to spend the month of August at her cottage in Sunningdale. Faith, who worked in Denise's beauty shop off Curzon Street, was going too.

After the first luxurious fortnight in the cottage something that I'd half-suspected was revealed to be true. Life at the cottage was luxurious indeed. There was an Indian chef. Every day the menu for lunch and dinner was a matter of long consultation. There was always a tray of drinks in the drawing-room. I discovered that Denise, reasonably enough, was making a charge of ten guineas a week for these joys.

I wrote to the Lord, asking him to let me have another £100 out of my legacy. "If war doesn't come," I told him, "I've got a good chance of a job in early September with the *Empire News*.

But at the moment, thanks to Beaverbrook lopping off my seven quid, things are pretty tight."

Through Robert Lynd I had, in fact, met the Editor of the *Empire News*. None the less, the job 'in early September' was rather far from definite.

On September 3rd we were having breakfast in the sun, in the garden. A large and genial B.B.C. man called Tommy had joined us a couple of days before.

Denise turned on the radio. The four of us looked at one another in plain terror as the voice of Neville Chamberlain told us that Britain was at war with Germany.

A couple of hours later I was driving Denise's car towards Holyhead. Denise and Tommy were going to stay with Roderick More O'Ferrall at his racing stables in Kildare. Faith was coming home with me to my father's house.

As far as I can remember it was a unanimous decision. We opened a lot of bottles of champagne. There was a good deal of hysterical laughter. Denise set the key for the rest of us when she said, "I'm certainly not going to be bombed until I'm ready for it."

We all pretended that we had to have at least one quiet week in which to gather ourselves together, before returning to face the raids which would surely begin at any moment.

I drove quickly towards Holyhead. We kept all the windows open, listening for the sound of German bombers.

At one moment, as we breasted a hill outside Kidderminster, I saw with an agonising twisting of my guts a long plume of black smoke mounting into the sky.

"Christ," cried Tommy, sitting beside me in front, "they can't have got Kidderminster—already!"

I stopped the car on top of the hill. We looked down upon the town in its peaceful, summer valley. The plume of black smoke rose densely from a factory chimney on the outskirts.

We had some more champagne from the supply in the boot.

We left the car in a garage in Holyhead. I told the proprietor I'd be back to collect it in about a week, and that I'd pay him then.

There were queues of people waiting to get aboard the mail boat, refugees as premature and as nervous as ourselves. The name of Lord Glenavy, coupled with the dispensation of a number of pound notes, got us aboard ahead of them. I settled down with Tommy in the bar to drink my way home.

At Dun Laoghaire the following morning Tommy and Denise hired a car to take them to Kildare. Faith and I went home to my father's house by taxi.

My sister's bedroom was available for her, because Biddy was staying with friends in the West of Ireland.

Faith went into Biddy's room, to unpack her suitcase, and the Lord followed me into mine. He looked grim and determined.

"No one knows how long this business is going to go on for," he said. "It may be years. If that girl is going to stay here she'll have to get a job. I can't support her—and neither can you."

The next two days must have been misery for Faith. She'd been the only one who had had doubts about running away, and now the Lord would neither speak to her nor look at her.

My mother did her best. She was very kind and gentle to Faith, but the situation was clearly impossible.

The two of us went to stay with some friends of mine in Foxrock, to get away from it, but another couple of days was enough for Faith. Her father, mother and sister were still in London. She told me she had to go back, to be with them.

"All right," I said. "Perhaps you'd better do that."

Then I said, "I'll follow you in about a week. I haven't really seen my mother at all."

She wouldn't look at me. Her face was sad. It was such a poor, thin lie.

I bought her ticket back to London on the pier at Dun Laoghaire. She said, "I'm terribly sorry you have to pay for my ticket, but I haven't any money."

I said, "That's all right. It's the least I can do."

We said goodbye to one another at the end of the pier. It was a cold, grey morning, with the seagulls quarrelling raucously over the garbage from the Mail Boat.

I told Faith I'd see her in London soon. "I suppose," I said, "I'd better join the Irish Guards. I'm about the right height for it, anyway."

It was the least I could say.

But Faith didn't smile.

I started home before the mail boat left the harbour, and was having breakfast when the Lord came into the dining-room.

"Someone rang up late last night from the More O'Ferralls," he said. "They wanted to know if you were going back to London, because they had no one to drive the car. I said you'd probably be staying here for a while."

"Thank you," I said, unable to say anything else.

The Lord tried to give me some consolation. "It's going to be pretty tough here," he said, "even if we do manage to keep out of the war. England's not going to be able to send us much in the way of food or coal or petrol. We'll just have to see what happens."

"That's right," I said.

I couldn't think about the future. I was trying very, very hard to forget the past.

Chapter Eight

I WAS twenty-six years of age, a large part of the world was at war, and I was living at home, without a job, in neutral Ireland. But after a week or two this situation seemed not to be so disgraceful after all.

Dublin was full of interesting refugees from London. The Shelbourne Hotel was alive with people trying to rent houses and to fiddle their Bentleys aboard the B & I boat in Liverpool.

I forgot that I'd run away. The terrifying war had settled down into uneventful stagnation. It seemed to me to be the business of people who had nothing better to do, or hadn't the imagination to get away from it.

There was a party somewhere in Dublin every night. The English refugees lined up the bottles and we brought our friends along to drink them. While the English bought the bottles we, the native inhabitants, were the hosts. We knew the interesting pubs. We knew the owners and the trainers and the jockeys. We were able to show the English a better time than they could have found for themselves. And every day more were arriving so that we could reject the dull ones, and choose the most amusing—and the most generous.

It felt as if this kind of life could go on for ever. Dublin almost seemed to have a special duty, in a world gone grey and regimented, to preserve the gaieties and the pleasures that we felt had vanished from everywhere else.

Then, one morning, the Lord came into the bathroom while I was shaving. I had a sense of foreboding. The bathroom was one of his favourite places for straight talks between us—or as straight as a talk could get.

He said, "I'm not being mean and I'm not criticising you, but the people you brought back here last night drank two bottles of whisky and a bottle of gin. I'm afraid I simply can't go on providing drink in that kind of quantity. The price of everything is going up—"

To forestall a lengthy explanation of the economic scene I said quickly, "I'm sorry about the drink. They were going to bring their own, but the pubs were shut."

The Lord shook his head. "It's not really the drink," he said. "I'm worried about you." He put the question deliberately. "What are you going to do?"

I said, instantly, "Write."

A mild feeling of optimism filled the house. My mother bought a card table and I set it up in my bedroom, with a box of typing paper. It was a pleasant room, overlooking the garden. It was a room in which anyone could work.

I sat looking at my Bluebird typewriter every morning for a week. I had no idea what I was going to write. After the *Evening Standard* and the *Express* an occasional article for the *Irish Times,* priced at a couple of guineas, seemed to be simply not worth while. A novel was beyond me. I told the Lord, "I'll probably try some short stories. The ones I wrote for the *Standard* went rather well."

I couldn't even begin. I played with paper fasteners and cleaned the typewriter. Sometimes, when I heard my father and mother talking in hushed voices in the hall so as not to disturb me, I wrote anything at all on the typewriter, to show them I was working.

"The cat sat on the mat wearing a paper hat. 'Hello', said the man to the cat, 'why are you wearing that hat . . .' "

At least, I could still type without looking at the keyboard. But I had nothing whatever to say.

During the weekend the Lord gave me his copy of *The Idiot*. "Dostoievsky's marvellous," he said. "You might easily get something out of him."

I read *The Idiot* right through, becoming more and more fascinated by every page. It wasn't always easy to follow. The Russian characters seemed to change their names at will, but I found a real excitement in Dostoievsky's incredible knowledge of the human mind.

After I'd finished *The Idiot* I read *The Brothers Karamazov*. It was simpler, and even more exciting, but it took up a great deal of time, sitting at the card-table in my bedroom with the book propped up against the typewriter.

I'd type out a page or two of *The Brothers Karamazov* every morning to let the sound of the typewriter be heard, but I was further away than ever from writing anything of my own.

Years later my mother said, "The typewriter started up every time I went past your door. I thought it was quite funny." But she smiled in a way that showed she remembered the anxieties of the time—a time when she must almost have been praying that 'everything would come right in the end'.

One day the Lord said, very tentatively, "If you'd like me to see anything you've written I might be able to give you a hand with it."

In desperation I wrote very quickly a thin little story about a golf match, where three men got tied up in the difficulties of scoring by points rather than by holes, and gave it to the Lord.

Next morning, in the bathroom, he talked to me about it. "The three men," he said, "don't have quite enough character. You could, perhaps, build one of them up by calling him 'the Sniffer'. He sniffs all the time."

The Lord stopped. There was nothing he could say to improve the story.

"I'll have a shot at that," I said. "It's quite a good idea."

The Lord hesitated. "I showed it to Beattie," he said. "She couldn't understand the point of it at all."

In my bedroom, I tore it up and went back to *The Brothers Karamazov*.

A couple of days later the Lord got me moving again, though it might have been by accident. He gave me his copy of Thoreau's *Walden, or Life in the Woods*.

I devoured it even more fiercely than I'd devoured Dostoievsky. Indeed, after Dostoievsky Thoreau was a crystal stream. The beautiful simplicity of his way of life could be, I suddenly knew, my own salvation. I, too, would get away from civilisation and live and write in a cottage on the shores of a tranquil brown lake in the West of Ireland.

I was full of Thoreau's lyrical love of nature. I was enchanted by his minute examination of the animal and insect life around his pond. A life of solitude in the cottage by the shores of the brown lake would also relieve me of the necessity of typing out pages of *The Brothers Karamazov* every time anyone passed my bedroom door.

Then I had an even better idea. I'd buy a boat and live in it, and write, on the River Shannon. A small boat could be made much more comfortable than a mouldering Connemara cottage. It would also be a great deal more fun.

There was still another advantage to a boat. The Lord loved boats. The idea of a boat would surely excite his enthusiasm.

It did. He said that a boat was a splendid idea, and began to make plans immediately. He said I ought to go down to Athlone for a couple of days and look around. Athlone was the yachting centre of the Shannon. He'd write to several yachtsmen he knew, to ask if they'd heard of anything suitable for me to buy.

Privately, no doubt, he was also thinking that a boat would get me out of Dublin and the all-night parties. It might also, just conceivably, provide me with something to write about, something that might turn into a whole, real book.

I took another couple of hundred pounds from my diminishing legacy, and moved into the Prince of Wales Hotel in Athlone.

It didn't strike me at the time that I'd already lived in a Prince of Wales Hotel—in London—perhaps because there was no resemblance of any kind between the two.

The Prince of Wales in Athlone was a meeting-place for everyone travelling between Dublin and the West, because the bridge over the Shannon here was the only one for miles to the north or the south. The hotel has since been demolished but in those days its gloomy little bar and shabby dining-room were usually filled to capacity with racing men or people crossing the river on their way from one big house to another.

It was a dangerous place for someone with my taste for parties, but for once I'd got something better to do. I'd bought a boat called the *Dinah*. It had been built by a local carpenter. It was powered by a Morris Cowley car engine and it was in the middle of a field. I paid £80 for it. The cabin was nine feet long by six feet wide but thanks to a greenhouse-like channel that raised the cabin-top to six feet six inches I was able to stand up inside.

I worked on the *Dinah* for a month, in the middle of the field. The previous owner had had her dragged up there, as a precaution against floods. She was clinker built and every plank had dried out so that the sun shone through the cracks into the cabin.

I caulked and painted twelve hours a day, while a monkey-like little mechanic called Mickey, knee-deep in tools in the cockpit, took the engine apart and put it together again. Several times a day Mickey, black with grease, would say, "Jaysus, there isn't room in here to change your mind."

Dostoievsky and even Thoreau had vanished. I couldn't remember the *Evening Standard* or the *Daily Express*. The war and Dublin and all the other complications had disappeared.

After working all day Mickey and I would get drunk on pints of plain porter in Ted Brown's pub on the quay, and meet again at six o'clock next morning. I began to grow a great, red beard. I was blissfully happy for what felt like the first time in years.

We launched the *Dinah* on a brilliantly fine day, easing her down to the Shannon on rollers which we'd borrowed from a boat-yard. She stuck for a moment, with her nose in the mud on the edge of the river, and then floated clear. Twenty minutes later she was resting on the bottom, with only the greenhouse arrangement showing above the surface of the water.

"We'll leave her there," said Mickey, as though this development were intentional, "an' let her suck up a dhrop or two."

Three days later we hauled her back into the field, with the help of a tractor, and began all over again. At the end of a fortnight we re-launched her. She floated and after some passionate winding of the starting-handle the engine fired.

Mickey revved it up. I leant over the side. Even the circulation pump was working.

"Jaysus," said Mickey, transported with delight, "there's nothin' the matther with it!"

We piled all the litter of six weeks work aboard and went down the river and under the bridge. We swung round in a wide circle and made fast outside Ted Brown's pub.

There was a great celebration that night. Someone said he'd heard that the Germans were advancing on Paris, but all that was a thousand miles away.

I stayed moored outside the pub for another couple of weeks. There were still a number of jobs to be done but, in fact, I was putting off the moment of departure into Lough Rea.

The expedition was beginning to feel dangerous. A number of old fishermen had warned me about losing the buoyed channel up the middle of the lake.

"You wouldn't see your nose in front of you," one of them said, "with the storms of rain that do be comin' down from the mountains an' there's a power of rocks outside of the buoys."

The most recent charts of the Shannon, even if I'd been able to get hold of them, had been made in about 1904. And then— I realised—I probably wouldn't have been able to read them with sufficient accuracy. Nor did I know nearly enough about the engine. Furthermore, I'd fallen overboard one night after coming back from Ted Brown's and had a moment of terror when I found that the side of the boat was too high for me to climb back in again. I nearly went over the weir before finding an iron ladder in the darkness, leading back up on to the quay.

Everything began to look very black. Despite all my caulking the *Dinah* still had to be pumped dry every morning. I realised I hadn't done the job properly, really knowing nothing about it. And I received a lot of warnings about the makeshift business of having a car engine in a boat. Mickey himself had told me to keep an eye on the circulation pump. The drive was his own invention—two sprockets and a chain off a bicycle. "You're banjaxed," he'd said cheerfully, "if the chain jumps off."

I began to foresee all kinds of disasters. The engine, over-heated, going on fire. Hitting a rock in a squall and falling over-board and not being able to climb back in again. The *Dinah* simply leaking more than usual during the night and sinking with me asleep in the cabin.

Then I had a letter from the Lord that contained a prevision of an even greater catastrophe. "The war," he wrote, "looks very bad for the British. It's not impossible that England will be invaded and then, of course, Ireland won't have a chance. If you haven't started already I'd get your trip in quickly. You want to get some value out of your boat."

I left Athlone by nearly going over the weir again, but this time in the *Dinah*. Mickey had done a job on the steering cables. I was out in mid-stream before I discovered he'd reversed them, so that when I turned the wheel to starboard the boat went to port. I zig-zagged wildly across the river until the current slammed me against the stakes guarding the weir.

I was there for twenty minutes or so, watching the stakes slowly giving way, wondering how I was going to get out from under the *Dinah* when she went over. I was rescued in the end by a couple of men from the harbour board, who winched the boat off with the help of a crane.

They were very angry about the damage to the stakes. "Bloody young eejit," I heard one of them say to the other. "I wouldn't let him loose in a rowin' boat."

I fixed the steering cables alongside the quay and started up-river at half-speed, terrified that the engine would conk out and I'd be down on the stakes again.

The voyage of discovery had started on a very muted note.

Within an hour the Shannon had begun to widen out into Lough Rea. It was a fine evening and I could see the black and red buoys marking the navigation channel for several miles ahead.

I hadn't the least idea what to do with the boat for the night. I was safe in the navigation channel, but I'd lose the buoys when it got dark.

I'd done it again. I'd gone flying off on a hare-brained scheme without any kind of serious preparation, and for the sole purpose of dodging responsibility. I'd also burdened myself with a very small kitten which mewed frantically unless I put it in the hollow of my neck.

It infuriated me so much that I threw it into the cabin and slammed the door. It went on scratching and mewing in blind panic for the next hour—an hour in which I approached the shore inch by inch, scarcely daring to use the engine in case I lost a blade of the propeller on a rock.

Ahead of me was a great bank of bulrushes stretching away to the fields behind. At least I'd be safe in there for the night. I revved up the engine and drove the *Dinah* into them. They stood six feet tall above the water. They scratched and tore at the cabin-top and then suddenly the engine stopped dead as weeds choked the screw. The bulrushes closed in behind me. There was dead silence, save for the kitten, going mad in the cabin. And I'd brought the whole lot on myself.

I slept between five and six the following morning, having been fighting the kitten all night. I put it on the opposite bunk. Time after time it fell off, to crawl up the side of mine and lodge itself on my face. I put it in the fo'c'sle and shut the door, until the mewing and scratching became intolerable. At one moment, in the black stillness, I stood in the cockpit with the kitten in my right hand, trying to find the courage to fling it away as far as I could into the bulrushes, but I knew it would come crawling back through the reeds, soaked and skinny, to climb over the gunwhale and sit on my face.

In the end I read for hours, holding the kitten away from me at the full stretch of my arm. Towards dawn both of us went to sleep.

It took me the whole of the next day to free the propeller. I stood in the stern in water up to my shoulders and cut the weeds away by feel. The kitten mewed continuously, balanced on the very edge of the counter, dabbing at me with one paw and then with the other. I was more concerned with the possibility of giant pike in the reeds, and slashed about with the knife every time something brushed against my bare legs.

The sun was going down when I pushed the *Dinah* out of the bulrushes with the boat-hook. I started the engine when I was well clear, and moved very cautiously away from the shore. In open water I let go the anchor and then for twenty minutes sat watching two trees in a field. They remained in line, so the anchor was holding. I had a huge supper of sausages and boiled potatoes and after it sat in the cockpit, smoking a pipe and holding the kitten firmly on my knee.

Everything was all right again. The *Dinah* swung gently on a wide arc on the anchor chain, the brown river water rippling like oil along her sides. I felt I'd already mastered the Shannon. If I was careful from now on, approaching the shore, there was no danger of hitting a rock. A hundred and fifty miles of river was at my disposal. I'd disappear into the Shannon and no one would find me—not even, perhaps, the Germans, if they came to invade.

The kitten mewed again and scratched my knee with its tiny, needle claws.

I held it up in front of me, and spoke to it aloud. I said, "If it wasn't for you, unfortunate kitten, everything would be absolutely fine."

I got rid of it the following morning, giving it to an old lady who ran a little grocer's shop in a village at the head of the bay in Lough Rea.

I opened up the engine as I left the miniature harbour. Enormous, tall clouds were sailing in from the Atlantic against a background of surprisingly—for Ireland—blue sky.

I'd got rid of everything, the kitten and the war and my father's sad face. Miles of Lough Rea lay ahead of me and even more miles of Lough Derg. I had rather more than £70 in a tin box in the cabin. I sang at the top of my voice,

> Come back to Erin, Mavoureen, Mavoureen,
> Come back to Erin, the land of the free . . .

My Bluebird typewriter and a box of typing-paper were in the special locker I'd made for them. I'd tried to open the locker some days before, but the door was swollen and stuck.

It didn't matter. There'd be plenty of time for all that.

In the next three months I never even tried to open the locker door. I'd settled into a life of complete and utter idleness, in which the days passed as amorphously as they had in Germany.

Every four or five days I'd boil a bucket of potatoes and chop them up, when they were cold, into an enamel basin. Then I'd chop up a tin of corned beef and half a dozen onions, add them to the cold potatoes and pour a bottle of salad dressing over the lot. Whenever I was hungry I dug into the basin with a spoon.

For days on end I saw no other human being. Whenever I came to a town I'd buy potatoes, and so on, and have a couple of bottles of stout in a pub, and then chug away again, wandering aimlessly up the river towards its source. I spent a lot of time combing and trimming my beard and moustache, both of which were parted in the middle and curled up at the ends.

Once, I spent a whole day sitting on the lavatory in the fo'c'sle, with my head and shoulders protruding through the for'ard hatch and my elbows resting on a cushion, watching three old men trying to raise a sunken launch alongside the quay in Rooskey, up in Co. Longford. The lavatory made a perfect ringside seat.

One evening I came into Lough Forbes, and anchored for the night off an island. The island looked artificial, as though it had been put there for some purpose. There was a large cleft in it, which might have been designed to shelter a cabin cruiser.

Next morning, when I was breakfasting out of the basin, I heard the sound of an engine. I went out on deck in my jersey and pyjama trousers and saw a small pinnace—there was no other word to describe its trim appearance—coming round the island towards me. A triangular standard fluttered in the bow.

Its brass-work blazed in the morning sun. At the wheel was an elderly gentleman in white flannels, a blue blazer and a yachting cap.

Urgently, I began to try to tidy the *Dinah's* cockpit, throwing old clothes and tools and bits of rope into the cabin.

The pinnace came lightly alongside. The elderly gentleman neatly grabbed my gunwale with a beautiful brass boat-hook.

"Good morning," he said. "I'm always glad to welcome visitors to my lake."

I suddenly guessed who he was. He must be the Earl of Granard, and the father of Arthur Forbes, whom Beaverbrook had so briskly dispatched to Moscow. Forbes was the family name, and Lough Forbes was undoubtedly his lake. And then I remembered something else. Lord Granard was also a director of the Bank of Ireland.

"Good morning, sir," I said. "You must know my father, Lord Glenavy."

"Indeed I do," said Granard. His manners were beautiful, but he couldn't conceal a look of mild surprise. The *Dinah's* cockpit was still a shambles, and my jersey and pyjama trousers were far from fresh.

"You must come to lunch," he said, "if you can spare the time."

I couldn't imagine what I was going to wear for lunch, in Castle Forbes.

"Thank you very much indeed, sir," I said. "I'd love to." Then I felt compelled to add, "I hope you don't mind me anchoring in your lake."

"Not at all," Granard said. "Shall we say twelve-thirty?"

The pinnace buzzed away. The Earl of Granard had not introduced himself by name. On Lough Forbes he didn't have to.

Lunch was not an easy meal. My sports jacket and flannel trousers were crumpled after weeks in a suitcase. Lady Granard, grey-haired and American, smoked cigarettes through a long holder and talked to the only other guest, who seemed to be the agent for the estate.

Granard, himself, scarcely spoke at all. I didn't tell him about my meeting with his son. It was quite possible that Arthur had already been killed in the war.

Just before the end of lunch Granard asked me, very politely, if I was on holiday, without enquiring from what. I said I was writing a book about the Shannon.

"How interesting," he said. "I shall look forward to reading it with pleasure."

The butler and two liveried footmen drew back our chairs as we rose to take coffee in the drawing-room.

Granard himself had picked me up at the jetty before lunch, in a small Morris saloon from which the doors had been removed. "We just use it on the estate," he'd said.

The agent drove me back in the same car. I rowed back to the *Dinah* in the dinghy, started the engine, pulled up the hook and left Lough Forbes at full throttle. Several miles farther up the river I tied up to a tree for the night, and then I did a strange thing.

I went ashore and ran as fast as I could for more than an hour through the woods and the scrub, fighting my way through the denser parts as though hurrying to an urgent appointment. Some indefinable instinct drove me on and on until suddenly my need to run was satisfied.

I turned and walked back to the *Dinah*, in the gentle and dreamy state that follows making love.

But probably I'd only been running away from the world, and the war and my father's anxiety—yet again.

But the war caught up with me.

I'd moored at the quay in Carrick-on-Shannon to buy supplies. In a pub I'd met the editor of the local paper. Throughout a long and boozy afternoon he tried to get me to write something for him, after I'd told him I was busy with a book.

Then someone turned on the radio behind the bar, to get the six o'clock news from Dublin. But in place of the news I heard a familiar voice, one that I'd often listened to in the Dail. It was the voice of Eamonn de Valera, leader of the Irish Government.

He sounded as deeply concerned as Neville Chamberlain had been in Denise's garden in Sunningdale. He spoke of 'our neighbour across the water' and her imminent danger of invasion by Germany. The British Army was home from Dunkirk, but at any moment the invasion fleet might sail from the Channel ports.

"And now," de Valera went on, "our own neutrality is threat-

ened. The Irish Republic may be attacked without warning from
the air or from the sea. Every able-bodied man must prepare
himself to defend our shores. The danger is very real."

Those were not his exact words. I was drunk and frightened,
and I don't remember them exactly. But this was exactly what
he meant.

At any moment German bombers might land at Baldonnell
Airfield. At any moment German submarines might surface outside the ports of Dublin, Cork and Galway.

"Sod it," I said to the newspaper editor. "I suppose I'd
better go and do something about it."

He was a genial old man, far gone in drink.

"Better you than me," he said. "Thanks be to Jaysus, I'm too
old." Then his face clouded over. The hand he put out for his
drink was suddenly shaky.

"What chance do we have, anyway?" he said.

We didn't seem to have any chance at all. The Irish Air
Force was almost non-existent. The Irish Army had never fought
against a mechanised enemy. And the British would have their
hands much too full to save us. Ireland would simply disappear.
She would become one enormous airfield for the Luftwaffe,
having no other purpose.

I rang my father from the pub. He said he'd heard Dev's
broadcast. He thought it was all a bit exaggerated, but if I did
want to join up a unit had been formed called the Irish Marine
Service. Their headquarters were in Cork Harbour, but there was
a branch called the Dublin Port Control, which would be closer
to home. He knew the commanding officer. He was sure the
Port Control would take me on.

I told him I'd take the *Dinah* back to Athlone, leave her there
and join him in Dublin as quickly as I could, probably in two
days time.

I went back to the newspaper editor, at the bar.

"I'm going to join the Irish Navy," I said. "The Dublin Port
Control Service. I'll be leaving here as soon as it's light tomorrow
morning."

But the shock of Dev's broadcast had already worn off. "The
Irish Navy," he said. "Bejaysus, I didn't know we had one."

"I wonder how long it's going to take you to realise," I said, "we're bloody nearly in the war."

It was the first time I'd been able to say that to anyone. For the first time since September 3rd my conscience was clear. It was true that if I'd been hurrying back to join the British Navy it would have been even clearer, but the Irish Marine Service was a great deal better than nothing.

It got better and better the longer I looked at it. I was, after all, an Irishman. If Ireland was about to be attacked it was my duty to be there to defend her in Dublin Bay, rather than in the North Sea or the Mediterranean.

I spent most of the night packing my clothes and books, throwing over the side all the junk that had accumulated during the months of idleness. The cupboard holding my typewriter was more tightly jammed than ever. I broke it open with a chisel. The cover of the typewriter was mildewed. I put it with the rest of my bags without bothering to wipe it clean. I knew it would be a long time before I'd be using a typewriter again.

I left Carrick-on-Shannon at dawn the next morning and carried on all day down the river and down through Lough Rea. On the way up I'd wandered all over the great lake. Now I kept to the buoyed channel down the middle of it, with the engine at full throttle, hurrying to join the Irish Navy, to defend my homeland.

I couldn't remember ever having felt so clean and so determined. I found I'd suddenly grown up, at twenty-seven years of age.

It was almost dark when I came under the bridge at Athlone, and tied up once again outside Ted Brown's pub. I didn't go in, but went into the town to buy all the newspapers I could find. I took them back to Ted's and read them in his dark little bar.

I hadn't seen a paper in weeks. They were full of 'the Emergency', as the war seemed to be called. In one of them I found a short piece about units of the Irish Army being stationed in motorboats to patrol the entrances to the harbours of Dublin, Cork and Galway.

"Those poor sods," I said to Ted, "rolling about in their green uniforms and blood-red ammunition boots. They needn't worry. The Marines are coming to the rescue."

Ted was more interested in the dog-racing results. I seemed to be the only person in Athlone who was seriously, and properly, concerned about the war.

Next morning I had my splendid red beard and moustache shaved off in a barber shop. I told the barber I was going to Dublin to join the Irish Navy.

"If I was you," he said, looking at my reflection in the big mirror, "I'd leave them whiskers be. They'd put the heart across Hitler himself."

"I don't know what the regulations are about beards," I said tersely. "Just take it off."

Once again I seemed to be the only one who was serious about the war.

I went back to Dublin by train, and took a taxi home, with all my battered luggage.

My father and mother were there to welcome me.

My mother said, "You've taken off your lovely beard! And I haven't even got a photograph—"

The Lord and I exchanged a stern look. There was no time for frivolity of this kind.

He said the Dublin Port Control would take me on immediately, as a Petty Officer. "The only thing is," he said, "you'll have to do three or four weeks training at Collins Barracks first."

"Collins Barracks!" I said. "That's the Army. What's all this training about?"

"I suppose arms drill and that sort of thing," he said, uncomfortably. "But you'll be all right. You did it at Rossall, didn't you, in the O.T.C.?"

"But I've forgotten the whole damn lot!" I said.

A large, grey shadow had suddenly been cast upon my gallant and praiseworthy rush to the Colours.

Chapter Nine

A SERIOUS woman, in search of the better side of my nature, once said to me, "What would you do now, if England became involved in another war?"

"I'd stay this time," I said, "and do what I could!"

"You said that so quickly you probably mean it." But she wasn't fully satisfied. "But what would happen," she wanted to know, "if you were in Ireland when war broke out?"

"I'd try to get back to London," I said. "England's given me a good living since 1947. I'd have to try to do something in exchange."

"If you'd still been working for Beaverbrook when the war broke out would you have stayed?"

"Yes—of course."

Her look of enquiry prompted me to think again.

"No, probably not. I'm not sure. At that time I felt I'd been rejected by England or, rather, by Beaverbrook. But even if I hadn't been seven quid a week isn't all that much."

"If you forgive me," the lady said, "I hadn't seen you as a soldier of fortune. You mean you're ready to sell your martial services to the highest bidder?"

"That," I said, "is too practical a way of looking at it."

In fact, I didn't want to talk about the war at all. It's an uncomfortable feeling, to say the least, to have missed a fearful experience that millions of other people endured—or failed to survive, including my own sister.

Some people gain a life-long inferiority complex from not having been to a public school or a university. Not having been in a war that nearly all one's contemporaries endured is a great deal worse.

Yet in Dublin, even in the black year of 1940, the war really didn't seem to have very much to do with us. There was no public opinion to shame young men into joining up. It seemed perfectly normal to be neutral.

Almost all the young men of my own age continued at their jobs, going racing on Saturdays and taking holidays in the West of Ireland, while Liverpool was being erased only a couple of hundred miles away.

A number of them, of course, did join one branch or another of the British Forces. Brian Inglis left the *Irish Times* to join the R.A.F., and a young reporter, who joined the British Navy, was on the *Prince of Wales* when she was sunk. Censorship, however, forbade all mention of their names in the Irish newspapers, in the interests of preserving our neutrality.

Bertie Smyllie, however, dealt with the loss of the *Prince of Wales* in elegant fashion. "All his friends," he wrote, speaking of the young reporter, "will be glad to know that he has now recovered from his recent boating accident."

But a lot of other young men lost their lives in the same boating accident, and even more terrible ways all over the world, while I was sitting safely in a small tug-boat in the middle of Dublin Bay.

The only way I can counter my own feelings about this, when people start talking about the war, is to say, "You don't know what suffering is until you've been the one Protestant among thirty-two Roman Catholics in the Dublin Bay Port Control."

But it isn't nearly funny enough, in the light of Buchenwald, Belsen and the London Blitz.

There were, however, some fairly acute physical discomforts attached to life in the Dublin Port Control, combined with a sense of purposeless futility which made them all the more difficult to bear.

We spent the first month or so in Collins Barracks, on the outskirts of Dublin, being drilled by N.C.O.s from the Irish Army.

There seemed to be no age limit in the new Marine Service. There were a number of boys of seventeen or eighteen whose fathers were fishermen or yacht hands from Dun Laoghaire. There were some elderly dockers who'd been put out of work by the war, and some equally elderly seamen in the same situation.

There were thirty-three of us and we all lived together in the same barrack room. Our uniforms were still being made, so in the meantime we wore navy-blue boiler suits and red Irish Army ammunition boots. There were all kinds of rumours about the uniforms and what they would look like when they were issued.

One of them was that Frank Aiken, the Minister for Defence,

was insisting that the new Marine Service should wear the same green material as the Army. The prospect of green bell-bottoms revolted the very souls of some of the old men who'd been in the British Navy in the first world war, but then everything else revolted them, too.

I had supposed that the other recruits to the new service would be as enthusiastic about it as I was myself but, in fact, though they'd joined of their own free will, they seemed to feel they'd been imprisoned in a singularly dirty and ill-run jail.

The N.C.O.s in charge of us were all 'muckin' eejits'. The food was only fit for 'muckin' pigs'. The arms drill was a 'muckin' waste of time'. The whole idea of the Port Control Service was 'the biggest muckin' lash-up' they'd ever seen.

The trouble was that we were all surprised at being subjected to army discipline. Nearly all of us had had some experience of the sea, and we all thought we'd go to sea immediately, in whatever sort of boats the Marine Service was able to provide.

We hadn't bargained for a month on the barrack square, nor had we bargained for the sudden irruption of the Irish language into our lives. After a couple of weeks of being drilled in English the N.C.O. in charge of us suddenly said, "From now on youse bowsies'll be doin' it in Irish."

There was a roar of outraged complaint. "Shure we can't even do it in muckin' English yet," was the burden of it, and many of us couldn't, indeed.

The next couple of weeks were plain chaos. The N.C.O. would bawl at us something that sounded like, "Mel—arrah!" and we'd stand there glaring back at him, having no idea what to do. There'd be a stream of querulous complaint—"What's the muckin' eejit on about, at all?"—and then some of us would come experimentally to attention, followed gradually by the rest.

The next order sounded like, "Go mere—marshawl!" Some of us marked time, others turned to the right, while the largest group went back to standing at ease.

Even the dimmest-witted among us became certain that the army was trying to drive us mad for some venomous purpose of its own, so much so that at the end of a month we were very nearly on the edge of mutiny.

Everyone was saying, "I'm goin' to walk owa this muckin' place an' let the muckin' army come an' muckin' find me, if it muckin' can."

Without warning, then, the army shifted us down to our own billet, a huge empty cargo-shed at the very farthest end of the North Wall, almost where the Liffey joined the sea.

Our first job was to erect a defensive system around the shed with sandbags and barbed wire. A warrant officer from the army was in temporary charge of us. I asked him what conceivable purpose the barbed wire could have. "It wouldn't hold up the German Navy for a single second," I said.

"To hell with the German Navy," he said. "It's the I.R.A. I'm worried about. I've got thirty-three rifles and three thousand rounds of ammo in there."

The army, in fact, was much more concerned about our ability to defend our weapons against raids by fellow Irishmen, than to defend the Republic against the invader.

As the weeks went by the confusion and our sense of futility became worse. One of our jobs was to patrol the North and South Wall on bicycles, and to go aboard each ship as she came in. They were nearly all colliers from the Welsh coal ports, and went back and forth as regularly as buses. We had, first, to ask the captain if he had anything to report, without knowing what kind of report it could possibly be. Then we had to ask him if he had any arms or ammunition, knowing perfectly well that he still had the two Lewis guns and the 2,000 rounds of ammunition he'd had the previous week. Also, a customs officer was there at the same time, to check that his seal was still intact, again from the previous week.

All this was, once again, intended to be a protection against raids by the I.R.A. The fact that they never made one was probably because they considered the Lewis guns to be out of date.

At the same time as this business was going on we were instructed not to have anything to do with certain British & Irish boats from Liverpool, which arrived at the North Wall in the middle of the night with what was called 'special cargo'. The special cargo was Bren gun carriers, anti-aircraft guns and similar items, provided by the hard-pressed British Government. They were shrouded in tarpaulins and quickly whipped away in army lorries before anyone could have a look, despite the fact that the B & I boats came up the Liffey with a red light at their mastheads, indicating that they had explosives on board.

While this was going on it was difficult to be patient with stories about German submarines openly refuelling at bases along the south and west coast.

Round about now I discovered a new source of irritation. I found, for the first time, that I could not be made an officer without a British Board of Trade certificate of navigation. Any certificate would do, even that of a Coasting Mate, which involved little more than the ability to read and write and to know that the sharp end of a boat went first, but without it I was stuck. And, furthermore, we didn't have a Board of Trade of our own.

I wrote, therefore, to the British Board of Trade, citing my yachting experience, the months on the Shannon and my present post as petty officer in the Dublin Port Control Service. "I hope," I said, "that this will qualify me to sit for your Coasting Mate's ticket."

The Board of Trade wrote back, with commendable speed, to say that four years service at sea was necessary before I could sit for the examination in question.

I made some more enquiries and found that the Marine Service might accept a Yachtmaster's Certificate as a qualification for promotion to Ensign, the lowest commissioned rank.

On my afternoon off I went for several weeks to the Nautical College near O'Connell Bridge, where I quickly discovered that the syllabus for the Yachtmaster's Certificate required, among other things, a fairly advanced knowledge of trigonometry.

I retired from the course without further delay.

As a reward, perhaps, for trying I received promotion, however, to the position of chief petty officer, and was put in charge of one of the watches on the Port Control Vessel itself.

She was called the *Noray*, and for years had been a kind of maid-of-all-work around the Port of Dublin. She was thirty-six feet long, with an elderly diesel engine that was started by a complex system of blow-lamps, hot bulbs and compressed air.

Six of us went to sea in her for twenty-four hours at a stretch, leaving the North Wall at eight in the morning to anchor a couple of miles out in Dublin Bay at the South Bar buoy.

Our job was to board and to search every incoming vessel, to check against the arrival of what Standing Orders called 'Unauthorised Persons'. The boarding party was armed with 1914

Lee-Enfield rifles and in the beginning we used a rowing-boat to cover the distance between the *Noray* and the ship.

It was dangerous and useless work. For myself, I'd never seen the inside of a tramp steamer and had no idea where to look for 'Unauthorised Persons'. Quite soon we gave up boarding the regular colliers and merely gave them the signal of the day by bawling through a megaphone.

By day, the signal was one of the International Code flags, and by night two red and two white lights in varying combinations.

Without the correct signal no ship was allowed to enter the Liffey. As a deterrent, there was a detachment of the Army stationed in a hut on the north side of the river, with a field gun.

It was fired only once. A collier forgot to hoist the signal and the army let fly with a blank across her bows. The noise frightened people for miles around. The crack of the field gun sounded just like war.

The collier came astern in a flurry of Liffey water, hoisted the signal and carried on up-river to her berth. Later on the owners complained, through their Dublin agent, about the Port Control delaying one of their ships.

My life settled into a pit of boredom and exhaustion. I'd take the *Noray* out to the South Bar Buoy at eight o'clock on Sunday morning, where we'd roll about to an anchor until eight the following morning, with nothing whatever to do except bawl at passing ships, and fish for dabs to supplement the army rations.

When I got ashore, to hand over to the next watch, I'd go home—by bicycle, after petrol rationing set in—to a small and decrepit flat I'd taken in Dublin, to go to bed round nine-thirty a.m. and get up some time during the afternoon.

I had to be back in the billet again by eight on Tuesday morning, and to remain there on what was called 'Shore Duty' until five-thirty that evening. I filled in the day by giving rudimentary instruction in navigation—a relic of my time in the Nautical College—to a number of old men and young boys who could have no conceivable use for the information I gave them, even if I'd known what I was talking about and they'd been able to understand it.

At eight o'clock on Wednesday morning I'd take the *Noray* out to the South Bar Buoy again, for another twenty-four hours.

I was earning £2 7s. a week. My clothes and my hands were permanently greasy with diesel oil, and the only thing I wanted to do was to sleep.

In this condition I got married. Sylvia had been Eileen Ascroft's secretary on the *Daily Mirror*. We met one evening in the Buttery bar, in the basement of the Royal Hibernian Hotel, and got married soon afterwards.

My father's wedding present was to insure my life for £2,000. It was plain that if he lost a son he had no desire to gain a daughter.

The war went on. Some things, like petrol, tea and tobacco were in very short supply, but there was always meat and drink.

The Guinness boats sailed once a week or so for Liverpool, heavily laden. As they passed us at the South Bar an old man in my watch would say wistfully, "There's a load of fockin' an' fightin' in that."

Some nights we'd hear the sound of airplane engines coming up from the south and turning east over the lights of Dublin. Those were the nights when Liverpool got it again.

And at the same time English people were coming to Dublin for a holiday from the war, and were openly grateful to us for providing the lights and the food and the drink that had vanished from Britain.

Sylvia and I went to live in a top-floor, furnished flat in Fitzwilliam Street. I used to leave it at seven o'clock every morning, carrying my bicycle down the front steps from its place in the hall, and ride down to the billet along the cobblestones of the North Wall. I'd spend every third night at sea and come home exhausted.

Unless I was on duty we'd go up to Rockbrook every Sunday after lunch. It was a long and uncomfortable journey in the bus, with a long walk at the end of it and the prospect of having to do it all over again that night. For me it was a relief to get away from the North Wall, to be able to play croquet again and to talk about golf with the Lord, but for Sylvia it must have been something of an ordeal.

She had no interest in games. I'd known all the other Sunday evening people for years. When, after supper, we played penny poker or mah jongh we used an almost private language that had first grown up at Clonard. Sylvia remained remote from it all. There was no attempt to exclude her but at Rockbrook, as at Clonard, you had to fight for your place, if you wanted to be part of the social scene.

Most Sunday evenings we'd walk in silence down the hill to the bus, to face the long journey back to Dublin and to the top-floor flat that wasn't big enough. Like a lot of war-time marriages ours had been preceded by rather too short an engagement. I hadn't known that she didn't want children, and she couldn't have known how gregarious I could be.

One evening I thought our marriage had ended in a tragedy for which I would never be able to forgive myself. I was cycling home up Fitzwilliam Street when I saw a couple of fire engines near the house in which we lived. Then I knew it was our flat that was on fire. There was a sudden gush of smoke and flame out of the bedroom window. I knew that Sylvia, with nothing to do, often went to bed in the afternoon. I was certain that she was being burnt alive.

I ran up the four flights of stairs, to find firemen round the door of our flat. They were excited, and shouting at one another. One of them raised an axe to beat the door in. I tried to get out my key, telling them it would be quicker.

"Get out of the way, you," cried the one with the axe. "There's two women in there!"

He splintered the thin door with the axe. I saw raging red flame as two of the firemen rushed in. Another one caught me by the arm and dragged me back downstairs. I found Sylvia and our old charwoman sitting on the pavement outside the house, both of them parchment-white and shaking. Sylvia's eyes were frighteningly bright. "We jumped out on to the roof at the back," she said. "The people next door got us in through their window." Then she said, "I hurt myself", and burst into tears.

We took a room in the Shelbourne Hotel that night, after I'd rung the Lord and told him what had happened.

Sylvia was still shaking violently and complaining about pains in her back. She found it almost impossible to move, but the doctor had been unable to find any injury.

Obviously she must have been suffering only from extreme shock, so next day I hired a nurse who was to become her insep-

A familiar expression on the face of Robert Maire Smyllie, listening
to yet another piteous appeal for an increase in wages.

My mother's illustration of a quotation from Sir William Orpen's autobiography. He painted her several times and they corresponded for years.

arable companion in the Shelbourne for the next three weeks.

In the middle of all this I got out of the Port Control.

I'd been angling for my discharge for some time. The Allied Forces had landed in Normandy. There was no longer any danger of Ireland being invaded. It was more futile than ever for me to continue rolling around in Dublin Bay. And now I wanted more than I'd ever wanted anything to get back on to the *Irish Times*.

To work for a newspaper again seemed to promise an almost miraculous liberation of the mind and the spirit, after the futile dirt and discomfort, the endless, querulous, fockin' this and fockin' that, of the Dublin Port Control.

I got Paul MacWeeney, the Sports Editor and a very old friend, to suggest to Bertie Smyllie that he might like to give me my old job back again.

Paul's first report was alarming in the extreme. He said, "The Editor burst at least three blood vessels when I said you'd like to come back. He said, 'Tell the shudderer to go back to England, where he came from.' "

It was the first time I'd really become aware that other people might have an opinion about my retreat from the war. I remembered how proud Bertie had been of Brian Inglis, and of the young reporter who'd had the boating accident. Suddenly, I saw the prospect before me of staying in the Marine Service for the rest of my life. When the war was over I'd be shifted down to headquarters in Cork, and spend the rest of my days on fishery patrol.

I begged Paul to try again. This time the message was still irascible in tone. "He said," Paul reported, " 'Tell that long sod he can't just come and go as he likes. Tell him there's a war on.' "

But I thought I detected a gleam of hope. It sounded as if Bertie didn't want to offer me a job, in case I couldn't get out of the Port Control. It felt like his devious mind, his eternal vigilance about his own *amour propre*.

If only I could get my discharge I was almost sure he would have me back. I made some oblique enquiries about how a discharge could be obtained, and found that there was no hope of getting one unless I had a firm offer of a civilian job.

It was like not being able to join the union unless you're working, and not being allowed to work until you're a union member.

I took a chance on catching Bertie in his office one evening round about six o'clock. I walked straight in on him, wearing my shabby, oil-stained uniform.

"Good evening, Mr. Smyllie, sir," I said.

Bertie looked at me over the top of his glasses, and then turned back to his typewriter.

"Lavatory attendants," he said, "and commissionaires are not required in the editorial sanctum."

It was a good sign.

"Mr. Smyllie, sir—please get me out of the shuddering Port Control. I'm going mad."

Bertie peered intently at the sheet of paper in his typewriter.

"Mr. Campbell."

"Yes, sir?"

"You're a sod."

"Yes, Mr. Smyllie, sir."

"You'd better come and do something about the Diary. It's a shower of lapidary crap."

I could have jumped over the Bank of Ireland. I could have run up the outside of Nelson's Pillar. It was the most beautiful moment of my life.

I bicycled like lightning back to the Shelbourne to tell Sylvia the news. Though I was leaping inside I told her my news composedly. It didn't seem to be the moment for making a lot of noise.

She said she was very glad, for me, but I knew it was really very bad, for her. Whatever discipline the Port Control had exercised over me, at least in the way of having to keep regular hours, had now gone for good, and now I was off on my own.

I had a bottle of champagne sent up to our room, and drank most of it myself. I kept saying, "Imagine—I don't have to bicycle down to the bloody North Wall ever again." Then I said, "Now we can live a proper life."

Two days later I handed in the remnants of my two uniforms, with my oilskins, rubber boots and the boiler suit in which I'd first trained in Collins Barracks.

I flew round the town on my bicycle looking for another flat and found one that was irresistible, and far too expensive. It was on the top two floors of a doctor's house in Fitzwilliam Square.

It faced south and the sun poured into the big living-room. Above the houses opposite I could see the soft line of the Dublin mountains.

The *Irish Times* was going to pay me seven guineas a week, which was very nearly what I was going to pay in rent, but the Lord seemed glad I was back on the paper again, and once again he was ready to help, having already paid the large bill from the Shelbourne Hotel.

Sylvia and I moved into Fitzwilliam Square, into a flat that was quite big enough for a family of six.

I turned myself to the *Irish Times*.

I began by looking up the word 'lapidary' in the dictionary, to see if it would give me a clue to the Editor's attitude towards the Irishman's Diary, a thousand-word column that ran every day.

I found that it meant, '(of style) suitable for inscriptions, monumental,' or else, 'a cutter, polisher or engraver of gems.'

'A shower of lapidary crap' might possibly mean that the Editor considered the Diary to be dull and heavy. But there was another problem. He did the Saturday Diary himself, under the pen-name of Nichevo, and I found it almost unreadable.

Nichevo's column often ran to a lot more than the required thousand words. It was chatty and parochial in the extreme. Almost every paragraph began, "I was talking to an old friend of mine yesterday and he told me—"

Quite often the old friend's name would be spelt wrong, and he'd be credited with doing a job he'd never held in his life.

It was clear I'd have to devise my own mould for the Diary. To get a thousand words out of Dublin life five days a week was obviously going to be a struggle, but at least it would be my own column. Furthermore, it should be fairly easy to make a success of it. Unlike the *Standard* and the *Express*, I felt there was no real competition from the other contributors to the paper.

Within a couple of weeks I was in deep trouble. The Diary had been a rag-bag for years, being made up from paragraphs from the reporters and from free-lance contributors who got 10s. 6d. to a guinea a time for their efforts.

I re-wrote any of this lapidary stuff that I thought was usable, and filled the rest of the column with pieces of my own.

Indignation broke out. The reporters complained that I was

cutting their stuff so much that their take was being reduced from a guinea to 10s. 6d., and the outside contributors protested that they were being hounded into bankruptcy because their paragraphs scarcely got in at all.

The atmosphere surrounding the Diary became so gritty that Bertie was forced to intervene himself—a notable occasion in that he scarcely ever made up his mind about anything.

"Mr. Campbell, sir."

"Yes, Mr. Smyllie, sir."

"Pismires and warlocks bedevil me on every side."

"I'm sorry to hear that, sir."

"I cannot come into the office without being assaulted by screeching crones."

"There's a lot of them about, Mr. Smyllie, sir."

"They complain that the way you're running the Diary is driving them to beg for bread in the streets."

"It's all a shower of lapidary crap, sir."

"I know it is. Do the shuddering Diary yourself."

The Editor removed his large, curved pipe from the shelter of his drooping, gingery moustache.

"Nemo me impune laccesit!" he thundered, and added, as he always did, "And give my regards to your Uncle Dick."

From then on the Diary was entirely my own. I fought for, and won, an office high up in an otherwise empty part of the rambling *Irish Times* building. It was furnished with a table and two chairs, and nothing else.

Every day I got back to it round about four o'clock to write my column, having cycled round the city all day to find something to write about. I worked harder than I ever had before, but no one inside the office seemed to like what I was writing.

One day, Alan Montgomery, the Chief Reporter, said to me, "This Diary of your doesn't look like a newspaper column at all." In addition to being Chief Reporter he was also the Dublin correspondent for *Time* magazine, and therefore tended to favour personalities and hard news. But I was writing about anything that interested me, and in a very personal way.

I did occasional interviews with visiting celebrities like Edith Evans, Irving Berlin, Orson Welles and Lord Mountbatten, but there was nearly always more of me in the interview than there was of them.

What I wanted to find was a situation, with a beginning and a middle and an end—almost a short story—with myself right in the middle of it, so that it was seldom indeed that I could find any meat in an idea given to me by someone else.

The Irishman's Diary shaped the pattern by which I was later to work for the *Sunday Dispatch*, *Lilliput* magazine and the *Sunday Times*.

For me the most important part of the pattern was to have as little to do with the office that employed me as they were prepared to tolerate. In my bare room in the empty part of the *Irish Times* I scarcely saw anyone from day to day. Sometimes, I was lucky enough to have finished a column before lunch, so that I was able to leave it on Alan's desk and go home.

But, as I've already said, to get a thousand words a day out of Dublin, working by my own choice entirely alone, was very hard work indeed. I'd store away the most trivial happening in my mind, in the hope that it would eventually turn into a paragraph. Quite often I'd wake at three o'clock in the morning, after a nightmare in which the *Irish Times* came out with a blank space where the Diary should have been.

Once, to try to relieve the pressure, I wrote a spare column, one of a timeless nature which could be pushed in to fill the gap when, as seemed inevitable, I broke down. It was set, and the galley proof held in reserve. A week later I wrote something about Belfast which Bertie must have found offensive, because my spare column was used in the Northern Edition. I had two different columns in the *Irish Times* that day. From then on I kept nothing in reserve, but worked from hand to mouth in increasing desperation. I combed the city of Dublin from end to end. I used to say to people, "I even know the names of the dogs in the streets."

And then I took on another thousand words a week.

Charles Eade, the editor of the *Sunday Dispatch*, arrived in Dublin, to try to increase the circulation of the Irish edition. I interviewed him, and suggested that the Irish edition might benefit by my writing a column for it.

Charles turned down the idea, on the grounds that the Irish edition had enough Irish stuff in it already.

He went back to London. A week later I had a letter from him inviting me to write a column for the Irish edition, for eight guineas a week. I shall never know what caused him to change his mind. It couldn't have been my Diary column, because he'd already told me it wasn't the kind of thing they could use in the *Dispatch*.

But eight guineas a week, for only one column, more than doubled my salary. I had no idea what kind of column I would write, but the offer was much too good to turn down.

I approached Bertie as circumspectly as I could, knowing that my earlier departure to Lord Beaverbrook would certainly loom large over the new proposition.

It didn't please him at all.

"It's fouling the nest, Mr. Campbell," he cried. "The *Sunday Dispatch* is a shuddering awful newspaper. The thought of a member of the *Irish Times* working for it pollutes my mind."

"But, Mr. Smyllie, sir, I need the money. And I don't suppose the *Irish Times* can pay me any more."

I hoped that that would find an exposed nerve, and it did.

For years Bertie had been fighting an evasive war with the Dublin branch of the National Union of Journalists and their plans for a union rate. Everyone on the *Irish Times* was underpaid—a grievance which Bertie countered, when he countered it at all, with the announcement, "It is a privilege, gentlemen, to be on the staff of a literate newspaper."

Now he said, "If you could allow, Mr. Campbell, the white light of your intelligence to play more generously upon the job you're doing you'd have no need of foreign pelf."

Quite suddenly, he gave in. He was a very generous man.

"All right," he said. "Do the shuddering thing. You're probably half way back to London already."

I had exactly the same thought in my mind.

From then on it was a struggle between the *Dispatch* and the Diary. I was now writing six columns a week out of the little that Dublin could provide, and keeping the best of it for the *Dispatch*.

London, I felt, was coming closer and closer—as it did in a physical sense, too.

The war was over. A lot of English people were arriving to taste the pleasures of a city that hadn't been bombed.

I interviewed all the interesting ones for the Diary and the *Dispatch*, with Dublin becoming more and more cosmopolitan all the time.

Among the arrivals was Frank Launder, to make the film *Captain Boycott*, on locations around Dublin and in the West of

Ireland. The stars were Stewart Granger and the Irish actress, Kathleen Ryan.

Bit by bit I became more entangled with the unit. I was delighted by the private jokes and by the apparently irresponsible fooling about that suddenly gave way to a hard, hushed concentration when the actual filming was going on.

Then Frank hired me to write some additional dialogue for the Irish actors. He didn't use a word of it but he paid me £25.

"You're the most highly paid screenwriter I've ever had," he told me. "There's an 'and' of yours in there somewhere."

That week, with the Diary and the *Dispatch* and the additional dialogue, I made £40 15s.

Dublin, once again, was getting too small. Sylvia and I were drawing further and further away from one another. The parties and the general disorder created by the film unit brought us to breaking point.

A week after the unit left for London Sylvia and I followed them. She'd packed all her clothes. We knew that our marriage was over, but I still pretended I was only going to London for a couple of weeks holiday.

We parted company at Euston. She went to stay with some friends, and I went to Frank Launder's house in Park Street.

That week I wrote a column for the *Sunday Dispatch* which was used in all the editions, not merely the Irish one. I was paid thirty-two guineas. The following week I wrote another piece about London, and received another thirty-two guineas.

I didn't hesitate. I wrote to Bertie Smyllie, telling him what had happened. I told him how grateful I was for all his help and advice, and for the way in which he'd rescued me from the Marine Service. Then, I said I'd have to resign from the *Irish Times*, and accept the job with the *Dispatch*. I went on to tell him about the size of my overdraft—'honourably earned, sir, while working for you'—and made a joke about the bank manager, who had urged me to emigrate before I went bankrupt.

'This *Dispatch* job,' I wrote, 'is my big chance. I've got to take it.'

Someone from the front office answered my letter. He said that the Editor had accepted my resignation, and would be glad if I could let the *Irish Times* have my cheque for a year's salary, in lieu of notice.

It sounded less like a final demand than Bertie, wounded, trying to get his own back.

I didn't answer the letter, and never heard another word about the year's salary I owed the *Irish Times*.

In the next couple of years I returned several times to Dublin, on holiday, without finding the courage to go and see him. Then, suddenly, he died, and it was too late.

But now the war was over and I was back in London, earning thirty-two guineas a week for writing one column.

My sister and her husband were buried side by side in Putney Cemetery. Biddy had married an Englishman and had gone to London to work with him in the Ministry of Aircraft Production. They were killed by a flying bomb in 1944.

I had no children, and I was separated from my wife.

But I was staying in the house of a film director and keeping a bundle of ten shilling notes in my breast pocket specially for taxis.

I hadn't had a 'good' war, but I was alive.

Chapter Ten

FOR a young man with my record—in those days one was still young in one's early thirties—the *Sunday Dispatch* job seemed to be a miracle.

The two columns I'd written that had earned me thirty-two guineas apiece would only just have got by, I thought, on a thin day for the Irishman's Diary, yet here they were handsomely displayed in a London Sunday newspaper with a circulation of more than half a million.

The first column was about the rigours of travelling with a trunk, in the absence of a suitcase. The second dealt with confusion in a nightclub. With the whole of London at my disposal I felt I could go on with this kind of thing for ever, particularly as it was only once a week.

My triumph would, of course, have been greater if the *Dispatch* had been a rather better newspaper. At the end of the war it looked about ten years out of date, seeming to depend for its survival on the serialisation of stuff like *Forever Amber*. On the other hand I realised that a rather better newspaper would probably not have hired me to write a column about a trunk and given me, at the same time, an astonishingly generous contract— a year's notice on either side for an indefinite period—so that the contract renewed itself every day.

Furthermore, as an outside contributor, I wasn't subject to P.A.Y.E., so that every week I collected the 32 guineas in cash.

I should have done a number of things to consolidate my extreme good fortune. With plenty of money in my pocket I should have found a flat, and made it into a home. I should have set aside at least £10 a week against income tax. I should have begun buying National Insurance stamps and, most of all, I should have gone to the *Sunday Dispatch* office, to attend editorial conferences and to dig myself into the life of the newspaper.

I did none of these things. For a month I stayed with Frank and Ailie Launder in Park Street. Frank used to leave very early in the morning for Pinewood, often not coming back until late at night. Ailie and I used to have our first gin and tonic round about 11 a.m., almost always being joined by various discontented ladies whose husbands were also in the film business, so that by lunch time it was plain that yet another day had been lost.

Some afternoons—those that I didn't spend in a drinking club —I went to the cinema by myself, but almost every evening found me in Olwen Vaughan's Petit Club Français, in St. James's Street. The club was a meeting place for film people, including a number of the Irish actors from Frank's film, *Captain Boycott*. By the end of each week there was nothing left of my thirty-two guineas.

The mornings in Park Street were miserable. I usually had a hangover, and the noise of the traffic outside was deafening. I wanted a home. Despite the savage quarrels that Sylvia and I had had I was missing the big sunny flat in Fitzwilliam Square, and even the regular work on the *Irish Times*.

I knew she was living in Artillery Mansions, in Victoria, and several times I almost rang her up to ask if I could come back, being afraid at the same time that it wouldn't work.

The private life of two people is entirely their own affair. The cause of their quarrels can only be of morbid interest to outsiders, so that I do not wish to write about the scenes that took place between Sylvia and myself, except to say that my nature gave her good grounds for fury.

I've been in love with many women, and have made the same mistake with them all. Each time I begin too protectively, too adoringly, seeking their company to the exclusion of everyone else, so that within a month we're wrapped in a cocoon of pet names and love-making that seals us off almost hermetically from the outside world.

Then the outside world and other people—and other women —regain their absorbing interest for me, so that the person I've been clinging to suddenly believes that our earlier happiness was a fraud. The feeling of having been tricked, been betrayed, becomes unendurable. She taxes me with it and I try to lie my way out of it, so that very soon, then, our relationship is devoid of all trust and mutual self-respect. The only thing I can do to try to hold it together is to make her laugh, literally and in the most commonplace sense to try to make her forget her troubles in laughter, so that we can go on living—at least on the surface —in our old warm and cosy and irresponsible way.

But there had been too many accusations between Sylvia and myself to make this possible.

I went on living in Park Street, drinking too much and spending every penny of my new salary. The only consolation was that the *Sunday Dispatch* column was going well. People were already writing in to ask, "Who is Patrick Campbell?" and "Why have we never heard of him before?"

I felt I could be very happy, if only I had a home.

Then I got beaten up outside a night-club. A man attacked me, while his friend mysteriously held his hat and overcoat, like a valet. He almost broke my jaw and then stole my signet ring and my wallet. The two of them disappeared into the fog, leaving me lying in the gutter in Little Compton Street. When the police car arrived they advised me to go home and sleep it off.

I got back to Frank's house round about six o'clock in the morning, with my jaw so swollen I could scarcely speak. The signet ring had been a twenty-first birthday present from my father. I couldn't bear the thought that I had let it be stolen. I seemed to have lost all contact with the decent, ordinary world.

That morning I rang up Sylvia and begged her to have me back. I said I'd had a small accident and was feeling rather low, but that it wasn't that that had made me ring her. I said I'd been thinking for some time we ought to try again.

She was kind enough to believe me. That morning she found a larger flat in Artillery Mansions, and we began living together again.

The beating-up outside the night-club made quite a funny piece for the *Dispatch* that Sunday.

The reunion was not a success. The flat was ancient and gloomy and it overlooked a fire-station, which erupted into the clanging of alarm bells and the roar of engines at all hours of the day and night.

Now that I had the opportunity to get away from them I rather missed the raffish life of Park Street and the French club. I didn't feel it would be wise to introduce Sylvia to either of them, since she would be bound to hear stories and gossip of the high old time I'd been having, and certainly compare it with the bleak and cheerless life of Artillery Mansions. Now that I had rent to pay and food and drink to buy I was being a great deal more careful with my money.

We went back to the sealed-off life that I'd imposed upon us when we were first married, except that now we were sealed-off from one another as well as from the outside world.

The swelling on my jaw had gone down and I was hardly drinking at all. Physically, I was feeling better than I had for weeks, and beginning to get restive at the discipline imposed upon me by having a wife.

Then something happened that gave me a valid reason for getting away from the flat. Richard Bennett, the editor of *Lilliput* magazine, asked me to come and see him, with a view to writing an occasional piece. After we'd talked we had lunch together, and then I went back with him to the office. By the time the pubs opened that evening he'd offered me a regular job, at £1,000 a year, plus twenty guineas for anything I wrote for the magazine. The rest of my work would be caption-writing and editing the work of outside contributors. This would leave me, Richard explained generously, as much time as I wanted for my *Dispatch* column, which I could write in the office, if I liked.

If I'd invented it myself I couldn't have thought of a better job. *Lilliput*, in those days, was still its crisp, satirical, intelligent and very funny self. The other members of the staff—Kaye Webb, James Boswell, Mechtild Nawiasky and John Symonds— were individually cleverer and more professional than anyone I'd ever worked with before. Writers like Betjeman, Pritchett, Sansom and Maurice Richardson—soon to join us—were regular contributors. Here was the kind of competition that I knew would put me on my mettle. And with the *Sunday Dispatch* salary I'd be making something like £57 a week—more than I'd ever earned before, and coming in regularly, every Friday.

After some celebratory drinks I got back rather late for dinner to Artillery Mansions and, playing it down a little, told Sylvia the good news. We both knew what it meant as far as we were concerned. It meant that she would be waiting all over again for me to come home, and telephone calls from the office at six o'clock, saying I had to go and meet someone and would be back as soon as I could.

I took her out to dinner that night, but failed to interest her in Richard and the splendid day I'd had with all the other remarkable people on the magazine.

From then on I left the flat at 9.30 every morning and came home, usually late for dinner, after drinks in the cathedral-like Henekey's, in Holborn. I didn't try to talk any more about *Lilliput*, except to underline the exhausting difficulties of trying to hold down two jobs at the same time.

In fact, of course, working for *Lilliput* didn't feel like work at all. The office was in an alley overlooking a bomb-site, well away from the management's headquarters in Shoe Lane, and they, in any case, were much more concerned with *Picture Post*, the leading magazine in the Hulton group.

It almost seemed that we owned *Lilliput* ourselves, that we could do exactly as we liked with it. There were no set conferences. We wandered in and out of one another's offices, presenting the most extraordinary ideas for the coming issue.

Soon after I arrived John Symonds, the very image of a literary man with his long grey hair in a Lloyd George bob, came into my room and said, very seriously, "I think I've had the best idea that has ever been conceived for a magazine. It is, simply, a piece entitled, 'What it's exactly like to be the King'."

I said it seemed to be fine, if we could get the right person to do it. I asked John if he had anyone in mind.

"I thought the King himself," he said intensely. "But, of course, I'm not sure if he does that sort of thing."

After a day in *Lilliput* it became harder and harder to face the gloom of Artillery Mansions. Unforgiveably, I found myself possessed of an extraordinary kind of malevolence against Sylvia —a kind of freezing of the spirit that scarcely allowed me to look at her, never mind talk to her.

One evening, so set was my face, so iron my silence, that she actually laughed out loud and said, as cheerfully as though to an old and comfortable friend, "You could at least afford one smile."

I became colder than ever, on being laughed at, and a row developed which led to my taking the trunk down yet again and throwing my clothes into it. At the front door, I told Sylvia I was going for good and started to drag the trunk down the endless corridor leading to the lift. It became heavier and heavier. I turned to see what was the matter and found that the trunk had become entangled in the coconut matting on the floor and that I was pulling miles of it behind me.

Sylvia was standing at the door of the flat with a look almost

of pity on her face. I picked up the trunk by its one handle and
threw it into the lift. Sylvia went back into the flat and shut the
door.

It was the final end of our marriage.

I took a taxi out to Dicky and Betty Massingham's house in
the Vale of Health, in Hampstead. Dicky was a lovely, big,
lumpish, shy and funny man who made documentary films, often
appearing in them himself. One of them, made for the G.P.O.
about posting early for Christmas, is still remembered as a perfect
little comic masterpiece.

I'd met the Massinghams in the French club, and taken to
them immediately. They were kind and gentle, thoughtful and
hard working, where nearly everyone else seemed to be as wild
and as dissolute as myself.

They took me in that night, asking no questions and not even
flinching at the sight of the trunk. It was a charming little house
and the Vale of Health was almost like the country. Dicky drove
to his office every morning and I went with him, leaving him in
Trafalgar Square to go to *Lilliput*. He drove me home again in
the evening, to a beautiful dinner cooked by Betty.

I stayed with them for a week, thinking that their life in the
Vale of Health and their deep affection for one another was the
kind of thing I could have had if I'd been more careful—except
that I wasn't sure what I should have been more careful about.

At the end of the week I found a bed-sitting-room in Hertford
Street, almost on the corner of Park Lane, unpacking my trunk
for the fourth time in a matter of weeks.

Lilliput now became my whole life. I wrote a short story for
the magazine every month, unconsciously building for myself a
reputation as a humourist that was to stand me in very good
stead. In fact, if it hadn't been for the stories that Richard
Bennett encouraged me to write I'm certain that later on I
would never have been employed by the *Sunday Times*.

The stuff I was writing, at the same time, for the *Dispatch*
would not, I'm afraid, have encouraged any other newspaper to
bid for my services, but it was only rarely that Charles Eade took
me to task about it.

Apart from *Lilliput* I was leading a lonely life, a bachelor
again at thirty-four, eating by myself every evening in small

restaurants in Shepherd's Market, just round the corner from my bed-sit, in Hertford Street.

Then, one evening in the French club, I found a very small and astonishingly pretty girl trying to buy a drink with an Irish half-crown. I started talking to her about Ireland. I found that her name was Cherry Lawson. She introduced me to her husband. The three of us got drunk together and I spent the night on the sofa of their flat in Chepstow Place, just north of Bayswater Road and about ten minutes walk from my own place in Hertford Street.

I should have gone home, but I didn't. Cherry was the prettiest and tiniest girl I'd ever seen, and I was already passionately in love with her.

Everything happened very quickly after that. Sylvia cited Cherry as co-respondent in her divorce case, and Cherry's husband cited me. Cherry and I got married and settled down in Dolphin Square, and here Brigid, my first and only child, was born. Soon, she was crawling like lightning all over the flat, with one little leg tucked in underneath her, and never in all my life had I lost my heart so completely to another human being.

I got back from *Lilliput* as soon as I could each evening to play with her. We invented an elaborate acrobatic game in which she stood wobbling on my hands, as I lay in an armchair, screaming delightedly to be put down. At the weekends, when we left her in her pram in the gardens, I'd watch her continuously from our fourth-floor window to make sure she came to no harm.

It was for Brigid's sake that we decided to buy a small house in the country, and found one in Bourne End, close to the Thames in Buckinghamshire. It was a delightful little house with a sheltered garden, a huge weeping willow and a small stream, at the end of the lawn, that was choked with weeds.

I was already in trouble with the Inland Revenue over back taxes on my *Dispatch* salary and had already, indeed, laid the foundations of an overdraft that was to get bigger and bigger over the next ten years, so I appealed to the Lord for the £1,000 deposit that was necessary before we could get a mortgage.

He provided, as usual, and for the first time I wasn't paying rent but living in my own house, with my own new furniture around me, with a very pretty wife and an absolutely beautiful child. I began to clear the stream and remake the garden.

My life had achieved a rational and estimable pattern at long last.

The only snag was that I had to catch the 8.40 train at Bourne End every morning, change at Maidenhead, arrive at Paddington at about 9.45 and then struggle into the Underground, to emerge at Farringdon Street station shortly after ten. From there there was quite a long walk to the offices of *Lilliput*. In the evening I caught the 5.45 p.m. from Paddington and arrived at Bourne End at seven, with another half mile to walk to get home.

For the first six months or so I almost enjoyed the discipline of commuting. It gave me a stable feeling to be one of millions of men hurrying to London every morning to provide for their wives and families, and then hurrying back again in the evening to see how the vegetables were doing in the garden. And the weekends, of course, particularly in the summer, were marvellous, with two whole free days ahead of me to work in the garden and to watch Brigid slowly beginning to walk and talk.

Then, gradually, the commuting seemed to become a fearful waste of time. Three hours of the day were being spent in trains. Richard and I often took authors out to lunch, to discuss something they were writing for us, and that seldom occupied less than another three hours, so that six hours of the working day were gone before I could settle down to doing anything useful.

I suggested to Richard that it might be more practical if I worked at home, coming up perhaps on Tuesdays and Thursdays to collect stuff for captioning or re-writing.

He was very good about it. He even tried to make it sound like an intelligent idea by telling me that one of the management's complaints about us was that we lived too much in one another's pockets, that we were all too much of the same mind.

"Perhaps," he said, "if we all got out and about more it might help to broaden the magazine."

My contribution towards broadening the magazine was to buy a prefabricated potting shed, nine feet by six, and to turn it into an office for myself, with a telephone and electric light, at the far end of the garden.

Here, I wrote my *Dispatch* column in a morning and, once a month, my short story for *Lilliput*.

Every Thursday I dropped into the office for a couple of

Rockall. My mother cheating herself inexpertly at patience. She painted the table on which she is playing.

Piling on the power and hitting it a mile down the middle—or, more probably, over the road on the left.

hours, before going on to have lunch with the Thursday Club on the top floor of Wheeler's, in Old Compton Street.

I'd just been elected to the Thursday Club. It was a breath of strong and heady air after the suburban-rural domesticities of Bourne End.

The President was the Duke of Edinburgh, and he appeared occasionally with Mike Parker. On a good day we might also have Arthur Christiensen, the editor of the *Daily Express*, Larry Adler, James Robertson Justice, Michael Pertwee, the Marquis of Milford Haven, Baron, the photographer, Donald Ogden Stewart, Tibby Clarke, Tony Wysard, Vasco Lazzolo and guests ranging from Ian Macleod to Charlie Chaplin and Orson Welles.

The lunch parties were a riot of bread-throwing, story telling and the singing of bawdy songs. Towards the end each lunch-party would be formally christened with a name that indicated the major event of the day, and it would be entered in the Thursday Club Book, together with a variety of rude drawings and the signatures of all present.

Owing to its nature, and the distinction of its members, the proceedings of the club were naturally kept as confidential as possible, but to give a little of the flavour of the Book I might reveal that on one occasion a member, having heard that the Duke was coming, invited his bank manager to be his guest, in the hope of fortifying his overdraft.

There were twenty-two other members present that day. The offender was ordered to go out and buy twenty-two twopenny stamps, to paste them into the Book and to sign his name across every one of them.

That lunch was christened something like, "I Promise Never To Do It Again Thursday".

As these lunches, ostensibly at least, were private parties the licensing laws seemed not to apply, and sometimes we rose from the table as late as six o'clock in the evening—much too late for me to catch the 5.45 for Bourne End.

But I found the Thursday Club irresistible. It provided exactly the kind of life that I most enjoyed. Famous or notorious people at their ease, drink flowing, no office to go to and inside gossip that the newspapers—including my own—would have paid a fortune for.

It had an adverse affect upon my private life. Quite naturally, Cherry, left alone all day with a small child, and waiting for me to come home, began to feel that she was living less than half a life herself. It was the familiar pattern establishing itself all over again, and then something happened to make things even more difficult between us.

The Rank Organisation at Pinewood Studios began to pay me a retainer of ten guineas a week for my exclusive services as an additional dialogue writer, together with another £35 if I did any actual work. The contract was for a year.

Now I had three separate pay-packets, amounting to a total of nearly £70 a week, no need to go to the offices of any of my employers, and an absolute minimum of work to do. Except that I did go to Pinewood. I'd bought a second-hand car and Pinewood was only twenty minutes away, through Burnham Beeches, from Bourne End. I went to Pinewood not to write scripts, but to revel in the glamorous life of the bar.

At that time Pinewood was bursting with activity and every evening the bar would be crowded with stars, producers, writers and directors, all engaged upon the inside gossip that I adored. I used to go over there two or three times a week before lunch, spend the afternoon watching some film being shot and then join in the evening session at the bar. From time to time I was asked to contribute to some screenplay, and I made this the justification for my long absences from home.

Then I found another diversion that took me away for even longer periods. I began to play golf on the days I didn't go to Pinewood or to the Thursday Club. I'd become a member of Temple Golf Club, near Hurley, and I'd also joined the Press Golfing Society and the Newspaper and Advertising Golfing Society, to play other teams at courses all over the Home counties.

Sometimes I left the house at eight in the morning to drive, perhaps, to Walton Heath or Addington, to play a match and not come home again until long after dinner.

I'd scarcely touched a club since leaving Dublin, but soon found I was able to play down to my comparatively expert handicap of two.

It was marvellous to leave the house—and Cherry's justifiable recriminations—early on a summer morning and drive to some beautiful course like Wentworth, Sunningdale or the Berkshire, knowing I'd be locked away in the private world of golf until dusk.

It was the Lord, who loved all games, who introduced me to golf, but most of all he taught me to play it without reverence, to set out upon every round with a high sense of adventure, so that often we laughed so much that we were unable to play the next shot.

He himself had been a fine player in his youth and had once won an Irish Close Championship at Lahinch, in the West of Ireland. In telling the story he sometimes only reached the semi-final, so that I never really knew what had happened, but one factor remained constant. On the night before the dramatic match he'd cut his thumb to the bone on a glass jug and, out of respect for this injury, devised a method of hitting the ball which came to be known, for ever after, as 'the Lahinch dunch, with tuck-in'.

Only he knew what the Lahinch dunch with tuck-in meant, but he would always resort to it in moments of crisis, particularly on the first tee on a cold morning, when his head was reeling from the after breakfast whizzer and his eyes running water.

In the interests of economy he always hired the smallest and youngest caddies he could find. It was marvellous to watch their bewildered and terrified little faces as Lord Glenavy, with extreme dignity, said to them, "Stand well back. We're doing the Lahinch dunch with tuck-in."

He would then hit the ball fifty yards straight along the ground. As it came to rest he would look at it expressionlessly, and finally make his comment. "Which fruddles."

'Fruddling' was an onomatopoeic term from our games of croquet, and had the general sense of making a mess of something. The children who carried his clubs for him treated him warily, believing him to be stone-mad.

But for me I couldn't have had a better introduction to a game which many people treat almost as a religious exercise, a rite to be performed silently and devotedly, one in which laughter is blasphemous.

Sometimes they have taken up the game because their doctors have recommended exercise. Sometimes they play it for business reasons, or just to get away from home. A lot of the time they're simply trying too hard to win.

They make deadly companions on the golf-course, where 50 per cent of the pleasure of the game lies in playing it with the right people.

The other 50 per cent of the pleasure is divided between striking the ball properly and winning—but winning, of course, in a way that makes it seem that one has scarcely been trying at all.

I once played a member of the Oxford University team in a match at Temple, a powerful young man who was a very accomplished player indeed. Walking up the second fairway he revealed a surprising interest in painting. For the rest of the round I chatted to him about my mother's activities in the world of art, how she made a class of students go away to get their hair cut, their fingernails clean and their clothes pressed before daring to return to receive instruction in the hard discipline of drawing; how she had told them, "Learn to draw the bones in your little finger perfectly before you even begin to dream of painting like Picasso."

The young man became interested in this close-up of the artistic life, and was astonished to find that I'd beaten him three and two. "I thought you weren't even trying, sir," he said.

It gave me a warm glow that lasted for the next two days.

Winning is of the greatest importance to me and, indeed, quite a lot of my merry laughter dies if I don't, but the real joy of golf lies in this feeling of being in a private world.

As soon as you've stepped off from the first tee no one can get at you for the next two or three hours. You're in open country with a different shot to play every couple of minutes and the certainty that the next one will be a miracle—perhaps a three-wood out of heavy rough that flies two hundred yards dead straight to the distant green.

There's an extreme sensual pleasure in hitting a golf shot properly, to time it so perfectly that there seems to be all the time in the world to swing the club back, to pull it down again slowly and then to pile on the power, as you come into the ball, so that as you hit it the shaft seems to shimmer in your hand. There's no need to look where that one has gone. It's gone a mile down the middle like a bullet out of a gun, and you know you're going to put the next one three feet from the pin.

And it's only the third hole, and the sun is coming out and there are fifteen more to go. Then a lazy, boozy lunch and out

again for another scheming victory, and possibly the course
record this time, locked away from the world and all its worries
in the easy companionship of four good caddies and three
amusing friends, all equally devoted to the game . . .

While all this was going on it crossed my mind only infrequently that the *Sunday Dispatch*, *Lilliput* and the Rank
Organisation were paying for it, and getting almost nothing in
return.

I placed great faith in my own anonymity, and used to tell
people—almost believing it myself—"It's only if you go to the
office, so that they can see what they've hired, that you're liable
to get the sack."

Ironically enough it was Pinewood, in spite of my fairly regular attendance at the bar, who rumbled me first. At the end of
the year my retainer was not renewed, but this—in fact—was
not a very serious blow. Whilst being paid £500 to do so I'd
met a large number of producers and directors who subsequently
made the error of taking me at my face value, and hiring me for
quite solid sums to work on various scripts. Very little of it ever
appeared in the final versions, for the reason that I had no
knowledge of the craft of writing for the screen. This, however,
is a deficiency that doesn't always deter producers from hiring
writers, and at one moment I was professionally concerned with
no less than five films at the same time.

Then, one Monday morning, a letter in a brown envelope
arrived from the Personnel Manager of the Hulton Press.

Incredibly, he said he'd been instructed to give me six months
notice, and that furthermore I would be required to work out
this notice by attending the offices of *Lilliput* five days a week,
and writing whatever might be requested by the Editor.

It was a horrible shock. I'd never been formally sacked by
anyone. It gave me a cold and frightened feeling to learn that
Lilliput, after eight years, found I wasn't worth the money it
was paying me.

It shouldn't, of course, have been so much of a surprise.
Richard had long since been sacked by the same totally unexpected kind of letter, and there had been three other editors after
him. Admittedly, I'd heard rumours of falling circulation and

advertisers shying away, but it never occurred to me that I could be personally affected.

I drove up to London that day to see Vernon Holding, one of the management veterans, to tell him I couldn't possibly work out my notice. "Have you ever seen a writer working out his notice?" I cried. "He just writes the same filthy word over and over again."

Vernon Holding agreed with me. A couple of days later I received a cheque for six months salary, and my long—if tenuous—connection with *Lilliput* was at an end.

There was still no real emergency, so far as money was concerned. I was doing more and more work for films—and television—and staying away for longer and longer periods from home, until finally the beginnings of a break came with Cherry.

Our interests had become so different that it seemed to be beneficial to both of us for me to take a flat in London and live there during the week, returning to Bourne End only at the weekends.

There was still no question of a legal separation, or a divorce, but to all intents and purposes we had begun living apart.

Now I began to miss the Rank retainer and the salary from *Lilliput*. I was running two homes, with a car in London and another one in Bourne End. The flat, off Notting Hill Gate, was only two small rooms, with a kitchen and bathroom, in a basement, but I was paying rent for it, while maintaining the household in Bourne End.

My bank manager was beginning to ask me what plans I might have for the future. I assured him that I was learning rapidly how to write for films and television and that all kinds of major prospects were both in hand and in store.

"At least," he said, looking for something concrete, "your salary from the *Sunday Dispatch* is always there."

It was, and by now it had been increased to £42 a week, but unfortunately without any elevation in the quality of the column.

I wrote it mechanically, every week of the year, but found TV and films much too exciting to give it more than a fleeting thought. I was getting further and further away from journalism, which I'd always regarded as my true profession, while remaining uncertain about the mark I was making as a dialogue writer, so that I was very grateful to Brian Inglis when he invited me to write twelve pieces for the *Spectator*, of which he had become the editor.

Brian followed me on the *Irish Times* as the writer of the Irishman's Diary and under his guidance for the *Spectator* I found myself concerned for the first time in years with the long-lost graces of style.

He not only suggested subjects for me to write about, but also returned a number of them to be re-written when he felt that I'd crept back into my old refuge of automatic writing.

They turned out to be the best thing I'd done for a long time. Then, just as I was beginning to feel a revival of interest in journalism, a series of crises developed on the *Sunday Dispatch*.

The circulation had been falling for some time, and now the management decided to do something about it. Charles Eade became a director, after nineteen years as editor, and in alarmingly quick succession Wally Hayes, Bill Hardcastle and finally Bertie Gunn took over.

Wally had sent me all over the country, writing descriptive pieces about pony-trekking and similar adventures, but without much success on my part, so that during the three weeks that Bill Hardcastle was editor I slipped back again into the old form of a very slight humorous account of some social mishap. When Bertie Gunn arrived, and asked me what plans I had for giving the column a lift, I was unable to provide an answer of any kind.

I simply didn't know what to do with the column. The thought of the football-pool fans and the greyhound racing enthusiasts who, I believed, formed the bulk of the *Dispatch* readers, lay on me like a dead weight. It was as though I was writing in a language that they didn't speak, and one that I had no great mastery of either. I felt I had fallen into a pit of grey, hostile gravel, and that any attempt I might make to get out would simply bring more of it showering down on top of me.

Bertie Gunn did his best. He'd read my *Spectator* pieces and suggested it would be fine if I could get some of the flavour of them into my *Dispatch* column. I pointed out that the *Spectator* provided a rather different audience. Bertie said he couldn't quite agree.

The situation was hopeless for both of us. I struggled on with the column for another six weeks, often having it rejected and writing another one, to find it used only in the Manchester edition or not appearing in the paper at all.

Bertie had one last proposal to make—that I take a year off from the weekly column and write or, at least, plan about six big feature stories instead, on full salary.

I couldn't even begin to think how I could set about such a project. I'd never written a big feature story, and was unable to imagine how to go about finding one, never mind six. And, most inhibiting of all, was the certainty that I'd lost all contact with the readers of the paper. I couldn't guess what would interest them.

I said I couldn't do it. We'd have to think of something else.

Ten minutes later I'd ceased to be employed by the *Sunday Dispatch*, with a year's money by way of compensation.

It was quick and clean and at least I was out of the gravel pit.

For the first time in twenty years I was without a regular income. Where once I'd had three pay packets, now I had none.

For the first three or four months, which was the length of time it took for the year's money to disappear, I continued to be as affluent as before.

I had enough TV and film work to keep my bank manager happy, but more and more quickly I was becoming aware how my situation had changed.

I realised, with the beginning of genuine panic, that all the money I'd earned from TV and films had been a bonus, a large bonus, but something quite separate from my regular income.

It had been spending money, pure and simple, or so I had regarded it; so much so, indeed, that I'd never bothered to fill in the counterfoils on the cheques I wrote, relying on the bank manager to tell me how I stood. But now, looking more closely at my finances, I saw that the so-called spending money had, in fact, gone to pay tax on my *Dispatch* salary. And that, further-more, it had sooner or later to pay the tax on itself.

Suddenly, I knew I was up against it for the first time in years. Two homes, two cars, a daughter to educate, my income cut in half and a lot of back taxes owing. I couldn't understand it. I had three suits and I was living in a basement. What could possibly have been going on?

Looking back on it now I realise that by the beginning of the sixties there had been a complete change in the whole structure of newspapers, entertainment and the means of communication. The change was all about me, and yet I was scarcely aware of it.

Commercial television had loomed up to grab advertising revenue away from newspapers and magazines and, in particular, from those that hadn't come to grips with the changing scene.

Teenagers had money in their pockets and wanted to spend it on something more exciting to them than the rather recherché humour of *Lilliput* and the imitation pornographic-romantic serials in the *Dispatch*.

The Swinging Age was under way, and any publication whose image was in the least old hat hadn't got a hope of survival.

A more sentient—and more industrious—journalist than myself would certainly have seen all this coming, and taken steps to try to attach himself to a newspaper or magazine with some foreseeable future.

I didn't. I let the two jobs that I'd held for a long, long time just crumble away beneath me, relying on the old familiar hope that everything would come right in the end.

Six months after leaving the *Dispatch* I became convinced that my career in journalism was over, that Fleet Street had finished with me for ever. Not only had no other newspaper approached me; it also seemed that the funny writer was no longer required. At one time every national daily and Sunday had their resident comedian. Now the great herd had dwindled down to about three, at least one of whom seemed to be in his death throes.

So that when my brother Michael rang me to say, "Rather a nice woman called Irene Josephy wants to meet you—I think she's some kind of agent", I wondered for a couple of days whether I could be bothered even to talk to her on the telephone. As far as Fleet Street was concerned I knew I was a dead horse, and that flogging me for ten per cent wouldn't even pay her for the postage.

I did ring her up in the end, mainly out of curiosity, wondering what marketable value she thought I had.

We met in El Vino's one morning, and I liked her immediately. While not exactly young, she wore gay and youthful clothes with an air. She was very much alive. When it came to newspapers and magazines she seemed to know exactly what she was talking about and talked about them with highly intelligent irreverence, bursting into sudden loud and unexpected laughter.

I felt there might be some hope of getting back into journalism, and agreed to let her see what she could do for me.

"Splendid," she said immediately. "We won't sign anything. We'll just see how it goes."

The following week she got me commissions to write for a couple of trade papers I'd never heard of, and for a great deal more than I thought they'd be able to pay. More equally unlikely commissions followed, and then several pieces for *Punch* and even the *Sunday Express*.

I was back in business again, thanks to Irene's skilful blend of flattering, coaxing and nudging, with always at the back of it the faint but unmistakable sound of the cracking of the whip.

We quickly established a relationship which I found to be full of delicate nuances.

I very much liked her tentative method of laying a new project before me. On the telephone, she would say, "I was talking to someone the other day at lunch—rather a nice man, really—and he was wondering if perhaps we might be able to do a little something for him. Of course I told him we were terribly busy, but we might just be able to find time to fit him in . . ."

At this point she would pause, and I could almost see her at the other end, testing the temperature of the water. Then I only had to say something like, "Well, we might be able to do a bit, if the money's right," to start her off on an enthusiastic soft-sell of the new idea.

I always had the feeling that she had a whole file of plans and projects for me that she kept to herself, whilst letting some of them out for a brief airing from time to time, just to see if they'd take.

It was a pleasant relief from responsibility to feel that I was an instrument which would go to work if the right button was pushed, and that someone else was busily looking for the right kind of work for the instrument to do.

Then, one of Irene's casual telephone calls gave me a much more personal stake in our affairs.

"By the way," she said, "the *Sunday Times* seems to be interested in us, but of course we'll just have to wait and see."

"The *Sunday Times*!"

I couldn't believe it. What did they want? Who had she been

talking to? Was it just an occasional piece? Or a regular job? Why did they want me?

I couldn't persuade her to be more specific. Perhaps she was merely trying to damp down my excitement, in case nothing came of it, and the disappointment would be too great for me to bear.

She rang off, saying she'd let me know the moment she heard something more definite.

I began pacing round my basement living-room, equally divided between two violent emotions.

It would be quite something to write for the *Sunday Times*. I'd be writing for an élite audience. I'd meet people at dinner parties who would say, "But you're not *the* Patrick Campbell— the one who writes for the *Sunday Times*?"

I couldn't remember meeting anyone who read the *Dispatch*.

Then the other emotion, one of plain terror, took over. In the scarcely conceivable event that the *Sunday Times* wanted me to write a regular column what in the name of God was I going to write about? If I hadn't been able, for months on end, to find anything to interest the *Dispatch* readers what hope would I have of arousing laughter or even mild amusement among the infinitely more sophisticated and intelligent people who bought the *Sunday Times*?

Then I remembered the *Spectator* pieces. I knew they'd held up well in comparison with the work of the other contributors, and many of them had been distinguished writers. Perhaps the *Sunday Times* had been encouraged to hire me because of them? And a lot of people still remembered my short stories in *Lilliput*. Perhaps I could do it.

But—Christ—what was the first column going to be *about*?

I spent the next few days divided between exultation and fear, with fear gradually being overcome by my old arrogant certainty that given the right medium, the right encouragement and the right audience I could be funnier than anyone else.

When Leonard Russell, an old friend and Literary Editor of the *Sunday Times*, asked me to lunch I went bounding off to meet him in Scott's, certain that this was it. The first column would write itself. I had only to get the job and there would be nothing more to fear.

I began by congratulating him effusively on the new look of

the sports pages. "Chris Brasher," I said, "is particularly good."

"He's particularly good in the *Observer*," said Leonard resignedly, "but I know what you mean."

The lunch ended on a curious anti-climax. Leonard wanted to know if I'd like to review some books for him. And that seemed to be all.

Suddenly, all the wind was let out of me. If the *Sunday Times'* interest in me was confined to reviewing books they could keep it. I'd never been able to review books and the few guineas it would bring in simply wouldn't be worth my while.

Now all the arrogance and the exultation had gone. The drivel I'd written for the *Dispatch* had been my own undoing. No newspaper would ever take me on as a regular contributor again.

"Well, sod them anyway," I said to myself, "there's always films and television."

I began knocking newspapers and the hopeful illiterates who worked for them. "The newspaper industry is dying," I announced to people who would listen. "It's television for me. That, at least, is expanding, getting bigger and better all the time."

When Irene rang to say, "The editor of the *Sunday Times* wonders if you'd be free for lunch next Tuesday", I couldn't think at all for a moment. Then, I believe I asked her, rather truculently, "What does he want?"

"I think," she said, "he wants to give us a job," and there was an undercurrent of excitement in her voice that convinced me it was true.

All my earlier terrors came flooding back. I wanted desperately to write a column for the *Sunday Times*. A credit on a film or television play seemed to me to have nothing like the kudos of my name at the top of a newspaper column. However good the film or play might be so many other people contributed to it that I could never regard it as being my own work. With my own newspaper column I was out on my own, fully exposed to blame —but much more probably to praise.

I went to lunch in Crockford's almost praying that by three o'clock I'd be a columnist for the *Sunday Times*. I got the job rather earlier, round about 2.15.

The editor was then Harold Hodson. He brought Pat Murphy with him, who was then the managing editor.

Throughout the lunch Harold Hodson scarcely spoke. Pat Murphy and I chatted about rugby, golf and tennis, games in which we had a mutual interest. Indeed, he harped so much on sport that I suddenly got the idea that he wanted me to join the sports staff, but he wouldn't come to the point.

I could bear it no longer. "Look," I said, "do you want me to come and work for you or not?"

Pat looked mildly surprised. "But, of course we do," he said. "But doing what?"

"Just your usual feet-off-the-ground column, old man," he said easily. "You know the kind of thing."

The incredible luck that had supported me throughout the whole of my working life had come to my rescue once again.

Only lately I was surprised to learn that my father, throughout his long and distinguished career, had felt that he, too, had been blessed in the same inexplicable way.

From hospital, during his last illness, he wrote to Francis Stuart, the Irish novelist, one of the few friends whose intelligence and perception he respected. Francis let me see the letter. In part, it read:

"The special feature of my progression has been the sustained good luck which has accompanied it, unsupported by any aims or ambitions on my part. Practically nothing happened in my life otherwise than I would have had it happen. In my various occupations I have found myself very briefly near the top of the ladder at an early stage, fear then dictating a prompt retreat. It has left me with the superstition that there was some function or significance which I was being facilitated to discharge but of which I have never been able to conceive."

I had certainly inherited my father's sustained good luck, but there was still a difference between us.

I knew it would always be indolence, not fear, that would dictate my retreat from the top of the ladder.

Nor would I ever have a superstition that there was some function I might have discharged, had I known what it was. I know what my function is only too well—the simple one of having a nice, easy time.

Chapter Eleven

AT the back of my basement flat in Campden Hill there was a yard just big enough to hold a table and two chairs. When the sun shone I lived and worked out there until the sun was hidden by the roof of the house. Even in high summer it was gone by two o'clock in the afternoon, leaving the yard in shadow that I found more and more unbearable.

I knew I had to move, to find a flat with a terrace or a balcony that would get the sun all day.

I couldn't now remember ever having been happy, living below ground. The basement was mixed up with the loss of two jobs, sleepless nights worrying about money—all the things I wanted to erase from my memory.

It was a familiar reaction. At one time the flat had been a God-given haven from domestic quarrelling. It had given me the extreme pleasure of being able to come and go as I liked. I'd woken in the little bedroom with the sun streaming in, delighted to know that I'd signed a contract the previous day to work on another film. Or, even better, knowing that I'd just finished one and that the next three or four days and nights could be given over entirely to pleasure, with no one to get in my way.

I'd enjoyed the flat so much that I'd redecorated the whole of it myself, taking immense pride in doing the job as professionally as possible.

Now, I couldn't stand it. It was too small. It was damp and dingy. I hated the rented furniture. I couldn't bear the thunder of the traffic above my head.

Once again I'd found a number of satisfactory reasons for turning ruthlessly against something that I'd loved. And, more particularly, because I'd found the place where I wanted to live.

Sometimes, when the sun had left the yard, I'd follow it into Holland Park, and on my way there I'd see people browning themselves on a terrace on the roof of a building at the very top of Campden Hill.

That was the place for me. When the sun shone I'd have it

all day long. Whoever owned the terrace seemed to have done nothing with it. But I would make a garden. In the summer it would be like living in the country again, with all the noise and stench of London far below.

I thought of going up to the flat and knocking on the door and asking if it was for sale, but I knew it wouldn't be. The owner would inevitably have it on a ninety-nine-year lease. And, worst of all, I knew he'd show me up to the terrace and I'd have a view all over London that would be the most splendid thing I'd ever seen—and couldn't have.

At a party I met a South African novelist called Rayne Kruger. He said he believed we both lived in Campden Hill.

"If you live in Campden Hill," I said to him, "perhaps you know the name of the bastard that owns that beautiful flat, the one with the terrace at the end of Airlie Gardens."

"I do," said Rayne. "I'm the landlord. In fact, I own the house."

I seized him by the arm, afraid that in the crowded room he might get away from me. "Who's living in it now?" I said. "Is there any conceivable chance of getting him out?"

"A Miss Forster," said Rayne, "is the tenant at the moment, but she's leaving soon. I'd prefer to let it unfurnished, on a fairly long lease—"

It was like living on top of the world.

The sitting-room and the bedroom had enormous windows pivoted in the middle so that they opened horizontally. With nothing between me and them I could watch the pigeons flying from tree-top to tree-top down below.

I bought furniture and crockery and pictures and carpets. For the first time in years I had a real home of my own, and it was unique.

From the terrace I could see Hampstead Heath and Kenwood to the north, and to the south the Surrey hills. To the east, beyond the unbroken green of Hyde Park, were the Post Office Tower, the Hilton Hotel and the dome of St. Paul's. Jet liners from America, using the Campden Hill water-tower as a mark, swung west over my head, and I could follow them all the way down the sky into London Airport.

I was entranced by my new home, so much so that I was easily able to overlook its disadvantages.

There was, for instance, no doubt that the sitting-room was rather small, so that I would have to work and eat at the same table. There was also no doubt that the terrace above was very big—as big, in fact, as the sitting-room and bedroom put together—and that the wooden staircase leading up to it was very steep and narrow. Furthermore, on all but the calmest days the wind up there was very brisk indeed, so that even if the raw materials of a garden could be imported in sufficient quantity the result would be somewhat exposed.

In time these minor disadvantages were going to cause me to move yet again, and into another basement at that, but for the next two years I wouldn't have lived anywhere else in London.

Everything had elevated itself. From grinding out a piece for the *Dispatch* in a cellar at the bottom of Campden Hill I was now writing a column for the *Sunday Times,* in a penthouse on top of it.

Now I had every incentive to work hard and well. The *Sunday Times* had the same effect upon me as Bertie Smyllie had had so many years ago.

I began to enjoy writing a column again, to look forward to the genuine sense of joy that comes from suddenly getting a good idea.

The good ideas do come suddenly, and almost always out of something that has happened to me personally. The experience might be of the most fleeting kind but it becomes instantly luminous, a lovely ready-made piece. Like the time I was sitting outside a café in the South of France, with the mistral howling out of a clear blue sky, and the large domineering lady drove up in a very small car with her elderly parents in the back of it.

She left them there while she went into the hairdresser's. The old people began to try to get out of the car, but the mistral kept banging the doors in their faces. I helped them out, holding on to them to prevent them being blown away. The domineering lady suddenly reappeared, very angry indeed. It seemed that both her parents were partially crippled. It had taken her the best part of half an hour to get them into the car—and now look what I'd done!

That happened on a Saturday, when I'd already written my column for that week, so that without warning I had a beautiful nut to cherish for the following Sunday.

When I've got an idea to cherish—one that arrives in good time—it gives me a glimpse of the warm contentment of pregnancy.

When I haven't got one, and it's already Wednesday morning, it's like a nightmare, in which I cannot move or run or speak or think and yet I've got to do so, because something fearful is rushing towards me for the kill.

I go out to the shops, to buy something I don't want, in the hope that something will happen. Panic-stricken, I cry aloud to the human race, "Do something, for God's sake!"

These empty weeks are a torment to all about me. I stalk about in grim and silent fury, which becomes all the grimmer when someone, trying to cheer me up, says, "I'm sure you'll find something—after all, it's only eight hundred words."

I explain to them bitterly that it isn't 'only' eight hundred words—that the piece must have some social or topical significance, that it must reflect or illuminate some contemporary attitude—and then I write a column about how not to bake a ham.

Only people who know me very well indeed can really help, and for them it must be like trying to tune in to a distant, foreign station on an obsolete radio. And when they do get through, with the beginnings of an idea, they must withdraw immediately, so that I can make it my own.

Helpers who don't understand the technique are in for a hard time. These are the well-meaning ones who give me an idea— usually a half-remembered incident from another newspaper— with the comfortable assurance, "It's right up your alley, Pat."

It's usually some farcical and totally unlikely event, like an elephant de-railing a tram, and it causes me to believe they've never read a word I've ever written. I demolish them and their suggestion with a ferocity that surprises both of us.

From the beginning I've been antagonised by their very form of address. A number of acquaintances, trying to be friendly, have an incurable tendency to address me as 'Pat'. I can't stand Pat, probably for the reason that I have a secret fear that Pat may have a real, physical existence. Pat the broth of a boy, Pat the red-nosed clown.

In my earlier years my father's apparently effortless ability to hold an audience, and to make them laugh uncontrollably, created in me a highly competitive desire to do likewise, so much so that I'm always tempted to give a 'live' performance of an idea that I've been saving to commit to paper, and extracting so much juice out of it that there's nothing left.

Far from being a clown who wants to play Hamlet, I'm more than happy to go on playing the clown, so that when Ned Sherrin asked me to appear on his TV show, 'Not So Much a Programme, More a Way of Life', I accepted the offer instantly, being filled at the same time with a dread of making a fool of myself that still wasn't strong enough to overcome my desire to become a public performer.

It was Kenneth Tynan who introduced me to Ned, over lunch at the Café Royal. For the first half-hour or so I thought Ned wanted me to write for the show. Then I realised he wanted me to appear in person as one of the 'talkers', and for the rest of the lunch I talked without stopping, to show him what he was going to get.

Despite this over-heated performance he invited me to appear on a closed-circuit trial run for the show, with a studio audience which contained a number of television critics. The other two 'talkers' were Norman St. John Stevas and the playwright, Alun Owen. David Frost was the chairman.

Before we went on he'd asked me if I'd like him to say something about my stammer, when he was introducing me. I agreed with him that it might be a good idea to prepare the audience for the shock of being faced with a talker who couldn't speak, for by now I was certain I'd be unable to articulate a single word.

I'd have given anything to be able to get up and walk out of the studio. I felt sick at the thought of my own vanity, the vanity that had led me to believe I could perform with professionals, in public.

The show began. David introduced me by saying something like, "And now here is Patrick Campbell, who may or may not be able to speak," and suddenly I got the most extraordinary feeling of euphoria. I was still tense and excited, but I couldn't wait to try to get the first laugh from the studio audience. I felt they were warm and friendly and on my side.

I can't remember how badly I stammered, or whether I stammered at all, but the audience did laugh. By the end of the show I felt completely happy and relaxed, and even impatient that I hadn't been given more to do.

When 'Not So Much a Programme—' went on the air, I became one of the resident talkers, every Friday night.

Before the show began we had dinner at Television Centre, to find what Donald Baverstock, who was then in charge of Channel One, called 'areas of conversation'.

The areas were in the main political or sociological, and I quickly found I was unable to make any serious contribution to them. The other guests varied from show to show. There were clergymen, university dons, Members of Parliament, writers and industrial tycoons—all experts in their own particular field, and eager to make their opinions known.

It wasn't long before Donald Baverstock discovered that I had no opinions of any kind, or at least no serious ones. We came to the understanding that I'd 'probably be able to think of something to say when the time came', and left it at that.

Every Friday night, just before we went on the air, I got the same feeling of euphoria—a delightful sensation of pleasurable excitement that I'd never known before. It was gratifying to find that the other talkers—nearly all of them public figures well accustomed to addressing large audiences—were almost invariably more nervous than myself. This, of course, was because they set store by their own opinions, and were deeply concerned with getting them across, whereas for me the whole thing was just a lark. I wasn't even dependent on television for my living. Once again I was able to regard the handsome fee paid for each performance as a bonus, over and above my regular income.

It's fair to say, however, that even now I cannot bring myself to contemplate how furious and disgruntled I would have been if I'd failed. And I might have failed if I'd ever been aware of the real size of the audience that regularly looked at the show. As it was I was conscious only of the small group of people in the studio, and among them it was always possible to pick out a couple who seemed specially well disposed towards me, and to play to them.

Ned Sherrin's warm-up before the show was a great help. He made everyone shake hands with the person behind him, so that by the time we went on the air it was almost as though we were having a private party. Furthermore, with the whole programme on the back of his neck, he always had a suggestion for something I might say, or remembered an anecdote I might tell, to get me off to a good start. With the exceptionally warm-hearted help of David Frost, I felt the first half-dozen shows were a breeze.

Then, as the weeks went by I began to reach the end of my store of comic incident, and to become concerned about my lack of knowledge of the subjects that we—or, rather, the other guests—discussed. I would sit there while they argued about Vietnam, primary education or the divorce laws, and could find no opinion about any of them that seemed to me to be worth delivering.

Instinctively, I began to make a corner of my own. It came quite easily—the sudden derisive and probably irrelevant interruption that made no contribution to the discussion, but at least got me back into it again, however briefly.

It worked, in the most unexpected way. I started getting letters from viewers commending me on my commonsense and the rational quality of my mind! They thanked me, sincerely, for the breath of fresh air that I intruded into overly pompous and opinionated argument. They couldn't know that I'd been doing it for years, long before I'd appeared on television. I was merely following my mother's example.

Her passion for life, for art, for the exercise of the imagination was so strong that she was incapable of listening for more than a few minutes to self-aggrandisement, or to what she believed to be second-hand opinions. She could not stop herself leaping on the offenders and putting them straight with a fury which she regretted afterwards only if they were so small-minded as to take offence.

Her interruptions and objections were much more passionately felt than mine, but at least the technique I'd inherited from her enabled me, on television, to keep up with some very distinguished thinkers!

On the night before each show the script of the sketches, played by John Bird, Eleanor Bron and the others, would be delivered to me by taxi from Television Centre, together with a number of empty pages menacingly headed 'Chat'. To assist with the 'Chat', however, Ned enclosed some notes about subjects and the lines on which they might be developed.

The talkers were supposed to study them and to make further notes of their own. Many of them did, in copious measure. The only thing that interested me, however, about these scripts was

the identity of the other guests and their possible reaction to a
light roasting.

Soon, I found I was appearing more and more regularly with
Malcolm Muggeridge. At least I had the sense not to try to go for
him, or I'd have been left for dead. Instead, I joined forces with
him in pursuit of such monuments to sincerity as Barbara Cartland and Godfrey Winn.

David Frost and later, on 'B.B.C.3', Robert Robinson would
begin by asking the potential victims some general questions about
their work and their general attitude towards the world and then,
when they'd started to talk, leave them to the mercies of Malcolm, with interruptions by myself.

Usually, the sides turned out to be much more evenly matched
than they looked on paper. Godfrey Winn, his sincerity as luminous as a halo, rose effortlessly above all our attempts to needle
him and finally won the trophy outright by thanking us very
generously indeed, when the show was over, for our kindness in
helping him through a frightening ordeal.

Barbara Cartland was equally successful. She'd been speaking
at some length in support of her own romantic style in fiction-
writing, paying no attention at all to Malcolm as he finally buried
his face in his hands, piteously complaining he could no longer
go on listening to such nonsense. Undismayed, Miss Cartland said
it was love that made the world go round and, in a sudden sideline, that her mother thought so, too. "My mother," she said,
"only likes stories and plays that have a happy ending."

Privately, I agreed with her—and was surprised to hear myself
saying, in a bitter, angry voice. "Then your mother must be a
very foolish old woman."

Miss Cartland lost not an ounce of dignity. She invited me to
repeat my remark. I did so.

"That," said Miss Cartland, "is not at all a nice thing to say.
My mother is watching this programme and I'm sure she will feel
very hurt."

At once, she regained her good humour, and went on talking
about her books. I didn't open my mouth again.

When the show was over I went up to her to apologise and
before I could do so Miss Cartland threw her arms around me.
"Thank you so much," she said, "for being so nice to me. I
thought you were marvellous."

The following evening an emissary delivered in person a bottle of some vitamin mixture, together with a note from Miss Cartland urging me to take it for the good of my health, with her compliments. The note repeated her thanks of the night before, with every appearance of sincerity.

There was another occasion when I became involved in an altercation with Bernard Levin about whether or not it was proper for him to refer to Sir Alec Douglas-Home as 'a cretin'.

The other guest that evening was Ian Macleod, and I'd taken very little part in the discussion, apart from silently mouthing the words from time to time, "Macleod for Leader".

This had been Ian's own suggestion. It was impossible to tell if he was serious when he suggested that I should try 'some subliminal advertising' on his behalf, but at any rate I did try to shape the words at intervals, at least giving myself something to do, while the other two ranged knowledgeably over the political field.

Then, suddenly, Bernard used the word 'cretin 'and before I knew what I was doing I'd jumped on him, for once with a feeling of absolute conviction. Making it up on the spur of the moment, I said that a 'cretin' was a medical term denoting total mental and physical incapacity and consequently was an unforgivable insult to be applied to Sir Alec Douglas-Home.

Bernard, taken by surprise, began to defend himself wildly and for several minutes the audience must have been looking forward to an actual exchange of blows.

When I got home that evening two newspapers rang me to ask if it was true that I had refused ever to appear again on television with Bernard Levin. I replied, with an enjoyable feeling of calm, that Mr. Levin was an excitable young man with an occasionally hysterical way of talking and that I would be glad to appear with him again at any time, as by now he had undoubtedly seen the error of his ways.

The 'cretin' business survived for nearly a week as an almost country wide controversy and did a lot for my growing reputation as a person of gentlemanly instincts and sound commonsense.

In fact, of course, this kind of television programme could have been tailored to fit me, demanding as it did only short and isolated bursts of highly pleasurable and often irresponsible showing-off.

As a result of television I began to receive half a dozen invitations a week to speak at lunches and dinners, and to take part in debates or hold discussion groups with students. I had the good sense to turn them all down, writing to the organisers to tell them that I was incapable of addressing an audience for more than three minutes at a time, and that on TV, if they watched closely, they would see that everyone else did most of the work.

When, however, I was asked to make six commercials for Schweppes ginger-ale I leaped at it as eagerly as I had leaped at Ned Sherrin's first invitation. The commercials were to be fifteen seconds in length each. The whole proposition sounded like a pushover. A lot of money for only two days filming and I'd known the director, Michael Truman, for many years.

After the first three or four takes on the first commercial I found I was up against something requiring a technique that was so far beyond me that I wanted to abandon the whole enterprise there and then. It was, in fact, the technique of acting, of performing a set of prescribed moves in front of a camera and speaking perhaps fifty words with the same degree of excitement as though they'd come to me on the spur of that very moment. And doing it over and over again.

When I'm thinking hard about something my face gets grimmer and grimmer. My lower jaw protrudes with such belligerence that strangers shy away from me in the street, though I might only be wondering if I'd forgotten to post a letter. Now, trying to remember the fifty words, and the constricted movements that accompanied them, my expression was homicidal at the moment when Michael said, "Action . . ."

He was patient in the extreme. He tried to get me laughing just before each take, so that some appearance of animation might at least remain for the first few seconds, before the murderous look set in again.

There was, of course, the additional problem of my stammer. Fifteen seconds, in which to deliver some fifty words, scarcely allowed of any hesitations at all. Time after time I broke down in the middle of a take, after getting held up too long over a word and knowing I was going to overrun. Sometimes, I couldn't even start.

By the end of the second day Michael was almost more exhausted than I was myself.

While making the ginger-ale commercials I looked upon my stammer as a nuisance that would have to be played down as much as possible, if we weren't to have endless takes. I thought that Schweppes had hired me to make them because my face was familiar to millions of people, and because I seemed to have been able to generate a feeling of warmth and goodwill.

Although I didn't care to think about this aspect of it too much, I did realise that my stammer fitted rather neatly into their campaign, the essence of which was never to mention the whole word 'Schweppes', but merely to present the first syllable, 'Sch—', and that was quite enough for me, in every way.

It wasn't until a year later that I realised my mistake.

In that year I'd forgotten the agonies of making the Schweppes commercial, and when the Butter Information Council offered me a great deal more money to make six for them I accepted the offer instantly.

With the Schweppes experience behind me I felt I was almost a professional actor and, indeed, had come to believe that if I were asked I would be able to play a small, cameo part in a film.

The new director was Michael Law, another old friend, but as soon as I began the first take I knew I was hopelessly out of my depth, all over again.

The old belligerent look was back, the stilted walk and the stammer that was suddenly worse than it had been for weeks.

After the first half-dozen takes Michael said, "That's coming along nicely—let's try it just once more."

We tried it several more times, but I could see that Michael was unhappy. I was trying desperately hard to give a perform-ance and had even nearly got the stammer under control, but something wasn't right.

Suddenly, Michael said, "Let's have a little chat."

I followed him apprehensively into an empty corner of the studio. He turned to face me, but seemed to be finding it difficult to put his thoughts into words. I knew I could have done it for him.

He wanted to say he couldn't go on with the commercials, that he was unable to direct someone who couldn't act. I was about to tell him I understood when he said, "I don't quite know how to put this—but could we have a little more of your trademark on the word 'butter'."

A combination of a number of things caused me to laugh out loud. There was relief that the whole enterprise wasn't going to be cancelled. There was Michael's extreme embarrassment. There was my own private knowledge that I'd been trying to suppress the very thing it seemed that everyone wanted.

"Well, sod it," I said. "And there was me trying to talk nice."

Michael grinned. "I know," he said. "But if you could just give us a little bit more. You see, the housewives seem to like it."

I found it almost impossible to believe him. Whenever I've seen myself on a recorded television programme I'm appalled by the contortions I go through in trying to speak. Though the effort to avoid stammering is exhausting, I never feel I'm having quite as tough a battle as it looks to be on the screen. I can only regard the fact that some people find these struggles endearing to be further evidence of my sustained good luck, except that it's a little hard to take the thought that people are more amused by how I speak than by what I say.

If I was offered, by some miraculous over-night cure, the opportunity never to stammer again, I'd accept it without hesitation, even though it meant the end for me of television.

This stammering business has got out of hand. Newspapers have written about the new hope I've given to stammerers all over the country. A speech therapist approached me to make a television series with him, presumably to bring about a mass cure. An extremely intellectual magazine published a long article entitled, "The Stammerer as Hero". A gossip column announced that, "Stammering is In." A television critic spoke of, "The shameful commercialisation of Patrick Campbell's stammer."

He was referring to the butter commercials, but it seemed to me he might as well have been complaining about the shameful commercialisation of Mr. Pastry's moustache in the Golden Wonder Crisps advertisements.

The stammer is as much part of me as Pastry's moustache or Harold Wilson's pipe or Lady Godiva's hair is of them.

After my little chat with Michael Law there was no need for me to put it on. Every time I thought of the word 'butter' looming up ahead of me I became so tense that in take after take I was unable to say it at all.

Seeing that my stammer is very probably here to stay I'm delighted to know that the housewives like it. Their liking it has provided me with a great deal more money than I could ever have earned by writing, and at the same time, of course, it's given a notable boost to the sales of my books.

It's a little sad to think, however, that I'm going to be left with my stammer long after the television audience has got tired of it, and fallen in love with a new personality with a slight cast in one eye and an entirely bald head. It's the audience who create the gimmick, and they like a new one at regular intervals.

Looking back now on the past three years I continue to be astonished by what television has done for me.

Never having been aware of more than the studio audience at the time, I find it incredible that so many people should recognise me in the street. The symptom, mostly, is the half-turn of the head, the pause if they're talking, the nudge to their friend and then they both turn to look after me with a degree of curiosity which, coming from total strangers, makes me feel uncomfortable —almost as though I should do something for them, like turning back to introduce myself formally, and to enquire after their health.

On the other hand it's both pleasant—and useful—to be recognised by head waiters, commissionaires and policemen, and to receive consideration from them that I never would have had in the days when I was only writing a column for a newspaper.

Among the many other things for which I'm indebted to Ned Sherrin was his ingenious title of, 'Not so much a Programme, More a Way of Life.'

It gave everyone a chance to get in on the act, even the police. Once, when I'd left my car too long outside a shop, I came rushing out to find a policeman standing guard over it. I launched out into the usual apologetic gabble, only to be halted by the policeman touching his helmet. "Shall we say, Mr. Campbell," he said, "it's not so much a parking offence, more a way of getting into trouble if we do it again."

Coming on top of everything else—the public recognition and the surprisingly kind remarks of the television critics—I felt I'd really arrived, that I'd made my mark on the huge city of London which I'd been trying to impress for so long.

Then I went back to Dublin to see my mother. She had just designed and caused to be erected a plaque beside the front door of the house in which George Moore had lived in Ely Place, on the grounds that no one else in Dublin was liable to remember him, even if they'd ever heard of him.

We went to look at the house and the plaque, and I found that the house was now used as a club by the staff of Irish Television.

I went into the bar, surrounded by the radiance of being a nation-wide personality on the infinitely bigger and more glamorous B.B.C., and met an old friend who used to be with me on the *Irish Times*.

He had the usual corrosive Dublin comment to make about a number of B.B.C. programmes, despite the fact that he, like thousands of other Irish citizens, received them free of charge, and eventually came round to my own contribution to television.

"I suppose," he said, selecting the least tolerable aspect of it, "you're making a fortune."

"I am, indeed."

"Good luck to you." But he was unable to leave it at that. The inevitable Dublin reduction gear had still to be engaged.

"All the same," he said, "we know who'd have been the best hand at it."

"My father?"

"Who else?" he said. "He'd have been a grand man on the telly."

I was quite surprised to feel pleased that I was still in the shadow of the Lord.